THE HEALTHY
SLIMMING
Handbook

First published in 1986 by
Octopus Books Limited
59 Grosvenor Street, London W1

Printed and bound in Great Britain
by Collins, Glasgow

ISBN 0 86273 212 3

Editor: Sybil Greatbatch
Nutritionist: Dr Nigel Dickie
Home Economists: Helen Mott, Glynis McGuinness,
Victoria Anthony, Alison Graham, Jennifer Craw
Consultant: Patience Bulkeley, Editor, Slimming Magazine

Illustrations: Caroline Bays

THE HEALTHY SLIMMING Handbook

by the experts of Slimming Magazine

Editor: Sybil Greatbatch

CONTENTS

INTRODUCTION

Not long ago anyone even contemplating going on a slimming diet would be met with cries of horror from friends and relations: 'Good Heavens, you can't cut down on your food – you'll ruin your health!' Fortunately that attitude has changed, due in large part to the greater publicity about the ill effects that being overweight has on our health. Nowadays, most people realize that the right kind of slimming diet must be *good* for their health.

However, some doubts still linger on. One that is frequently expressed concerns age: 'Am I too old to diet?' or 'Is he too young to diet?'. The answer to both questions is that excess weight is just as unhealthy for the elderly as for the young. Getting down to the right weight on a well-balanced diet can and probably will increase the life-span and will make you feel better. Older people tend to have a lower calorie requirement than younger people because they are less active, but their nutritional needs are very similar.

One of the most common causes of life-long weight problems is that parents 'left it too late' before deciding to help their child to slim. A fat child is likely to grow into a fat adult. Obesity is a sign of malnutrition, not good nutrition. It isn't kind to allow a child to remain very overweight, and it certainly isn't healthy.

In modern western society very few people go short of calories. On the contrary, the main nutritional problem arises from the fact that many people consume an excess of energy. Despite what some manufacturers would have you believe, energy is exactly the same as calories. When you decide to lose weight, calories are the essential factor to consider. As described in Chapter 2, the average woman uses up about 2,000 calories a day, a man uses up 250 calories more. If you consume the correct amount of calories each day your weight will remain steady; consume more and the excess will be stored as fat. Thus in order to reduce your fat store you need to eat less than you are burning up.

Although we run the risk of eating certain food elements (such as fat and salt) in excess, in this country we do not normally suffer nutritional deficiencies. This is because in eating the usual generous quantity in the normal haphazard way, most people end up eating a wide variety of foods which provide a wide variety of nutrients. By good luck, rather than good management, we usually end up getting adequate quantities of all the nutrients we need. When you are dieting there is more possibility of error, because you may be restricting the range of foods you eat, or eating less than before. Therefore greater care must be taken in choosing a diet that is nutritionally balanced. The advice in Chapter 2 tells you how to construct a healthy diet plan, and all the diets we have devised have been thoroughly checked to ensure they are nutritionally sound.

In general, the foods to avoid when dieting are those which supply a large number of calories but few nutrients. Sugar is the prime example here; whether it is white or any shade of brown, it only supplies unwanted calories, and no vitamins, minerals and protein at all. The calories in sugar are often called 'empty calories' for this reason.

The other aspect of slimming is the way in which you can speed up your weight loss by becoming more active, that is by increasing the number of calories you burn up. This doesn't necessarily mean you have to take up tennis or join a keep-fit class. For instance, if you are sitting down, watching TV or reading, you are burning up far fewer calories than if you are walking home from the shops carrying a heavy shopping basket, so you can increase your daily calorie expenditure simply by sitting less and moving more. Never send the children to fetch and carry for you; go yourself, especially if it means running up and down stairs, which is an excellent calorie burner. Walk whenever you can, rather than taking the car. To help you on your way, there are exercises in Chapter 4 which you can easily incorporate into your normal day.

Looking good is as important as feeling good. Following the beauty care and clever dressing advice in Chapter 6 will make you feel much more confident throughout your bid to slim. Low self-esteem is depressing and being depressed makes it much more difficult to maintain a slimming campaign. It is much more likely that you will keep to a diet if you are proud of your appearance.

Are you ready for take-off? If so, turn to the first questionnaire in this book. As you move on to each chapter, first answer the questions which will help you to assess your diet needs, pinpoint any specific problems and highlight where you may have gone wrong up till now. Following the advice in this book will benefit your figure, health and looks.

CHAPTER 1

*R*EADY FOR TAKE-OFF

ARE <u>YOU</u> OVERWEIGHT?

Start by answering this questionnaire. Your answers, together with the hints which follow, will help you to assess your weight problem and your reasons for wanting to slim.

1. What is your present weight? ....
Do you think you have a weight problem?

2. What do you consider to be your ideal weight? ....

3. Why do you want to slim? Tick any of the following reasons for losing weight that apply to you:
   a. To be more healthy ☐
   b. To look more attractive ☐
   c. To wear fashionable clothes ☐
   d. To be more active ☐
   e. Because the family would like you to be slimmer ☐
   f. To get a new job ☐
   g. To be more confident ☐
   h. To change your lifestyle ☐
   i. To look good on holiday ☐
   j. Because you're getting married ☐

4. Now ask yourself if there are any reasons why you want to remain overweight. Write them down below. You may not at first be able to think of any advantages in hanging on to excess weight, but read this chapter, then ask yourself the same question again. ....
....
....
....
....

5. Are there any reasons why you think you can't lose weight? If so, list them below.

....

....

....

Check your answer to question 1.
TIME TO BE HONEST: Do you avoid looking at yourself full length in a mirror or catching a glimpse of yourself in shop windows? If so, the chances are you are trying to avoid facing up to a shape you don't admire. Take a good look at yourself in a mirror from all angles, standing relaxed without holding your breath. Remember that however weighty your problem you *can* do something about it now that you have admitted it is there.

Check your answer to question 2.
WHAT YOU SHOULD AIM AT: Use the charts below as a guide rather than a rigid rule. Your personal ideal weight could be 4.5 kg (10 lb) or so either side of the medium-frame figure given for your height. Heights are minus footwear; but these ideal-average weights include an allowance of 2 to 3 lb (about 1 kg) for light indoor clothing.

IF YOU'RE A WOMAN			IF YOU'RE A MAN		
4ft-10 (1.47 m)	**7st-7**	(47.5 kg)	**5ft-2** (1.57 m)	**9st-0**	(57 kg)
4ft-11 (1.50 m)	**7st-9**	(48.5 kg)	**5ft-3** (1.60 m)	**9st-4**	(59 kg)
5ft-0 (1.52 m)	**7st-12**	(50 kg)	**5ft-4** (1.63 m)	**9st-7**	(60.5 kg)
5ft-1 (1.55 m)	**8st-1**	(51.5 kg)	**5ft-5** (1.65 m)	**9st-10**	(61.5 kg)
5ft-2 (1.57 m)	**8st-4**	(52.5 kg)	**5ft-6** (1.68 m)	**9st-13**	(63 kg)
5ft-3 (1.60 m)	**8st-7**	(54 kg)	**5ft-7** (1.70 m)	**10st-3**	(65 kg)
5ft-4 (1.63 m)	**8st-11**	(56 kg)	**5ft-8** (1.73 m)	**10st-8**	(67 kg)
5ft-5 (1.65 m)	**9st-0**	(57 kg)	**5ft-9** (1.75 m)	**10st-12**	(69 kg)
5ft-6 (1.68 m)	**9st-5**	(59.5 kg)	**5ft-10** (1.78 m)	**11st-2**	(71 kg)
5ft-7 (1.70 m)	**9st-9**	(61 kg)	**5ft-11** (1.80 m)	**11st-7**	(73 kg)
5ft-8 (1.73 m)	**9st-13**	(63 kg)	**6ft-0** (1.83 m)	**11st-11**	(75 kg)
5ft-9 (1.75 m)	**10st-3**	(65 kg)	**6ft-1** (1.85 m)	**12st-1**	(76.5 kg)
5ft-10 (1.78 m)	**10st-7**	(66.5 kg)	**6ft-2** (1.88 m)	**12st-6**	(79 kg)
5ft-11 (1.80 m)	**10st-11**	(68.5 kg)	**6ft-3** (1.90 m)	**12st-11**	(81 kg)
6ft-0 (1.83 m)	**11st-1**	(70.5 kg)	**6ft-4** (1.93 m)	**13st-2**	(83.5 kg)

FORGET ABOUT BIG BONES: The size of your bones is not a good indication of whether your frame is small, medium or large. Neither are your wrist, hand or shoe measurements. Consider instead your skeleton's spread. If you have a rangy frame it will need more flesh to cover it than if you have a narrow frame.

PREVENTION IS BETTER THAN CURE: Even if you have decided that you really have too little excess weight to worry about, check the list below. These are the most frequent times that weight gain occurs, even in women who have never suffered a surplus-weight problem.

Getting married

It's very natural when you are setting up home that you want to show off your cooking skills, or perhaps you have always left that sort of thing to Mum and now you need to experiment for yourself. Most people, men and women, enjoy cooking for others more than they enjoy cooking for themselves, so the early years of marriage are one of the prime times when weight gains occur. Remember that good food doesn't have to be fattening. Get yourself a low-calorie cookbook or try out some of the recipes given in the diets in this book. Read the Calorie Cutter's Guide starting on page 172 and you will see how very simple changes can save you hundreds of calories without you – or your partner – feeling in any way deprived.

Becoming a Mum

If you eat for two when you are pregnant, you'll probably end up with a post-birth bulge that you didn't bargain for. Here's some advice to help you avoid this.

EAT WELL, BUT WISELY: It is more important that you make sure you are eating a very healthy diet while you are pregnant than to increase the quantity you eat. See 'Improve Your Diet', page 40, for a list of the basic food groups. The basis of good nutrition is to eat a varied diet that will supply you with all the vitamins and minerals you require. When you are pregnant and breast-feeding you need more calcium and iron than usual. Gradually increasing your consumption of high-fibre foods will help if you are suffering from constipation (see High-Fibre Diet, page 50). To increase your calcium intake drink at least 600 ml (1 pint) of milk a day (skimmed milk is just as high in calcium as whole milk). Also choose extra portions from the milk and cheese list on page 40. The easiest way to increase your iron intake is to eat a liver or kidney meal two or three times a week. All meat contains iron, although it is not as rich a source as offal. Many breakfast cereals can also provide iron. As vitamin C aids iron absorption, you may get more out of your breakfast if you drink a glass of fresh fruit juice with it or add fruit to your cereal bowl.

KEEP AN EYE ON YOUR WEIGHT: Experts estimate that you should gain 0.6 kg (1½ lb) during the first 10 weeks of pregnancy and 2.5 kg (5½ lb) during the next 10 weeks, that's just half a stone over the first 5 months. Gaining another 6.8 kg (15 lb) fairly evenly over the final 20 weeks of pregnancy adds up to a total of 9.9 kg (22 lb). This weight is made up of the baby, surrounding fluid, items such as the umbilical cord and placenta, and a small amount of fat. If you seem to be gaining more than this, take a look at your food intake. The recommended calorie requirement for a pregnant woman is 2,400 calories a day, so don't try to reduce your food intake too severely, but follow the healthy eating advice above, and make sure you are not eating lots of sugary or fatty foods. Discuss any weight control plan with your doctor first. Make sure that any weight control regime you follow is devised especially for pregnant women by reliable medical experts.

BABY BULGE

❛During my pregnancy, my weight soared to 13st-7, and when I left hospital after baby's arrival I was still very heavy. Quite how heavy only struck me when, having had to leave baby in hospital for a few extra days, I found that kind people kept asking me when my baby was due.❜

DON'T DO AEROBICS! You are likely to get less active as you get further into pregnancy which could be the cause of an excess weight gain. But now is not the time to look for an exercise solution to the problem. Exercises can be very beneficial to your well-being and help with the birth of your baby, but you need to do the special ones taught at ante-natal exercise classes. These exercises are mainly for stretching and strengthening muscles, correcting pregnancy posture and helping you to relax; they are not the sort to burn up lots of calories.

Middle Age

Reaching any particular age is no excuse to become heavier. But many people find that as they get older they have more difficulty staying in trim. There are a number of reasons for this. From the early 20s onwards everyone's metabolism starts to slow down a little, which may mean that you will not burn up the same number of calories that you did when you were younger. Also as you get older you may well become less active – you start walking rather than running up the stairs, spend fewer evenings at the disco and more time entertaining friends to dinner. However, there is absolutely no reason why you shouldn't be just as trim when middle-aged as you were when you were 20. You can decrease your calorie intake (and that needn't mean decreasing the amount you eat) or increase your calorie expenditure by taking more exercise (see the exercise chapter, starting on page 210), or a bit of both.

Going on the Pill

Some women experience a weight gain when they start taking oral contraceptives, other women have no problems at all. When a woman starts taking the Pill her body is to some degree permanently in an artificial state of pregnancy and there may be an increase in body fluid or protein tissue, although this could not account for a weight gain of more than 4.5 kg (10 lb). Signs of fluid retention are a bloated feeling and sometimes puffiness in legs, arms and fingers. If fluid retention is the problem, then your doctor may suggest switching to another pill. But some research suggests that for a number of psychological and physical reasons, some women just start to eat more when they start taking oral contraceptives. A slight increase in food consumption often goes unnoticed, but if you have been eating exactly the right number of calories to keep you slim that increase could be enough to cause a steady weight gain.

The menopause or hormonal changes

The menopause can make your hormone balance go somewhat haywire for a while, and because of this, weight control may be a bit more difficult temporarily. Another time hormonal changes can affect weight is after a hysterectomy if the operation involves the removal of the ovaries. It's possible in this case that your doctor may give you replacement hormones, gradually tapering off the dosage to mimic the effects of the natural menopause. It is difficult to do this in a precisely balanced way and your metabolism may be temporarily altered to some extent. If you find yourself gaining weight you may need to control your food intake more carefully or increase your activity, or both. The good news is that your hormones and metabolism will eventually settle down.

Giving up smoking

It is true that some people who give up smoking develop weight problems. Smoking leads to a number of changes in the body's chemistry, including an increase in the amount of some of its hormones. When smoking stops, it seems that it takes some time for this effect to wear off and in the meantime the body demands more food to satisfy this disturbed chemistry. Another reason is that putting food into the mouth satisfies part of the basic 'cause' of smoking, which is what the psychologists call oral satisfaction. A cigarette or sweet may be a sort of adult 'dummy' serving to pacify stress or boredom. There is also the fact that food tends to taste much more appetising when your taste buds are no longer 'kippered'. Fortunately, any proper diet plan will reduce surplus weight just as effectively for an ex-smoker as for the slimmer who has never indulged in tobacco.

CHEW ON IT! There is a special chewing gum which slowly releases nicotine from a resin and so allows for a gradual reduction of nicotine levels in the blood; this reduces the risk of withdrawal symptoms. It is currently available only on prescription from a doctor. If the withdrawal symptoms are not too severe, however, it is better to chew on a stick of sugarless chewing gum which will supply oral satisfaction for just 10 calories a stick.

GETTING MOTIVATED

Check your answers to question 3 on the questionnaire.

GIVE GETTING SLIM TOP PRIORITY: It seems cruel to say this, but unless getting slim is one of the most important things in your life, then you may be wasting your time. It takes determination to slim and unless you give your campaign top priority, you will find all sorts of excuses for giving up.

DON'T DO IT TO PLEASE A PARTNER: Slim for yourself. A weight loss programme which is designed to please a partner is doomed to failure. Sooner or later an apparent ingratitude, lack of understanding or tact will disappoint or infuriate you into abandoning your diet. You must do it for yourself.

KEEP A GOAL IN MIND: Without some sort of motivation you will have no reason to exert the self-discipline that dieting inevitably involves, so set yourself a target. You may want to get slim for a summer holiday, or be a slender bride. Whatever the goal is, make sure it is achievable.

ABANDON SELF-DISGUST: Dislike of your own appearance can be a major motivation for starting a diet, but if it is prolonged and excessive it may prove a serious drawback to sustained slimming. The woman who holds a low opinion of herself will give up her diet when she is faced with a tiny setback.

KEEP BATTLING ON: Few slimmers succeed in keeping to their diet without ever cheating. Remember that if you eat an extra slice of toast and jam, all you have done is eaten a hundred or so extra calories. You will just have to work harder the next day to undo the damage.

SWITCH FROM WILLPOWER TO SELF-CONTROL: An example of willpower is drooling in front of the baker's shop window and resolving not to buy your favourite cake. Self-control consists of sending someone else to buy your bread, while you shop in less dangerous zones.

LOSE YOUR OLD HANG-UPS: Start seeing yourself as a worthwhile person who can cope with the ups and downs that life inevitably throws your way. The old you probably faced a blue day with a binge: the new you will find other cheer-up tactics, such as making an appointment to get your hair restyled, or calling a friend and suggesting a trip to the theatre or to see a film.

REWARD YOURSELF FOR SMALL SUCCESSES: To make sure your diet doesn't seem endless, give yourself small treats for weekly weight loss – but make sure your rewards are non-food ones. Your weight problem may well have started when your mother gave you sweets and chocolates as a reward for being good, or as a comforter when you were upset.

SUCCESS ENCOURAGES SUCCESS: There are many things you can reward yourself for when you are dieting apart from a good weekly weight loss. Give yourself points for sticking to your diet for one day, for resisting a particularly tempting food offering, or even succeeding in limiting your food indulgences on a day out. When you have accumulated a certain number of points you can promise yourself some kind of treat. (See page 27 for how to chart your weight loss, and pages 200 to 201 for keeping a record of your eating habits.)

ACCEPT THAT SOME DAYS WILL BE DIFFICULT: Your moods often change and problems, large and small, may arise. If you expect every day to be plain sailing, you will founder at the first little ripple, let alone the storm that is bound to come.

Check your answer to question 4.

DON'T USE BEING FAT AS AN EXCUSE: If you have ever said to yourself 'I'll get myself a job as soon as I've lost some weight', or 'When I'm slimmer I'll go to an exercise class', you could well be using your excess pounds as an excuse for not doing either. If you are using a weight problem as a convenient way to avoid taking positive action, your diet campaign doesn't stand a chance.

TAKE COURAGE AND CROSS YOUR WEIGHT-LOSS BARRIER: Many people claim that they can't slim below a certain weight, and that barrier will often be located at a weight at which they are just approaching slimness. The fear of getting slim and becoming an extra-attractive woman can be a major factor in creating this barrier. Over the years you may have opted out of making an effort to be in the swim. Relationships with other women have developed on a comfortable, uncompetitive basis. Fears that getting slim will change all this often stop you trying.

DON'T FEAR CHANGE: A fear of change is not an unusual human trait. It may be particularly strong among many overweight people. There is a general feeling that however bad the present may be, the future is still an unknown quantity and may be even worse. But if you are not prepared to take the risk and change your shape, you'll never know how good it could have been.

Check your answer to question 5.

STOP MAKING EXCUSES: Research on overweight people shows that those who put the cause of their problem squarely where it belongs and admit honestly that they have been eating too much, are more likely to succeed in getting slim than those who cite other people or such uncontrollable factors as 'glands' or 'fluid retention' as the reason for their being overweight.

DON'T BLAME YOUR LIFESTYLE: Overweight people often use their circumstances as an excuse not to lose weight: 'I eat because I'm under pressure at work'; 'I have to attend lots of business lunches'; 'My husband's often away and I can't be bothered to cook well-balanced, low-calorie meals just for myself'. However, if you are determined enough, there are ways round these problems. Identify your problems from those listed below and see our tactics for success. See also 'Turning Over a New Leaf', starting on page 161, for hints on how to break bad eating habits.

YOUR PROBLEM: You're in a job where your diet must survive trolley snacks, canteen lunches, stodgy sandwiches, frequent birthdays, lack of shopping-time.

YOUR TACTICS: Plan ahead with your calorie guide at the back of this book. Do one big weekend shop. Stock up with crispbreads, low-calorie fillings for slimline packed lunches, low-calorie drinks and soups, low-fat yogurt, lots of fruit. Aim to prepare an enticing lunch-box each morning, but avoid crisis if your early-rising system breaks down by keeping a basic stock of crispbreads, small jars of spread, and so on in a plastic box at work. Top up with natural yogurt or fruit from the canteen.

When the birthday tray comes round, choose the least destructive cake – meringue or éclair – and count it into your daily calorie allowance as a legitimate treat.

Realize in advance that your time of least resistance is likely to be when you stagger home. So plan to meet it with ready-prepared raw vegetable nibbles waiting in the fridge and low-calorie soup needing only to be heated to help tide you over until you've had time to prepare supper.

YOUR PROBLEM: You're stuck for hours each week in the kitchen, with wall-to-wall food, children, leftovers, orange juice, crisps, chocolate, biscuits, etc.
YOUR TACTICS: Stop trying to fit your diet into the family catering. For as long as it takes, treat yourself as an individual. Plan out a week's main meals for yourself (if eating baby portions of the family's meals hasn't worked for you before, it won't work for you now). Build a personal programme of simply-prepared, substantial meals, with large quantities of unrestricted items, such as vegetables, salads, low-calorie drinks. Shop for nourishing, no-bother, boil-in-the-bag meals and individual frozen packs. Have your day's diet sheet pinned up to greet you each morning. Prepare main items and accompaniments early in the day, when your morale is high.

Savour your meals before the family has theirs; then you can serve them with no fierce hunger pangs calling for superhuman control.

When it comes to buying family treats, beware the bumper pack of choc-bars with two or three 'to spare' or the iced bun rings with two more portions than there are people! Buy singly, allocating just one per person.

YOUR PROBLEM: You live alone – along with boredom, lack of encouragement and the temptation to pick and eat your way through the day.
YOUR TACTICS: Turn your slimming campaign into a full-scale, time-absorbing project. Prepare a detailed programme of your meals for the coming week. Consider a diet involving five or six mini-meals a day to absorb your time and attention. Check calories carefully.

Keep a food diary, giving blow-by-blow descriptions of your battle progress: time of meals, where you ate them, how long they took, temptations met and overcome, temptations met and not overcome, suggestions for side-stepping them in future. Save your daily treat until the end of the day to act as both a goal and a reward. Choose something you particularly enjoy.

Keep as busy as you can. Look for extra interests, new hobbies. Get out of the house as much as you can. If you're stuck for something to do, offer your help in some charity scheme.

YOUR PROBLEM: Your job involves unsociable hours and, consequently, peculiar meal-times – a changing pattern of shifts, perhaps.

YOUR TACTICS: Accept that you'll be eating at off-beat times. Remember it's *what* you eat within 24 hours, not *when* you eat it, that decides your shape. Find a flexible diet, offering interchangeable, quickly-prepared meals. Map out a programme for seven 24-hour periods. Make use of boil-in-the-bag packs, calorie-conscious sandwiches, meals on toast, single frozen portions. Eat your meals in whatever order happens to suit your work-pattern. If it helps, forget labels like breakfast, lunch and dinner: your digestion registers food, not names. Have quick, low-calorie life-savers at hand to keep binges at bay when you're tired.

YOUR PROBLEM: Lack of cash for 'special dieting'.

YOUR TACTICS: Your top priority is to learn more about nutrition, then you will soon see that old ideas about dieting on expensive steak, etc, never had genuine validity and are, in any case, completely outdated. Aim at a low-fat, low-sugar, high-fibre regime: it's by far the best for your health, shape – and purse.

Now do your homework. Read through the calorie and dieting lists to find low-cost foods which you enjoy.

Make the most of crispbreads, bread, baked or boiled potatoes, baked beans and other pulses, fish portions, curd and cottage cheeses, all varieties of pasta. Count the calories and see the difference!

DIET ONE DAY AT A TIME: Don't start worrying about what is going to happen tomorrow or next week. Dismiss what happened yesterday as a thing of the past and start each day with new resolve.

READY FOR TAKE-OFF ▼

HOW LOW SHOULD YOU AIM?

CHECK YOUR TARGET WEIGHT on page 11. Remember that your personal ideal may be 10lb more than the average given, or 10lb less. If you were once slim, you will know at what weight you felt best. If you have never been slim, then aim for 10lb more than the weight given and reassess your figure when you get there. Weights can be deceiving and a much better guide to excess fat is the simple pinch test. If you can grab handfuls of flab round your middle, at the tops of arms, at tops of legs, then you still have a way to go.

SET SMALL TARGETS: If you have a lot of weight to lose it is more encouraging to set yourself small targets to achieve so that the task doesn't seem endless. Aim at first to lose, say, 1 stone, then when you have achieved that goal, set yourself a new target. Give yourself a reward when you reach each target.

GET READY TO READJUST: If you need to lose several stones, wait until one or two of those have disappeared before setting your final target.

DON'T SLIM TOO FAR: If you have set your ideal weight too low and start to look a bit bony, don't go any further. You may have the sort of frame that can carry an extra 4 or 5lb.

DON'T EXPECT TO LOSE THE SAME EVERY WEEK: Weekly weight losses tend to fluctuate so keep in mind that any weight loss is good, even if it is not quite what you were expecting. Learn to look on the positive side of even the smallest loss.

DISCOUNT FOR PMT/PMS DAYS: For many women a small weight loss may correspond with pre-menstrual tension, or pre-menstrual syndrome as it is now called. During this time temporary fluid retention will often cause the scales to register little, if any, apparent weight loss. Emotionally this may be a bad time to keep smiling, but try. Next week the scales could well register a much larger weight loss than you expect.

STOP WORRYING ABOUT WATER RETENTION: The retention of small amounts of water during a woman's natural menstrual cycle is temporary. It is not necessary to take normal fluid retention into account when dieting: healthy kidneys do a remarkably good job of keeping the body's water level exactly right.

DON'T TRY TO BE PERFECT: It is unrealistic to expect a perfect weight loss every week and the person who sets up this goal is doomed to disappointment. A natural consequence of this is depression and depression leads to giving up dieting.

A 2 TO 3LB WEEKLY LOSS IS A GOOD AVERAGE: Many people, particularly those with a considerable amount to lose, report quite dramatic weight losses in the first week. This can happen because you are losing a store of excess water along with the fat. However, this weight-shedding will probably slow down to a more normal 2-3 lb a week later on.

EXPECT TO SLOW DOWN AS YOU GET SLIMMER: Heavily overweight people can lose weight faster initially simply because, being so heavy, they burn up more calories in moving their bodies about from place to place. As you get slimmer you lose this calorie-burning advantage and either need to cut calories or increase your activity to maintain the same weight loss.

MAKE SURE THAT YOUR BATHROOM SCALES STAND EVENLY: A slight sloping surface literally tips the scales – sometimes in your favour, sometimes against it. Scales also need to stand on a hard surface: so if your bathroom is carpeted, make sure you put a piece of wood under the scales.

BATHROOM SCALES CAN BE INACCURATE: You can check them by weighing yourself on a balance scale at the chemist. But even if your scales are inaccurate, they are likely to show up the same discrepancy every time you weigh yourself, so they will still record weight loss.

STAND STRAIGHT ON THE SCALES: Have your weight evenly balanced on both feet and as close to the centre of the scale as possible. Rocking backwards and forwards can actually change a scale's reading – try yours and see the variation.

WEIGH YOURSELF UNCLOTHED: It is best to weigh yourself unclothed, but if you do wear any garments, make sure you wear similar ones each time. Of course, the less you wear, the less you weigh and that itself can be cheering. Slimming Club members have been observed shedding rings and jewellery before stepping on the scales and one anxious dieter admitted removing her false teeth! But remember that if you try to disguise a weight gain by weighing yourself in lighter clothing, you are only cheating yourself.

DON'T WEIGH EVERY DAY: It may be difficult to resist leaping on the scales each day to see if your diet is working, but because body weight fluctuates all the time you may well find that the scales don't register a loss. A once-a-week weigh-in is a much better indication of progress.

WEIGH AT THE SAME TIME OF DAY: Most people are 3 or 4 lb heavier at night than in the morning, and unless you have starved all day (not advisable) you will probably find this is true for you. The heavier evening weight is partly because of food eaten earlier; and partly because after you have absorbed this food into your body cells – especially the carbohydrate part of it – you retain some additional water. During the night your body will continue burning up that food and getting rid of water. Some will evaporate in your breath and some will be passed in your urine the following morning.

NO PERMISSION REQUIRED: If you are overweight and in normal health it is quite unnecessary to ask your doctor's permission to go on a reducing diet that is 1,000 calories or more. But make sure that the diet you choose to follow is nutritionally balanced and has been devised by experts who are concerned for your health as well as slimness.

DO ASK YOUR DOCTOR: If you have any health worries or a condition that requires a special diet, such as diabetes, ask your doctor before embarking on a reducing diet. If there is a particular diet you would like to follow, show it to him or her for approval. But take his/her advice on the eating plan that is best for your health.

STOP BLAMING GLANDS: If you have a glandular disorder then you will have already seen your doctor with more serious symptoms than overweight. Glands are the body organs which produce hormones and some disturbance or disease affecting, say, the thyroid gland could indeed cause a gain in body weight. But in such a case being fat would be the least of one's worries.

Chart Your Success
It is very encouraging to see proof of those excess pounds reducing. Draw up your own progress chart and pin it on your bathroom wall, or fill in the chart on the right. First write in the number of stones you now weigh at the chart's top left corner. Then ring round the pounds figure below, so that your precise starting weight is recorded. After each week's weigh-in, put a dot in the appropriate column. Join up the dots and see your weight come down. If it falls off the chart (congratulations!) it's easy to rule up another one and take it from the top again.

PROGRESS CHART

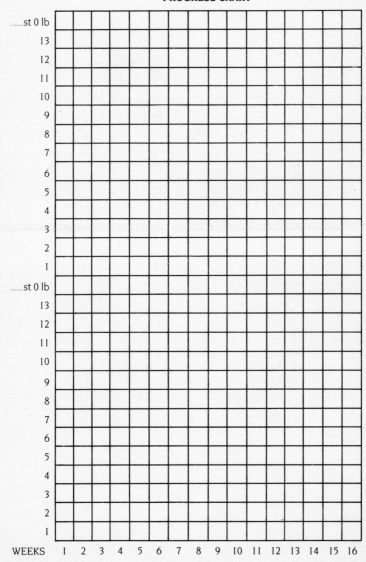

WEEKS	1	2	3	4	5	6	7	8	9	10	11	12	13	14	15	16

CHAPTER 2

THE DIET DILEMMA

WHICH DIET IS FOR YOU?

FILL IN THIS QUESTIONNAIRE. When you have filled in the
questionnaire you will be able to link your answers with the
hints which follow. These will help you to decide which diet
will suit you best. The questionnaire will also identify your
danger foods and assess if you should be following a healthier
pattern of eating.

1. In the past twelve months, have you dieted:
   a. Consistently? ☐
   b. Occasionally? ☐
   c. Only for a few days or not at all? ☐

2. How long ago did you start to put on weight?
   a. Twelve months ago or less ☐
   b. Overweight since childhood ☐
   c. Between 1 and 10 years ☐

3. Why do you want to lose weight?
   a. To be healthier ☐
   b. To look more attractive ☐
   c. To please family or friends ☐

4. On a normal day do you regularly eat substantial portions
   of any of the following:
   a. Fried foods? ☐
   b. Potatoes? ☐
   c. Bread? ☐
   d. Cheese? ☐
   e. Cream and milk? ☐
   f. Fruit and vegetables? ☐
   g. Cereals? ☐

5. Do you regularly eat any of the following as between-meal snacks:
- **a.** Sweets? ☐
- **b.** Chocolates? ☐
- **c.** Nuts? ☐
- **d.** Crisps and corn snacks? ☐
- **e.** Fresh fruit? ☐
- **f.** Raw vegetables? ☐

6. Do you drink alcoholic drinks:
- **a.** Every day? ☐
- **b.** Once or twice a week? ☐
- **c.** Very occasionally? ☐
- **d.** Never? ☐

7. Do you drink fruit juices or sugary, fizzy drinks:
- **a.** Every day? ☐
- **b.** Once or twice a week? ☐
- **c.** Occasionally? ☐
- **d.** Never? ☐

8. Do you take sugar:
- **a.** In tea? ☐
- **b.** In coffee? ☐
- **c.** In other drinks? ☐
- **d.** Not at all? ☐

9. If you have failed on a diet, was it because you were tempted by any of the following items:
- **a.** Sweet foods? ☐
- **b.** Savoury foods? ☐
- **c.** Alcohol? ☐

10. Is there any one food you find particularly difficult to give up during dieting? If so, what is it?..............

11. Please tick the description that most applies to you:
- **a.** I eat at roughly set times each day. ☐
- **b.** My mealtimes vary, depending on what I'm doing. ☐
- **c.** I eat little during the day and most food after 5.30 pm. ☐

d. I eat my main meal in the middle of the day and have
lighter meals in the evening. ☐
e. I eat little and often. ☐
f. I eat when I feel like it. ☐

12. Is there any particular time of day when you are most
tempted to cheat on your diet?..............

13. Do you go out to work:
a. Full time? ☐
b. Part time? ☐
c. Not at all? ☐

14. Are you married?..............

15. Have you any children?..............

16. In an average day, how much do you eat of the following foods:
a. Milk, cheese, yogurt, butter?...
b. Meat, poultry, fish, eggs, beans? ....
c. Vegetables and fruit? ....
d. Bread, cereals and pasta? ....

YOUR WEIGHT IS IMPORTANT: The heavier you are the more calories
you need to move your body from A to B, so your weight is a very
important factor in calculating the calorie total at which you will
lose weight. If you are Mr or Ms Average you need roughly
15 calories per pound to maintain your weight. So, if you weigh
63 kg (10 stones) you can eat about 2,100 calories without gaining
weight, and if you are 51 kg (8 stones) that figure will come down to
1,680 calories. But the calculations are complicated by the fact that
not every individual has the same basal or resting metabolic rate
(see below).

BREATHING BURNS UP CALORIES: Your basal metabolic rate is a
measure of the total energy (or calories) your body needs just to
stay alive. Even when you are lying in bed your heart is beating, you
are breathing in and out and automatically controlling your body
temperature. The average woman has a basal metabolic rate of
1,400 calories a day. But there is some evidence that BMR could be

as low as 800 calories for some women. An average man has a basal metabolic rate of 1,700 calories a day.

ACTIVITY COUNTS TOO: In addition to BMR calories, you burn up extra doing certain activities (see Chapter 4). Some activities, such as sitting reading, will burn up few more calories than if you were lying in bed, while a strenuous sport will burn up many more. The average woman will use up 700 calories a day in activity and a man will use up about 1,000 calories. But again.there are enormous differences between individuals. Some people rarely exercise, go everywhere by car, sit at a desk all day. Other individuals may cycle to work, have a physically demanding job, or exercise regularly. Here's an example of how the calorie balance sheet may look:

Ms A

Calories needed to keep the body functioning	1,400
Calories used in activities	700
Number of calories used up in a day	2,100
Number of calories eaten	2,100

Result: No weight gain or loss

Ms B

Calories needed to keep the body functioning	1,200
Calories used in activities	900
Number of calories used up in a day	2,100
Number of calories eaten	1,500

Result: Weight loss

Mr C

Calories needed to keep the body functioning	1,700
Calories used in activities	1,000
Number of calories used up in a day	2,700
Number of calories eaten	3,500

Result: Weight gain

CALCULATE YOUR OWN CALORIE ALLOWANCE: If you are overweight you have been eating more calories than your body needs so it has stored the fat surplus to call upon in times of food shortage. When you reduce your calorie intake you will be drawing on that store. All men and most women will start using up that fat store if they eat no more than 1,500 calories a day. But to achieve a speedy weight loss, some women may have to cut down to 1,000 calories.

Look back at your answers to the first three questions on the questionnaire. Here's how you can use them to calculate your own calorie allowance:

1. If you are a woman with 19 kg (3 stones) or more to lose, you will probably lose weight at a steady rate keeping to 1,500 calories daily. If you are a man you can allow yourself 1,750 calories. But if you have been dieting consistently for some time, check below.

2. If you are a woman with under 6.3 kg (1 stone) to lose, you may need to keep to a strict 1,000 calories daily to lose weight. Men with just a little to lose need go no lower than 1,250 calories.

3. If you have between 6.3 kg (1 stone) and 19 kg (3 stones) to lose, you should set your calorie limit halfway between these allowances, for example 1,250 for women, 1,500 for men.

DON'T CUT CALORIES TOO DRASTICALLY: Generally 1,000 calories a day is the lowest allowance that should be set for a diet followed without medical supervision. This does not mean that you are courting disaster by eating a couple of hundred calories less on days when you happen to find it easy to be very strict. However, if you are planning a prolonged slimming campaign at very low calorie levels, it is wise to get your doctor's permission first.

Check your answer to question 1.

ALLOW FOR SOME SLOWING DOWN: During prolonged periods of dieting the body shows a tendency to adjust to its lowered calorie intake and to burn up less calories. This was useful as a primitive survival mechanism, but makes life difficult for slimmers in modern-day Western societies! If you have been dieting steadily for twelve months or more, you may find it necessary to reduce your calories a little lower than the totals on page 34 (but not below 1,000, see next hint). If you have dieted occasionally or just for a few days your body is unlikely to have made any adjustment. If you dieted for a long period several months ago, then returned to 'normal' eating, your body will have re-adjusted to a higher calorie requirement.

Check your answer to question 2.

ASSESSING YOUR METABOLISM: If you have been overweight since childhood there is a strong possibility that you have a lower than normal metabolic rate. But this doesn't mean you can't lose weight – it just means that you may have to work a little harder and be a little stricter to get those pounds off. Do not cut your calories to below 1,000 calories a day (except as a short-term emergency measure), but work at increasing the calories you burn up (see Chapter 4). If you have recently put on weight it is likely that some changed habits have increased your calorie consumption (see pages 13 to 16 for possibilities). If your weight problem began during the last few years, sit down and try to work out what changed in your life a few months before you noticed you were putting on weight. Did you give up playing a sport? Did you start snack-eating when the family left home and it no longer seemed worthwhile cooking proper meals? Have you started a job which involves eating out regularly? If you can find a reason for your weight gain it is easier to work out a plan to resolve the problem.

Check your answer to question 3.
PAY ATTENTION TO WHAT YOU EAT: You want to be healthy as well as look more attractive when you lose weight, so it is important to pay attention to what you eat as well as counting the calories. The secret of good nutrition, to provide all the minerals, vitamins and protein we require, is simply variety.

CHOOSE GOOD AND SLIMMING FOODS: When you are dieting make sure you include some low-fat, protein-rich foods such as white fish, lean meat, offal, eggs, skimmed milk and cottage cheese. Eat plenty of vegetables and fruit and this should ensure your supply of nutrients. (If in answer to question 6 you have ticked that you want to lose weight to please family and friends, you will probably find it very hard to diet. Check the section on Getting Motivated, page 17).

Check your answer to question 4.
IDENTIFY YOUR FATTENERS: If in the course of a normal day you regularly eat substantial portions of fried foods, cheese, cream and whole milk, you can be fairly certain this is the reason for your weight problem. If you eat bread with lashings of butter or margarine, potatoes fried or mashed with butter, cereals served with full cream milk, or vegetables covered in buttery sauces, you can't expect to stay slim. Fatty foods are the highest calorie foods of all and need to be strictly limited if you wish to lose weight.

Check your answer to question 5.

MAYBE YOU DON'T NEED TO DIET: Quite minor modifications to a person's regular eating routine can mean really sizeable weight reductions. Over a year the number of calories saved can be staggering. If you regularly eat the following items, see how many pounds you could lose by giving them up (providing, of course, you don't substitute them with other high-calorie items).

Cut out one chocolate a day and you will lose 2 kg (4 lb) in a year: An average chocolate from a popular assortment amounts to 35 calories. If you just need something sweet to chew, consider swapping it for a wine gum (5 calories) or a stick of sugarless chewing gum (10 calories). Remember, though, that sweet things are bad for your teeth as well as your diet and are best avoided altogether.

Cut out one small packet of dry roasted peanuts every day and you will lose 13.5 kg (30 lb) in a year: Dry roasted peanuts don't look as though they can be very high in calories, but a small 50 g pack, which you could nibble without noticing, costs 285 calories. Switching from salted peanuts to a 50 g packet of mixed nuts and raisins would mean a daily saving of 120 calories and a loss of 5.8 kg (13 lb) in a year.

Cut out one small packet of crisps a day and you will lose 6 kg (14 lb) in a year: Though, at an average of 130 calories, a small packet of crisps isn't a large daily indulgence, giving it up can still mean losing a stone in a year. If a nibble of this kind means a lot in your life, you could halve its fattening potential by switching from crisps to a lower-calorie packet of corn snacks.

Check your answer to question 6.

Cut out one pint of beer a day and lose 8.5 kg (19 lb) in a year: This loss is based on an average figure of 180 calories for a pint of bitter or pale ale. Lager averages 170 calories a pint so a switch in this direction won't be much help and don't consider a change to diabetic lager which could cost 210 calories a pint. Examining your usual intake pays off, particularly in the case of high-calorie social habits. Just cutting two pints to one or a whole to a half could trim many a pub tum.

Cut out one glass of sweet white wine a day and lose 5.8 kg (13 lb) a year: If you average two glasses of wine a day, then cutting out one of them could mean almost a stone off in a year, just another illustration of the weighty price you pay for alcohol. Sparkling spa or mineral water served in a crystal glass with ice and lemon, looks special and tastes refreshing, yet contains no calories. Iced tap water plus lemon garnish is another alternative to consider. Cutting out half a glass of wine a day (i.e. drinking half wine and half water) amounts to a loss of 2.9 kg (6½ lb) a year.

Check your answer to question 7.

Cut out one pint of fruit juice a day and save 10 kg (23 lb) a year: Fruit juice always seems so innocent and it is easy to forget the calories in a drink. But give up just two long glasses of fruit juice a day and drink a low-calorie squash instead and you'll cut your calorie intake from about 110 calories a half-pint to no more than 10 calories.

Cut out one can of cola a day and lose 5.8 kg (13 lb) in a year: You don't have to give up drinking coke, just swap to a diet cola. A cola, depending on the make, costs from 130 calories for a 330 ml (11.6 fl oz) can, to 145 calories, but a diet cola contains no calories.

> **SPECIAL DRINK**
> Before each meal, I ceremonially pour a low-calorie cola or something similar into a tall, handsome glass and add ice – make it 'important', so to speak – then slowly savour it. This, I find, curbs my appetite enormously.

Check your answer to question 8.

Cut out two heaped teaspoons of sugar in six cups of coffee or tea a day and lose 29 kg (64 lb) in a year: Giving up two heaped teaspoons of sugar in six drinks a day is a pretty painless change when you see the result. You can soften the sacrifice by using artificial sweeteners, but there is an added bonus if you can do without them in that long before the year is up it's likely that your tastebuds will actually prefer drinks unsweetened. Even giving up just one heaped teaspoon six times a day equals an annual loss of 14.5 kg (32 lb).

Check your answer to questions 9 and 10.

IDENTIFY DANGER FOODS: If a previous diet failed because you indulged in certain foods, or if giving up some favourite snack makes dieting a particularly grim affair for you, it may be best to try

to incorporate some of your danger foods into your weekly menus. But make sure that just one bite won't start off a craving for more. Some chocolate lovers, for example, find a small bar will satisfy their craving; while other people find that just a taste of chocolate encourages them to indulge more. If you identify your danger foods before you start to diet, you can plan how you will cope with them.

Check your answers to questions 11 to 16.
PICK YOUR NORMAL EATING PATTERN: The diet that is successful for you is the one that most closely follows your normal pattern of eating. If you are an erratic eater, for example, it is unrealistic to start a diet that insists you eat three set meals a day. If you go to work you need to pick a diet that will allow you a packed lunch or a meal out.

*I*MPROVE <u>YOUR</u> DIET

A slimming campaign is an ideal time to start some healthy eating habits which you can continue when all those excess pounds have disappeared. Foods can be split into five basic groups. To ensure a nutritionally balanced diet you should eat some items from four of the groups (A-D below) each day – the fifth group consists of foods eaten mainly for pleasure that should be kept to a minimum because they have little nutritional value (see high-calorie, low nutrients group in the food chart on page 43).

A. Milk and Cheese
If your usual menus include some helpings of milk, cheese, yogurt, butter and margarine you will be getting some protein, vitamins A and D, B vitamins, calcium, phosphorus, magnesium and zinc. But you could also be consuming more fat than is considered healthy. Choose skimmed milk, low-fat cheese, low-fat yogurt and low-fat spread and you will halve fat and calories. All you will lose nutritionally are the fat-soluble vitamins A and D in whole milk (although some manufacturers now put these back into skimmed milk). In any event you will get A and D vitamins from cheese, low-fat spread and other diet sources. Vitamin D is also obtained from sunlight (ultraviolet rays enable the skin to form vitamin D). As a rough guide, allow yourself 2 portions a day from this group of foods. Here is a list of serving sizes:

300 ml (½ pint) skimmed milk
50 g (2 oz) low-fat hard cheese
100 g (4 oz) skimmed milk soft cheese
100 g (4 oz) cottage cheese
150 g (5 oz) carton low-fat yogurt
25 g (1 oz) low-fat spread

B. Meat, Poultry, Fish, Eggs and Beans
From this group of foods you will get protein, B vitamins, vitamins A, E, D and the minerals iron, phosphorus, magnesium, calcium, as

well as iodine and zinc. Seeds and nuts also come under this heading. To keep calories low, again choose the foods which are lowest in fat – white fish rather than oily fish; poultry instead of red meats; beans rather than nuts. Calcium is only available in fish when you eat the bones (such as canned sardines) and in some nuts. A rich source of iodine is seafood, and nuts supply a good amount of vitamin E, although you'll also get this vitamin from eggs, fatty fish and meat. Offal is particularly rich in vitamins and minerals and is one of the main sources of iron. Beans also contain fibre. For a healthy diet choose 2 servings a day from this group of foods. Here are some serving sizes:

1 *egg*
100 *g (4 oz) prawns or shrimps*
100 *g (4 oz) kidneys*
175 *g (6 oz) white fish*
75 *g (3 oz) lean red meat*
175 *g (6 oz) cooked beans*
2 *rashers bacon, well grilled*
225 *g (8 oz) can baked beans in tomato sauce*
100 *g (4 oz) roast chicken or turkey*
1 *lamb chop*
100 *g (4 oz) beefburger, well grilled*
25 *g (1 oz) nuts*
3 *sardines, canned in tomato sauce*
2 *pilchards, canned in tomato sauce*

C. Fruit and Vegetables
If you are already eating lots of fresh fruit and vegetables you will probably be getting a supply of vitamins A, C and minerals, calcium and iron. You will also be getting a good helping of fibre. With the exception of avocado pears, fruit and vegetables contain little fat and can be eaten in large quantities on a reducing diet. Allow yourself about 4 servings a day of fruit and vegetables; here are examples of serving sizes, but remember not to cook or serve with fat or sugar.

100 *g (4 oz) mushrooms*
4 *sticks celery*
Mixed green salad of lettuce, cucumber, cress and green pepper

175 g (6 oz) cauliflower
3 medium tomatoes
100 g (4 oz) carrots, cabbage, swede, turnips or runner beans
150 g (5 oz) broccoli
50 g (2 oz) sweetcorn
100 g (4 oz) peas
100 g (4 oz) potatoes
225 g (8 oz) slice melon
100 g (4 oz) raspberries, strawberries, blackberries or blackcurrants
1 medium grapefruit or orange
1 medium apple, pear, peach or nectarine
100 g (4 oz) grapes
1 small banana

D. Breads and Cereals

You will get the most nutritional benefit if you choose wholegrain bread and cereals, and in this group you can also include rice and pasta. Many breakfast cereals and breads are enriched with added vitamins and minerals and you will get some protein, B vitamins, folic acid, vitamin E, iron, phosphorus, magnesium, zinc and calcium from this group of foods. Wholemeal bread, bran cereals, wholemeal rice and pasta are also excellent sources of dietary fibre. Allow yourself 4 servings a day from this group.

25 g (1 oz) wholemeal bread
25 g (1 oz) breakfast cereal
25 g (1 oz) rice, weighed raw
25 g (1 oz) pasta, weighed raw
4 crispbreads

CALORIE/NUTRIENT VALUE FOOD CHART

		CALORIES		
		Low	**Medium**	**High**
NUTRIENTS	**High**	Boiled or poached egg Cottage cheese White fish Shellfish Skimmed milk Citrus fruit Yogurt	Chicken (no skin) Lean meat Oily fish Low-fat hard cheeses Medium-fat soft cheeses Whole milk	Fatty meat Cheddar and hard cheese Nuts
	Medium	All fruits other than citrus and avocado pear Salads (without oil) Green vegetables Crispbreads	Bread Breakfast cereal Pasta and rice Peas and beans Potatoes Dried fruits Low-fat spreads	Fried savoury foods Fish and chips Meat pies Scotch eggs Margarine, butter
	Low	Thin soups Tea and coffee Slimmers' drinks Over-cooked vegetables	Thick soups Jam and marmalade Sugar and honey Sweet drinks Avocado pear	Sweets and chocolate Puddings, cakes and biscuits Cream Oil Pastry Alcohol

*C*HOOSING <u>YOUR</u> DIET

Calories are what slimming is all about, but many people are still confused about this fact. You can cut down fats, control carbohydrates, increase fibre, eat just a narrow selection of foods, but every diet depends for its success on the fact that by following its formula you will reduce your calorie intake.

CALORIE COUNTING
To make up your own diet from a calorie guide you need to be very organized and prepared to do a certain amount of calculating. But the great advantage of counting calories is that you can eat absolutely anything you fancy as long as it does not exceed your calorie allowance and is nutritionally balanced.

DO YOUR SUMS: Recipes you cook regularly call for careful calorie counting because they could have a big impact on your get-slim sums. So you need accurate scales, a set of measuring spoons (it's unlikely that your heirloom silver, etc, was forged in standard sizes), a measuring jug for larger liquid quantities, a pen and paper. List all recipe ingredients, measure out accurately and, using the calorie chart on pages 342 to 371, calculate each quantity value and enter it alongside. Add up the total; divide this figure by the number of portions you intend the recipe to produce, then you'll know what's on your plate.

CHOOSE A DIET: If calorie-counting sounds like hard work to you, then there is an easier way to follow a calorie-controlled diet. If you choose one of the diets that follow, we do all the calculating for you. A calorie-controlled diet can be devised to suit all sorts of lifestyles. As they are nutritionally balanced, all of the diets in this book can safely be followed for as long as it takes to achieve your target weight.

▼
▼

*T*HE <u>ANYONE-CAN-DO-IT</u> DIET

The Anyone-Can-Do-It Diet is designed to be super-speedy, super-simple.

Here's what you do

1. Mix a week's supply of high-fibre cereal (see 'Breakfast Bowl', page 46) and store in an airtight bag or jar.
2. Make a great big panful of soup. Choose Chicken Soup, Curried Bean Soup or Leek and Potato Soup and freeze your choice in seven individual portions.
3. Cook a delicious vegetable mixture (see 'Vegetable Mix', page 48) and divide it into meals for the week. Research shows that if you eat the same sort of thing each day, you'll tend to find it a bit easier to eat less. And being able to keep out of the kitchen can do wonders for any slimmer's willpower!

Here's how you slim

1. Each day take a helping of cereal and serve it with one item from the Fruit Chart on page 46. You are allowed 300 ml (½ pint) skimmed milk each day which you can share between cereals and drinks.
2. Enjoy one portion of soup each day served with two 25 g (1 oz) slices of wholemeal bread. Toast the bread if you wish, but don't spread it with anything.
3. For your main meal of the day, eat one vegetable serving, either hot or cold, with one item from the Protein-Plus Chart on page 49.
4. In addition, you can eat any two items from the Fruit Chart as between-meal snacks or as a sweet finish to a meal.
5. Drink as much as you wish of water, unsugared coffee and tea (with milk from allowance) and low-calorie soft drinks. Each day you'll be consuming no more than 1,000 calories – low enough for anyone to lose weight fast.

BREAKFAST BOWL
4 *whole wheat cereal biscuits*
100 g (4 oz) *branflakes*
75 g (3 oz) *all bran*
90 g (3½ oz) *dried apricots*
75 g (3 oz) *dried figs*
65 g (2½ oz) *raisins*

▲ Break up the cereal biscuits into a large bowl and mix with the branflakes and all bran.
▲ Chop the apricots and figs, add these to the cereals with the raisins and mix well.
▲ Either divide into 7 portions and store in separate plastic bags or store in a jar and take one helping a day.

FRUIT CHART Add one of these items to your Breakfast Bowl each day:
1 *medium apple*
1 *medium orange*
1 *medium pear*
1 *small banana*
1 *large grapefruit*
2 *tangerines*
200 g (7 oz) *raspberries, fresh or frozen*
75 g (3 oz) *green grapes*
2 *peach halves, canned in natural juice*
2 *pineapple rings, canned in natural juice*
100 g (4 oz) *apricots, canned in natural juice*
150 g (5 oz) *pears, canned in natural juice*

CHICKEN SOUP
4 × 225 g (8 oz) *chicken leg joints*
4 *sticks celery, chopped*
2 *medium onions, peeled and chopped*
3 *chicken stock cubes*
1.75 *litres (3 pints) water*
bouquet garni
salt
freshly ground black pepper
65 g (2½ oz) *skimmed milk powder*
3 *level tablespoons cornflour*

▲ Discard the skin from the chicken joints and place the chicken in a large saucepan.

▲ Add the celery and onions to the pan with the crumbled stock cubes, water and bouquet garni. Season with salt and pepper.

▲ Bring to the boil, cover and simmer for 45 minutes. Discard the bouquet garni.

▲ Take the chicken meat from the bones. Discard the bones and roughly chop the chicken.

▲ Blend the skimmed milk powder and cornflour with a little cold water until smooth. Add to the soup with the chicken flesh and liquidize until smooth.

▲ Pour back into the pan and simmer for 1-2 minutes, stirring constantly.

▲ Divide between 7 freezer containers and leave to cool. Cover, label and freeze.

▲ Reheat from frozen in a small pan over a low heat, stirring continuously.

LEEK AND POTATO SOUP

750 g (1½ lb) leeks
750 g (1½ lb) peeled potatoes, chopped
1 medium onion, peeled and chopped
3 chicken stock cubes
1.75 litres (3 pints) water
2 bay leaves
salt
freshly ground black pepper
50 g (2 oz) skimmed milk powder

▲ Discard the roots and the toughest green leaves from the leeks and slice the remainder into rings.

▲ Place all the vegetables in a large saucepan with the stock cubes, water and bay leaves. Season with salt and pepper.

▲ Bring to the boil, cover and simmer for 30 minutes or until tender. Discard the bay leaves.

▲ Purée the soup in a liquidizer with the skimmed milk powder.

▲ Divide between 7 freezer containers and leave to cool. Cover, label and freeze.

▲ Reheat from frozen in a pan over a low heat, stirring the mixture constantly.

CURRIED BEAN SOUP

2 medium onions, peeled and chopped
3 × 450 g (15.9 oz) cans baked beans in tomato sauce
1½ level teaspoons curry powder
3 chicken stock cubes
1.2 litres (2 pints) water

▲ Place the onions in a large saucepan with the baked beans, curry powder, stock cubes and water. Bring to the boil, cover and simmer for 15 minutes. Purée in a liquidizer until smooth.
▲ Divide between 7 freezer containers and leave to cool. Cover, label and freeze.
▲ Reheat the soup from frozen in a small pan over a low heat, stirring constantly.

VEGETABLE MIX

750 g (1½ lb) courgettes, sliced
750 g (1½ lb) aubergines, sliced
salt
450 g (1 lb) carrots, peeled and sliced
225 g (8 oz) celery, sliced
2 green peppers, cored, seeded and sliced
2 red peppers, cored, seeded and sliced
2 medium onions, peeled and sliced
2 vegetable or chicken stock cubes
350 ml (12 fl oz) water
2 level tablespoons tomato purée
½ level teaspoon ground cumin
¼ level teaspoon cayenne
225 g (8 oz) sweetcorn
3 × 225 g (8 oz) cans red kidney beans, drained

▲ Sprinkle the sliced courgettes and aubergines with salt and leave to stand for 10 minutes.
▲ Rinse the courgettes and aubergines thoroughly and place in a large saucepan with the rest of the prepared vegetables, stock cubes, water and tomato purée, cumin and cayenne.
▲ Bring to the boil, cover and simmer for 15 minutes. Add the sweetcorn and drained beans. Cook for a further 5 minutes. Add a little water if necessary to prevent sticking.

▲ Divide between 7 freezer containers and leave to cool. Cover, label and freeze.

▲ Thaw for 4 hours at room temperature, or overnight in the refrigerator.

▲ Serve cold or reheat slowly in a covered pan.

PROTEIN-PLUS CHART

Choose one of the following each day to add to your main meal:

750 g (3 oz) prawns

2 rashers well-grilled streaky bacon

100 g (4 oz) cooked cannellini beans

2 grilled lamb's kidneys

100 g (4 oz) white fish fillet, grilled without fat

1 frankfurter

1 × 100 g (3½ oz) can tuna in brine

65 g (2½ oz) cooked turkey, without skin or bones

90 g (3½ oz) bacon steak, well grilled

25 g (1 oz) Double Gloucester cheese, grated and used as a topping

THE <u>HIGH-FIBRE</u> DIET

The High-Fibre Diet is ideal for your health and is comfortingly easy on your slimming willpower.

Dietary fibre is the natural substance which many manufacturing processes remove from food. Whether you eat it as it occurs naturally in wholegrain cereals, vegetables and fruit, or take it in the form of high-bran products (i.e. those containing added bran), dietary fibre absorbs water and grows bulky.

There's plenty of evidence to show that high-fibre foods are satisfying and filling to eat and so make a slimming campaign easier. Experts now recommend a daily intake of fibre of between 30 and 40 grams. Fibre counts are given for each meal in the High-Fibre Diet so that you can make sure you are getting a good daily intake.

The High-Fibre Diet gives you seven 1,500 calorie menus from which to choose. You can follow the menus from Day 1 to Day 7 if you wish or choose the three or four menus you like best and repeat them until you are down to target weight.

Not all calories in fibre are fully digested, so you should lose weight well on 1,500 calories a day. If, however, you wish to reduce your daily calories for a speedier weight loss, you can bring each day's total down to 1,250 by missing out the snack meal.

Diet Rules
1. You are allowed a milk allowance of 300 ml (½ pint) skimmed milk per day. (Milk in menus is additional to this allowance.)
2. The total calorie allowance per day is 1,500 (including milk); if you wish to reduce this, you may miss out the snack which amounts to 250 calories.
3. You may drink low-calorie squashes or sparkling drinks, tea or coffee (with milk from allowance), and water freely.

————————DAY 1————————

BREAKFAST

JUICE; ALL BRAN WITH APRICOTS AND RAISINS (15.5 g fibre)

120 ml (4 fl oz) unsweetened orange juice
2 dried apricots
40 g (1½ oz) all bran
1 level tablespoon raisins
150 ml (¼ pint) skimmed milk

▲ Drink the juice as a starter.
▲ Chop the apricots, mix with the all bran and raisins and serve
with the milk.

LIGHT MEAL

TUNA AND KIDNEY BEAN SALAD; BANANA (14 g fibre)

1 × 100 g (3½ oz) can tuna in brine
100 g (4 oz) red kidney beans, cooked or canned
1 tablespoon lemon juice
1 level tablespoon chopped parsley
lettuce, shredded
2 high-fibre crispbreads
1 level teaspoon low-fat spread
1 medium banana

▲ Drain and flake the tuna, then mix with the kidney beans, lemon
juice and parsley.
▲ Serve on a bed of lettuce with the 2 crispbreads and low-fat
spread.
▲ Eat the banana for dessert.

MAIN MEAL
STUFFED GREEN PEPPER; ORANGE (17.5 g fibre)
1 *medium green pepper*
150 *g (5 oz) minced beef*
1 *tomato*
25 *g (1 oz) onion*
25 *g (1 oz) mushrooms*
15 *g (½ oz) brown rice*
4 *tablespoons fatless beef stock or water*
salt
freshly ground black pepper
pinch of dried mixed herbs
175 *g (6 oz) frozen mixed vegetables*
1 *large orange*

▲ Cut the top off the pepper and remove the seeds. Place in a pan of boiling water for 3 minutes. Drain and stand the pepper upright in a small ovenproof dish.

▲ Fry the mince without added fat, until well browned, then drain off the fat.

▲ Chop the tomato and add to the meat in the pan with the chopped onion, mushrooms, rice and stock or water. Season to taste and add the herbs.

▲ Stir well, heat to simmering point, then cover and simmer for 30 minutes.

▲ Spoon the savoury mince into the pepper, cover with the lid or foil and bake at 190°C, 375°F, Gas Mark 5 for 20 minutes.

▲ Cook the mixed vegetables as directed on the packet and serve with the stuffed pepper.

▲ Eat the orange for dessert.

SNACK
PIZZA TOAST (4 g fibre)
1 *rasher streaky bacon*
1 × 40 *g (1½ oz) slice wholemeal bread*
1 *level teaspoon yeast extract*
1 *tomato*
25 *g (1 oz) Edam cheese, grated*
4 *olives, stoned and halved*

▲ Grill the bacon well.
▲ Toast the bread on one side and spread the untoasted side with the yeast extract. Slice the tomato and place on top.
▲ Sprinkle the cheese over, cut the bacon into strips and arrange on the cheese in a lattice pattern.
▲ Decorate the pizza with the olives and grill until the cheese has melted.

—————————————DAY 2—————————————

BREAKFAST

TOAST AND MARMALADE; APPLE (8 g fibre)
2 × 25 g (1 oz) slices wholemeal bread
2 level teaspoons low-fat spread
4 level teaspoons marmalade
1 medium apple

▲ Toast the bread and spread with low-fat spread and marmalade.
▲ Follow with the apple.

LIGHT MEAL

LENTIL SOUP AND WHOLEMEAL ROLL (18 g fibre)
600 ml (1 pint) fatless chicken or vegetable stock
25 g (1 oz) lentils
100 g (4 oz) carrots, chopped
100 g (4 oz) turnip, peeled weight, chopped
50 g (2 oz) leeks, chopped
50 g (2 oz) parsnips, peeled weight, chopped
salt
freshly ground black pepper
1 × 45 g (1¾ oz) wholemeal roll
2 level teaspoons low-fat spread

▲ Place the stock in a saucepan, add the lentils and vegetables and bring to the boil. Season to taste, cover and simmer for 20 minutes.
▲ Serve with the roll spread with the low-fat spread.

MAIN MEAL
HADDOCK AND COURGETTE BAKE; PINEAPPLE AND YOGURT
(11 g fibre)
200 g (7 oz) haddock fillet
1 tablespoon lemon juice
175 g (6 oz) potatoes, with skin
1 tablespoon oil
50 g (2 oz) onion, chopped
½ clove garlic, crushed
175 g (6 oz) courgettes, sliced
175 g (6 oz) tomatoes, canned or fresh
1 tablespoon parsley, chopped
2 pineapple rings, canned in natural juice, drained
3 level tablespoons low-fat natural yogurt

▲ Cut the fish into strips, sprinkle with lemon juice and allow to stand for 15-30 minutes. Boil the potatoes until tender.
▲ Heat the oil, add the onion and garlic and cook until golden. Add the courgettes, cover and cook for 5 minutes.
▲ Add the haddock strips and stir gently for 2 minutes or until cooked. Add the tomatoes and heat through.
▲ Sprinkle with parsley and serve with the boiled potatoes.
▲ Eat the pineapple topped with natural yogurt for dessert.

SNACK
EDAM AND SULTANA SALAD (7½ g fibre)
100 g (4 oz) carrot, grated
25 g (1 oz) Edam cheese, grated
25 g (1 oz) sultanas
1 × 25 g (1 oz) slice wholemeal bread
1 level teaspoon low-fat spread

▲ Combine the carrot, cheese and sultanas.
▲ Spread the wholemeal bread with low-fat spread and serve with the salad.

——————DAY 3——————

BREAKFAST

ALL BRAN WITH BANANA (16 g fibre)
1 large banana
40 g (1½ oz) all bran
120 ml (4 fl oz) skimmed milk

▲ Slice the banana and serve with the cereal and milk.

LIGHT MEAL

BUTTER BEAN AND BACON SALAD (12 g fibre)
50 g (2 oz) wholewheat macaroni or pasta shapes
1 × 223 g (7.9 oz) can butter beans
1 back rasher bacon, well grilled
50 g (2 oz) cucumber, chopped
1 level tablespoon oil-free French dressing
salt
freshly ground black pepper

▲ Boil the macaroni or pasta shapes and drain.
▲ Drain the butter beans and mix with the chopped bacon, cucumber and macaroni.
▲ Stir in the oil-free French dressing and season to taste.

MAIN MEAL

CHEESY SPINACH OMELETTE; APPLE (15.5 g fibre)
2 eggs, size 3, separated
100 g (4 oz) fresh or frozen spinach, cooked and chopped
salt
freshly ground black pepper
pinch of grated nutmeg
1 level tablespoon low-fat spread
25 g (1 oz) Edam cheese, grated
75 g (3 oz) button mushrooms, poached in fatless stock
1 × 40 g (1½ oz) slice wholemeal bread
1 medium apple

▲ Mix the egg yolks with the chopped spinach. Season with salt, pepper and nutmeg.
▲ Whisk the egg whites until stiff. Fold the whites into the egg yolk and spinach mixture.
▲ Melt 2 level teaspoons of low-fat spread in an omelette pan, pour in the mixture and cook for 3 minutes. Place the omelette under a hot grill and cook until set. Sprinkle with cheese and fold in half.
▲ Serve with mushrooms poached in stock and the slice of bread spread with the remaining 1 level teaspoon of low-fat spread.
▲ Eat the apple for dessert.

SNACK

BAKED BEANS ON TOAST (16 g fibre)
2 × 25 g (1 oz) slices wholemeal bread
2 level teaspoons low-fat spread
1 × 150 g (5.3 oz) can baked beans

▲ Toast the bread and spread with the low-fat spread. Heat the beans and serve with the toast.

---------------------**DAY 4**---------------------

BREAKFAST

FRUIT AND NUT YOGURT (6.5 g fibre)

1 *medium apple, cored and diced*
1 *medium banana, sliced*
150 *g (5 oz) low-fat natural yogurt*
4 *hazelnuts, chopped*

▲ Mix the fruit with the natural yogurt and sprinkle with the hazelnuts.

LIGHT MEAL

BAKED POTATO WITH CHICKEN AND SWEETCORN (9.5 g fibre)

1 × 200 *g (7 oz) potato*
75 *g (3 oz) cooked chicken*
3 *rounded tablespoons canned or frozen sweetcorn*
½ *small green pepper, cored, seeded and diced*
2 *level tablespoons low-calorie salad dressing*

▲ Bake the potato at 200°C, 400°F, Gas Mark 6 for 45 minutes or until soft when squeezed gently.
▲ Discard the skin from the chicken and chop the flesh. Mix with the sweetcorn, pepper and salad dressing.
▲ Score the potato, open up and pile the chicken mixture on top.

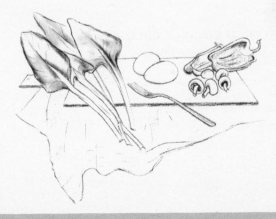

MAIN MEAL

STIR-FRIED LIVER; PEAR (11.5 g fibre)
40 g (1½ oz) long-grain brown rice
75 g (3 oz) lamb's liver
1 tablespoon oil
1 medium onion, thinly sliced
1 medium courgette, thinly sliced
25 g (1 oz) red or green pepper, cored, seeded and diced
50 g (2 oz) button mushrooms, sliced
50 g (2 oz) bean sprouts
2 teaspoons soy sauce
4 tablespoons water
salt
freshly ground black pepper
1 medium pear

▲ Boil the brown rice until tender.
▲ Cut the liver into small bite-sized pieces. Heat the oil in a non-stick wok or frying pan. Add the liver, onion and courgette and stir fry for 3 minutes.
▲ Add the pepper and mushrooms, stir fry for 1 minute, then add the bean sprouts, soy sauce and water. Season and stir well until almost all the liquid has evaporated.
▲ Serve the brown rice with the stir-fried liver mixture.
▲ Follow with the pear.

SNACK

CRUNCHY FRUIT COTTAGE CHEESE (5 g fibre)
100 g (4 oz) cottage cheese with pineapple
25 g (1 oz) peanuts and raisins
2 celery sticks

▲ Mix the peanuts and raisins with the cottage cheese and serve with the raw celery.

——————————**DAY 5**——————————

BREAKFAST

GRAPEFRUIT AND SULTANA BRAN (7.5 g fibre)
½ *large grapefruit, segmented*
50 g (2 oz) *sultana bran*
150 ml (¼ pint) *skimmed milk*

▲ Mix the grapefruit with the cereal and serve with the milk.

LIGHT MEAL

HAM AND COTTAGE CHEESE ROLLS; APPLE (10 g fibre)
2 × 40 g (1½ oz) *slices wholemeal bread*
2 *level teaspoons low-fat spread*
2 *slices lean cooked ham*
100 g (4 oz) *cottage cheese with chives*
1 *medium apple*

▲ Flatten the bread with a rolling pin and spread thinly with low-fat spread.
▲ Place the slices of ham on the bread and top with the cottage cheese. Roll the bread as you would a Swiss roll.
▲ Serve with the apple.

MAIN MEAL

SPAGHETTI BOLOGNESE (8 g fibre)
90 g (3½ oz) minced beef
25 g (1 oz) onion, chopped
½ clove garlic
1 × 225 g (8 oz) can tomatoes
pinch of dried oregano
pinch of dried basil
1 level tablespoon tomato purée
salt
freshly ground black pepper
50 g (2 oz) wholewheat spaghetti

▲ Brown the mince in a non-stick pan, then drain off and discard the fat. Add the onion and garlic to the mince and cook until soft.
▲ Chop the tomatoes and add to the pan with their juice, herbs, the tomato purée and seasoning. Bring to the boil, cover and simmer for 20 minutes.
▲ Boil the spaghetti and drain.
▲ Arrange the spaghetti on a plate and spoon the sauce into the centre.

SNACK

PEANUT COLESLAW (7 g fibre)
100 g (4 oz) white cabbage, shredded
50 g (2 oz) carrot, grated
25 g (1 oz) onion, finely chopped
1 level tablespoon low-calorie salad dressing
2 level tablespoons low-fat natural yogurt
25 g (1 oz) peanuts, shelled or roasted

▲ Combine the vegetables with the salad dressing and yogurt. Mix the peanuts in just before serving.

DAY 6

BREAKFAST

FRUIT MUESLI (20 g fibre)
40 g (1½ oz) bran muesli
1 medium pear, cored and diced
4 dried apricots, chopped
120 ml (4 fl oz) skimmed milk

▲ Mix the fruit with the muesli and serve with the milk.

LIGHT MEAL

PRAWN AND PEAR SALAD (9 g fibre)
2 level tablespoons low-calorie salad dressing
2 level tablespoons low-fat natural yogurt
1 level tablespoon tomato purée
1 level tablespoon sherry
1 level tablespoon lemon juice
100 g (4 oz) prawns, peeled
1 medium pear, cored and diced
salt
freshly ground black pepper
lettuce, shredded
1 × 45 g (1¾ oz) wholemeal roll
1 level teaspoon low-fat spread

▲ Combine the low-calorie salad dressing, yogurt, tomato purée, sherry and lemon juice. Stir in the prawns and pear and season.
▲ Serve on a bed of lettuce with the roll spread with low-fat spread.

MAIN MEAL

ROAST LAMB WITH VEGETABLES; BANANA AND GRAPE DESSERT (11 g fibre)

100 g (4 oz) carrots
200 g (7 oz) potatoes
75 g (3 oz) lean roast leg of lamb
1 tablespoon mint sauce
2 tablespoons fat-free gravy
1 small banana, sliced
100 g (4 oz) black grapes, halved and seeded
2 tablespoons unsweetened orange juice

▲ Boil the carrots and potatoes in separate pans.
▲ Discard the fat from the lamb and serve with the mint sauce, gravy and vegetables.
▲ Mix the banana and grapes, sprinkle the juice over and chill before serving.

SNACK

CRUNCHY DATE SANDWICH (7 g fibre)

6 peanuts, finely chopped
2 dried dates, finely chopped
1 celery stick, finely chopped
50 g (2 oz) low-fat soft cheese
2 × 25 g (1 oz) slices wholemeal bread

▲ Combine the peanuts, dates and celery with the soft cheese.
▲ Spread the mixture on the bread and serve.

----------DAY 7----------

BREAKFAST
POACHED EGG ON ROLL (4 g fibre)
1 egg, size 3
salt
freshly ground black pepper
1 × 45 g (1¾ oz) wholemeal roll
2 level teaspoons low-fat spread

▲ Poach the egg in boiling water and season. Serve on the roll, halved and spread with low-fat spread.

LIGHT MEAL
MACARONI MUSHROOM CHEESE (18½ g fibre)
50 g (2 oz) wholewheat macaroni
100 g (4 oz) fresh or frozen peas
50 g (2 oz) mushrooms, sliced
2 level teaspoons cornflour
150 ml (¼ pint) skimmed milk
25 g (1 oz) Edam cheese, grated
salt
freshly ground black pepper
25 g (1 oz) fresh wholemeal breadcrumbs

▲ Boil and drain the macaroni. Boil and drain the peas and mushrooms.
▲ Combine the cornflour with a little of the milk. Bring the remainder to the boil in a pan, stir in the cornflour mixture and bring to the boil, stirring constantly. Simmer for 1 minute. Stir in 15 g (½ oz) of the grated cheese, peas and mushrooms, then the macaroni.
▲ Transfer to an ovenproof dish, season and sprinkle the remainder of the cheese and the breadcrumbs on top.
▲ Brown under the grill until the cheese melts.

MAIN MEAL

PORK WITH APPLE; MELON (9 g fibre)

150 g (5 oz) lean pork leg or shoulder steak or fillet
100 g (4 oz) cooking apples, peeled weight, cored and diced
1 slice onion
salt
freshly ground black pepper
85 ml (3 fl oz) cider
50 ml (2 fl oz) stock
75 g (3 oz) cabbage
100 g (4 oz) potato with skin
225 g (8 oz) melon

▲ Remove and discard all fat from the pork. Put the pork in an ovenproof dish, add the diced apple, onion and seasoning.
▲ Pour in the cider and stock, cover and bake at 180°C, 350°F, Gas Mark 4 for 1¼-1½ hours.
▲ Serve with boiled cabbage and potatoes.
▲ Follow with melon for dessert.

SNACK

BANANA YOGURT WITH SULTANAS AND WHEATGERM
(5 g fibre)

1 medium banana, peeled and sliced
2 level tablespoons sultanas
1 level tablespoon wheatgerm
1 × 150 g (5.3 oz) carton natural low-fat yogurt

▲ Mix the banana with the sultanas, wheatgerm and yogurt.

THE <u>WORKING</u> WOMAN'S DIET

Whether you are married or single, if you are a working woman you probably don't have a lot of time to spend in the kitchen. Breakfasts are usually quick affairs, you may need to take a packed lunch to work and when you get home in the evening you almost certainly won't want to wait an hour or so for your meal to be ready.

The Working Woman's Diet is very flexible. You can make up your own daily menus, choosing meals to add up to your personal slimming total. If you have over 3 stones to lose start at 1,500 calories a day, if you have between 1 stone and 3 stones to lose, diet on a daily 1,250 calories and if you have a stone or under to lose keep to 1,000 calories.

Each meal section has a range of calories to choose from: this means that if you prefer a very low-calorie breakfast and lunch to enable you to eat more calories in the evening, then you have this option. Alternatively, if you find that a higher calorie breakfast keeps you from wanting much food later on, then you can spend your calories that way.

The Cereal Meals include recipes that are suitable for breakfasts, but they can also make satisfying evening snacks, too. The Sandwich and Salad Meals include recipes suitable for packed lunches. The Meat, Fish and Vegetarian Meals are most suitable for main meals, and Fruit Meals can either be served as light meals on their own or as desserts to supplement a main meal.

All the meals have been designed to be quick and easy to make and if you want to share an evening meal with family or friends you can easily increase quantities and serve them the same (with extra vegetables if you wish).

Variety is the basis of good nutrition so, if you can, choose meals from three different sections each day. You will also benefit from including a liver meal each week. The Working Woman's Diet is simple, flexible and effective. It will work for *you*.

Diet Rules

1. You are allowed 300 ml (½ pint) skimmed milk each day. This is in addition to any milk given in the recipes. Your milk allowance will cost 100 calories.

2. Choose any meals you wish to add up to your slimming calorie total (see introduction). Your strictest allowance will be 900 calories (plus 100 calories for milk) and your highest 1,400 calories.

3. Variety is the basis of good nutrition, so choose meals from different sections each day.

4. Drink as much as you wish of water, unsugared black coffee and tea (or with milk from allowance) and low-calorie soft drinks.

CEREAL MEALS

ORANGE AND OAT BREAKFAST Serves 1 (150 calories)

1 *small orange, segmented*
2 *hazelnuts, chopped*
15 *g* (½ *oz*) *rolled oats*
120 *ml* (4 *fl oz*) *skimmed milk*

▲ Mix together the orange, hazelnuts and oats and serve with the milk.

CEREAL WITH BANANA Serves 1 (150 calories)

1 *wheat breakfast biscuit*
1 *small banana, sliced*
85 *ml* (3 *fl oz*) *skimmed milk*

▲ Serve the breakfast biscuit with the banana and milk.

SLIMMER'S PORRIDGE Serves 1 (200 calories)

150 *ml* (¼ *pint*) *skimmed milk*
25 *g* (1 *oz*) *rolled oats*
2 *level teaspoons golden syrup or brown sugar*

▲ Bring the milk to the boil in a saucepan and stir in the oats. Simmer gently for 2-3 minutes.
▲ Pour into a serving dish with the golden syrup or brown sugar.

BRANFLAKES WITH BANANA AND APRICOT Serves 1
(200 calories)
2 *dried apricots, chopped*
1 *small banana, sliced*
25 *g* (1 oz) *branflakes*
120 *ml* (4 fl oz) *skimmed milk*

▲ Mix together the apricots, banana and branflakes and serve with the skimmed milk.

BRAN CEREAL AND APRICOTS Serves 1 (200 calories)
5 *dried apricots, chopped*
40 *g* (1½ oz) *bran cereal*
150 *ml* (¼ pint) *skimmed milk*

▲ Mix the apricots with the cereal and serve with the skimmed milk.

MUESLI AND YOGURT Serves 1 (250 calories)
4 *level tablespoons muesli*
150 *g* (5.3 oz) *carton low-fat raspberry or strawberry flavoured yogurt*

▲ Stir the muesli into the yogurt before serving.

WHEAT AND MIXED DRIED FRUIT Serves 1 (250 calories)
15 *g* (½ oz) *dried dates, weighed with stones*
1 *wheat breakfast biscuit*
1 *dried peach, chopped*
1 *dried fig, chopped*
120 *ml* (4 fl oz) *skimmed milk*

▲ Discard the stone from the dates and chop.
▲ Crumble the wheat biscuit and mix with the fruit.
▲ Serve with skimmed milk.

SANDWICH MEALS

PRAWN SANDWICH Serves 1 (200 calories)
50 g (2 oz) peeled prawns
1 level tablespoon low-calorie seafood dressing
2 × 25 g (1 oz) slices wholemeal bread

▲ Mix the prawns with the seafood dressing.
▲ Make into a sandwich with the bread.

BANANA AND HONEY SANDWICH Serves 1 (200 calories)
2 × 25 g (1 oz) slices wholemeal bread
1 level teaspoon honey
1 small banana, peeled and mashed

▲ Spread one slice of bread with the honey.
▲ Spread the banana on top and add the remaining slice of wholemeal bread.

CHICKEN AND CORN SANDWICH Serves 1 (250 calories)
2 × 25 g (1 oz) slices wholemeal bread
2 level tablespoons corn relish
50 g (2 oz) cooked chicken, chopped

▲ Spread corn relish on one slice of bread.
▲ Make into a sandwich with the chicken and bread.

EGG AND CRESS SANDWICH Serves 1 (250 calories)
1 egg, size 3, hardboiled and shelled
2 × 25 g (1 oz) slices wholemeal bread
1 tablespoon low-calorie mayonnaise
cress

▲ Mash the egg and mix with the low-calorie mayonnaise.
▲ Make into a sandwich with the bread and a little cress.

PEANUT BUTTER SANDWICH Serves 1 (300 calories)
2 × 40 g (1½ oz) slices wholemeal bread
1 level tablespoon peanut butter

▲ Spread one slice of bread with the peanut butter and top with the remaining slice.

CHEESE AND SALAD SANDWICH Serves 1 (300 calories)
2 × 40 g (1½ oz) slices wholemeal bread
4 level teaspoons low-calorie salad dressing
25 g (1 oz) fat-reduced Cheddar cheese, grated
1 medium tomato, sliced
1 large lettuce leaf
4 slices cucumber

▲ Spread the 2 slices of bread with salad dressing and make into a sandwich with the remaining ingredients.

NUTTY FRUIT SANDWICH Serves 1 (450 calories)
1 large banana
2 level tablespoons sultanas or raisins
1 level tablespoon walnuts, chopped
3 × 40 g (1½ oz) slices wholemeal bread

▲ Mash the banana and mix with the sultanas or raisins and walnuts.
▲ Make into a double-decker sandwich with the slices of bread.

SALAD MEALS

EGG SALAD Serves 1 (200 calories)
1 egg, size 3, hardboiled and shelled
75 g (3 oz) cooked peas
¼ red pepper, cored, seeded and diced
cress
2 level tablespoons low-calorie salad dressing
lettuce, shredded
¼ cucumber, sliced
2 tomatoes, sliced

▲ Roughly chop the egg and mix with the peas, pepper, cress and low-calorie salad dressing.
▲ Arrange the lettuce, cucumber and tomato on a plate and top with the egg mixture.

ORIENTAL PRAWN SALAD Serves 1 (250 calories)
100 g (4 oz) cooked or canned sweetcorn
¼ red or green pepper, cored, seeded and sliced
100 g (4 oz) bean sprouts
75 g (3 oz) peeled prawns
1 tablespoon white wine or cider vinegar
1 teaspoon soy sauce
1 level teaspoon honey

▲ Place the sweetcorn, pepper, bean sprouts and prawns in a bowl.
▲ Mix the vinegar, soy sauce and honey together, add to the salad and toss to mix thoroughly.

CHICKEN, CELERY AND APPLE SALAD Serves 1 (250 calories)
90 g (3½ oz) cooked chicken
1 medium apple, cored and diced
a little lemon juice
2 sticks celery, chopped
1 level tablespoon low-calorie salad dressing
2 level tablespoons low-fat yogurt
salt and freshly ground black pepper

▲ Discard the chicken skin and cut the flesh into bite-sized pieces.
▲ Toss the apple in the lemon juice.
▲ Mix all the ingredients together, season and serve.

CHEESE SALAD Serves 1 (300 calories)
¼ lettuce
¼ small cucumber, sliced
2 celery sticks, sliced
¼ red pepper, cored, seeded and diced
1 tomato, quartered
1 tablespoon oil-free French dressing
50 g (2 oz) fat-reduced Cheddar cheese, grated
1 × 25 g (1 oz) slice wholemeal bread
1 level teaspoon low-fat spread

▲ Make a salad with the vegetables and add the dressing.
▲ Serve with the cheese and bread spread with the low-fat spread.

COTTAGE CHEESE, PINEAPPLE AND NUT SALAD Serves 1
(300 calories)
100 g (4 oz) natural cottage cheese
2 rings pineapple canned in natural juice, drained and chopped
¼ red pepper, cored, seeded and diced
25 g (1 oz) dry roasted cashew nuts
50 g (2 oz) cooked peas

▲ Combine all the ingredients and serve in a bowl.

PARADISE RICE SALAD Serves 1 (400 calories)
40 g (1½ oz) long-grain brown rice
1 medium orange
1 small banana
1 tablespoon lemon juice
2 rings pineapple canned in natural juice, chopped
2 tablespoons pineapple juice from can
2 level tablespoons sultanas or raisins
1 level tablespoon desiccated coconut

▲ Cook the rice in boiling water, drain and leave to cool.
▲ Peel and segment the orange, saving as much juice as possible.
▲ Slice the banana and sprinkle with lemon juice.
▲ Mix all the ingredients together and serve.

HADDOCK AND PASTA SALAD Serves 1 (450 calories)
100 g (4 oz) smoked haddock
40 g (1½ oz) wholewheat pasta shapes
1 medium apple
1 tablespoon lemon juice
2 celery sticks, chopped
1 carrot, grated
100 g (4 oz) mushrooms
½ red pepper, cored, seeded and diced
75 g (3 oz) cooked peas
50 g (2 oz) canned sweetcorn
4 tablespoons oil-free French dressing

▲ Poach the haddock in simmering water for 10-15 minutes, or until cooked. Flake the fish, discarding the skin and bones.
▲ Cook the pasta in boiling water until tender, then drain.
▲ Core the apple, dice the flesh and sprinkle with lemon juice.
▲ Mix all the ingredients in a bowl and toss with the oil-free French dressing.

MEAT MEALS

GRILLED BACON STEAK AND PINEAPPLE Serves 1 (350 calories)
1 × 175 g (6 oz) potato
1 × 100 g (3½ oz) bacon steak
1 pineapple ring canned in natural juice, drained
150 g (5 oz) fresh or frozen peas

▲ Bake the potato in its jacket at 200°C, 400°F, Gas Mark 6 for 45 minutes or until soft when squeezed gently.
▲ Grill the bacon steak well. Grill the pineapple ring for 2-3 minutes.
▲ Cook the peas and drain.
▲ Serve the bacon steak topped with the pineapple ring and accompanied with the baked potato and peas.

SAUSAGE, BACON AND BAKED BEANS Serves 1 (350 calories)

2 *beef chipolata sausages*
2 *rashers streaky bacon*
1 × 225 g (8 oz) *can baked beans in tomato sauce*

▲ Grill the chipolata sausages and bacon until well cooked, turning frequently.
▲ Heat the baked beans and serve with the sausages and bacon.

CHICKEN LIVERS WITH RICE Serves 1 (350 calories)

40 g (1½ oz) *long-grain brown rice*
1 *small onion, finely chopped*
½ × 225 g (8 oz) *can tomatoes, roughly chopped*
pinch of dried mixed herbs
¼ *chicken stock cube*
100 g (4 oz) *chicken livers*
50 g (2 oz) *button mushrooms, sliced*
50 ml (2 fl oz) *water*
salt
freshly ground black pepper
1 *level teaspoon cornflour*

▲ Boil the rice until tender. While it is cooking, prepare the livers.
▲ Place the onion, tomatoes and their juice in a saucepan with the herbs and stock cube. Cover and simmer for 10 minutes.
▲ Cut each chicken liver into 2 pieces, discarding any greenish bits. Add the livers, mushrooms and water to the pan and season. Return to the boil. Cover and simmer gently for another 8 minutes.
▲ Blend the cornflour with a little cold water until smooth and stir into the pan. Stir until boiling, then simmer for 1 minute.
▲ Serve the livers with the rice.

CHICKEN WITH BAKED POTATO AND CARROTS Serves 1
(400 calories)

1 × 175 g (6 oz) *chicken breast*
2 *level tablespoons low-fat natural yogurt*
1 *level tablespoon tomato purée*
¼ *level teaspoon paprika*
salt
freshly ground black pepper
225 g (8 oz) *potato*
100 g (4 oz) *carrots*

▲ Skin the chicken and place in a small ovenproof dish.
▲ Mix together the yogurt, tomato purée and paprika. Season, then spoon over the chicken, making sure that it is completely coated. Cover the dish and cook at 180°C, 350°F, Gas Mark 4 for 45 minutes.
▲ Prick the potato and push a skewer through the centre. Bake with the chicken.
▲ Boil the carrots and serve with the chicken and baked potato.

BEEF AND CABBAGE STIR FRY Serves 1 (350 calories)

150 g (5 oz) *fillet or rump steak*
1 *tablespoon oil*
100 g (4 oz) *white cabbage, shredded*
50 g (2 oz) *red pepper, cored, seeded and diced*
50 g (2 oz) *green pepper, cored, seeded and diced*
1 *teaspoon soy sauce*
1 *teaspoon cider vinegar*
salt
freshly ground black pepper

▲ Discard any fat from the steak, slice thickly across the grain and cut into small pieces.
▲ Heat the oil in a non-stick pan or wok, add the cabbage and stir fry for 3 minutes. Add the pepper and stir fry for 3 minutes.
▲ Push the cabbage and pepper to one side of the pan and fry the steak for 3 minutes.
▲ Mix together the soy sauce, cider vinegar, salt and pepper and add to the pan. Stir until all the ingredients are coated.
▲ Check the seasoning and serve immediately.

MINCED BEEF AND BAKED BEAN CASSEROLE Serves 1

(450 calories)
100 g (4 oz) minced beef
50 g (2 oz) mushrooms, halved
1 × 150 g (5.3 oz) can baked beans in tomato sauce
pinch of chilli powder
100 g (4 oz) cooked potato, sliced

▲ Brown the minced beef in a non-stick pan and drain off the fat.
▲ Mix the minced beef, mushrooms, beans and chilli powder together and turn into an ovenproof dish.
▲ Arrange the sliced potatoes on top in an overlapping pattern. Cook at 190°C, 375°F, Gas Mark 5 for 20 minutes.
▲ Serve hot.

HAM OMELETTE AND ROLL Serves 1 (450 calories)

100 g (4 oz) frozen mixed vegetables
2 eggs, size 3
1 tablespoon water
salt
freshly ground black pepper
1 level teaspoon low-fat spread
40 g (1½ oz) lean cooked ham, visible fat discarded and lean chopped
1 × 45 g (1¾ oz) wholemeal roll

▲ Cook the mixed vegetables according to the packet instructions.
▲ Lightly beat the eggs, water and seasoning together.
▲ Melt the low-fat spread in a small omelette pan and brush all over the surface. Pour in the eggs and cook until lightly set.
▲ Place the ham in the centre of the omelette, fold over and serve with the mixed vegetables and wholemeal roll.

LAMB KEBABS Serves 1 (500 calories)
40 g (1½ oz) long-grain brown rice
200 g (7 oz) lamb leg steak, fat discarded, lean cut into bite-sized pieces
2 small tomatoes
4 pickled onions
¼ green pepper, cored, seeded and cut into squares
8 button mushrooms
4 bay leaves
100 g (4 oz) fresh or frozen carrots

▲ Boil the rice until tender.
▲ Thread the lamb, tomatoes, pickled onions, green pepper, mushrooms and bay leaves on to 2 kebab skewers. Cook under a preheated grill, turning occasionally.
▲ Cook the carrots in boiling water and drain.
▲ Serve the kebabs with the rice and carrots.

MIXED GRILL AND VEGETABLES Serves 1 (500 calories)
175 g (6 oz) fresh or frozen carrots
1 lamb's kidney
50 g (2 oz) lamb's liver
2 rashers streaky bacon
1 tomato, halved
100 g (4 oz) mushrooms
1 wholemeal pitta bread

▲ Cook the carrots and drain.
▲ Halve and core the kidney. Grill the bacon until well cooked, then grill the liver, kidney and tomato.
▲ Poach the mushrooms in a little water or stock.
▲ Serve the mixed grill with the mushrooms, carrots and pitta bread.

FISH MEALS

COD AND PEAS Serves 1 (350 calories)
175 g (6 oz) cod fillet
75 g (3 oz) fresh or frozen peas
1 × 40 g (1½ oz) slice wholemeal bread
2 level teaspoons low-fat spread
2 level tablespoons low-calorie seafood sauce or tomato ketchup

▲ Poach the cod in a little water for 10-15 minutes until cooked.
▲ Cook the peas and drain.
▲ Spread the bread with the low-fat spread and serve with the cod, peas and seafood sauce or ketchup.

SCRAMBLED SMOKED HADDOCK Serves 1 (350 calories)
150 g (5 oz) smoked haddock fillet
1 tomato, halved
2 eggs, size 3
1 tablespoon skimmed milk
salt
freshly ground black pepper
1 level teaspoon low-fat spread
¼ red pepper, cored, seeded and diced
50 g (2 oz) cooked peas

▲ Poach the haddock in a little water for 10-15 minutes until cooked, then flake and discard the skin.
▲ Grill the tomato halves. Beat the eggs, milk and salt and pepper together.
▲ Melt the low-fat spread in a non-stick pan and pour in the egg mixture. Cook over a low heat, stirring constantly, until the egg is just cooked and creamy. Stir in the haddock, pepper and peas.
▲ Check the seasoning and serve with the tomato halves.

TROUT WITH ALMONDS Serves 1 (400 calories)
1 × 225 g (8 oz) trout
2 level tablespoons flaked almonds
100 g (4 oz) fresh or frozen French beans
100 g (4 oz) canned sweetcorn

▲ Grill the trout without adding any fat, turning several times until cooked.
▲ Place the almonds on a piece of foil and grill until brown.
▲ Boil the French beans until tender. Heat the sweetcorn.
▲ Serve the trout sprinkled with almonds, with the vegetables.

FISH FINGERS, CHIPS AND BEANS Serves 1 (400 calories)
75 g (3 oz) frozen oven or grill chips
3 cod fish fingers
1 × 150 g (5.3 oz) can baked beans in tomato sauce

▲ Cook the chips as directed on the packet.
▲ Cook the fish fingers, without adding any fat, under a preheated grill, turning once until golden brown and crisp.
▲ Heat the baked beans in a saucepan and serve with the fish fingers and chips.

BAKED POTATO WITH BRIE AND PRAWNS Serves 1 (450 calories)
1 × 225 g (8 oz) potato
1 tablespoon skimmed milk
50 g (2 oz) Brie, diced
65 g (2½ oz) peeled prawns
salt
freshly ground black pepper

▲ Bake the potato in its jacket at 200°C, 400°F, Gas Mark 6 for 1 hour or until soft when squeezed gently. Cut the potato in half lengthways and carefully scoop out the flesh. Keep the cases intact.
▲ Mash the potato flesh with the milk. Stir the cheese and prawns into the mashed potato and season to taste.
▲ Pile the mixture into the potato cases and reheat in the oven for about 10-15 minutes.

CURRIED RICE WITH FISH Serves 1 (400 calories)
65 g (2½ oz) rice
¼ level teaspoon curry powder
¼ level teaspoon turmeric
pinch of salt
300 ml (½ pint) water
100 g (4 oz) white fish fillet, e.g. cod, haddock or coley, fresh or frozen
¼ small red or green pepper
2 level tablespoons sultanas or raisins

▲ Place the rice in a small saucepan with the curry powder, turmeric, salt and water. Add the fish if frozen, but not if fresh. Cover the pan, bring to the boil and simmer gently for 10 minutes.
▲ Discard the white pith and seeds from the pepper and dice the flesh. Add to the pan with the sultanas and fresh fish, if using.
▲ Cover the pan and simmer for a further 10-15 minutes, or until the rice is tender. At the end of cooking, the water should have been absorbed.
▲ Carefully lift out the fish and discard the skin and bones. Flake the fish and mix with the rice.

SARDINE-STUFFED POTATO Serves 1 (400 calories)
1 × 225 g (8 oz) potato
50 g (2 oz) cottage cheese with chives
50 g (2 oz) sardines in tomato sauce, drained
salt
freshly ground black pepper
100 g (4 oz) fresh or frozen peas

▲ Bake the potato in its jacket at 200°C, 400°F, Gas Mark 6 for 1 hour, or until soft when squeezed gently. Cut the potato in half lengthways and scoop out the flesh.
▲ Mash the potato flesh with the cottage cheese, canned sardines and salt and pepper.
▲ Pile the mixture back into the potato cases and reheat in the oven for 10-15 minutes.
▲ Cook the peas, drain and serve with the potato.

VEGETARIAN MEALS

BAKED BEAN AND VEGETABLE PIE Serves 1 (350 calories)
100 g (4 oz) courgettes, sliced
100 g (4 oz) button mushrooms
1 × 225 g (8 oz) can baked beans in tomato sauce
4 pickled onions, sliced
½ teaspoon Worcestershire sauce
1 tablespoon tomato ketchup
salt
freshly ground black pepper
25 g (1 oz) fresh wholemeal breadcrumbs
15 g (½ oz) mature Cheddar cheese, grated

▲ Boil the courgettes and mushrooms in 2 pans for 5 minutes.
▲ Drain and mix with the baked beans, pickled onions,
Worcestershire sauce and tomato ketchup. Season lightly and turn
into an ovenproof dish.
▲ Mix the cheese with the breadcrumbs and sprinkle the mixture
on top. Bake at 190°C, 375°F, Gas Mark 5 for 20 minutes. Brown
under the grill, if wished.

MUSHROOM AND TOMATO OMELETTE Serves 1 (350 calories)
100 g (4 oz) button mushrooms, halved
2 level teaspoons low-fat spread
2 eggs, size 3
1 tablespoon water
salt
freshly ground black pepper
2 medium tomatoes, sliced
1 × 45 g (1¾ oz) wholemeal roll

▲ Cook the mushrooms in a little stock or water for 5 minutes.
▲ Melt the low-fat spread in a small non-stick omelette pan, then
brush over the surface. Beat the eggs, water and seasoning together,
pour into the pan and cook to make an omelette.
▲ As the omelette begins to set, add the sliced tomatoes and
drained mushrooms.
▲ Fold the omelette in half and serve with the wholemeal roll.

WALNUT-STUFFED POTATO AND BEANS Serves 1 (400 calories)

1 × 225 g (8 oz) potato
100 g (4 oz) cottage cheese with chives
4 walnut halves, chopped
salt
freshly ground black pepper
100 g (4 oz) French beans

▲ Bake the potato in its jacket at 200°C, 400°F, Gas Mark 6 for 1 hour or until soft when squeezed gently. Cut in half lengthways and scoop out the flesh.
▲ Mash the flesh with the cottage cheese, add the walnuts, salt and pepper, then pile the mixture into the potato cases. Reheat in the oven for 10 minutes.
▲ Cook the beans, drain and serve with the potato.

TANGY BLUE CHEESE TOAST Serves 1 (400 calories)

50 g (2 oz) Danish Blue cheese
2 level tablespoons tomato chutney
few drops Worcestershire sauce
2 × 25 g (1 oz) slices wholemeal bread
2 large tomatoes

▲ Place the cheese, chutney and Worcestershire sauce in a bowl. Mix well with a fork.
▲ Toast the bread. Spread the cheese mixture on top and grill until bubbling.
▲ Serve with the tomatoes, raw or grilled without fat.

MACARONI CHEESE Serves 1 (450 calories)

50 g (2 oz) wholewheat macaroni
1 level tablespoon cornflour
150 ml (¼ pint) skimmed milk
pinch of dry mustard
40 g (1½ oz) mature Cheddar cheese, grated
salt
freshly ground black pepper

▲ Boil the macaroni in plenty of boiling water.
▲ Blend the cornflour with a little of the milk to make a smooth paste. Heat the remaining milk to boiling point, then pour on to the blended mixture, stirring constantly.
▲ Return to the saucepan, bring to the boil and simmer for 1-2 minutes. Remove from the heat and stir in the mustard, cheese, salt and pepper and macaroni.
▲ Serve hot.

CREAMY BAKED POTATO AND SALAD Serves 1 (450 calories)

1 × 225 g (8 oz) potato
1 egg, size 3, hardboiled and chopped
½ green pepper, cored, seeded and diced
1 level teaspoon chopped chives
1 level tablespoon low-calorie salad dressing
50 g (2 oz) skimmed milk soft cheese
100 g (4 oz) white cabbage, shredded
75 g (3 oz) carrots, grated
2 level tablespoons low-calorie salad dressing

▲ Bake the potato in its jacket at 200°C, 400°F, Gas Mark 6, or until soft when squeezed gently.
▲ Meanwhile, mix the egg, pepper, chives, salad dressing and soft cheese together.
▲ When the potato is cooked, cut in half lengthways and top each half with the cheese mixture.
▲ Mix the cabbage and carrots with the low calorie dressing and serve with the potato.

BROWN RICE RISOTTO Serves 1 (450 calories)
50 g (2 oz) onion, finely chopped
3 tomatoes, roughly chopped
50 g (2 oz) long-grain brown rice
400 ml (14 fl oz) water
½ teaspoon mixed herbs
salt
freshly ground black pepper
100 g (4 oz) mushrooms, chopped
75 g (3 oz) fresh or frozen peas
50 g (2 oz) fat-reduced Cheddar cheese, grated

▲ Place the onions, tomatoes, rice, water, herbs and salt and
pepper in a small saucepan. Cover the pan, bring to the boil and
simmer gently for 30 minutes.
▲ Add the mushrooms to the pan with the peas and simmer for a
further 15 minutes, stirring occasionally. Add a little extra water if
the mixture becomes too dry.
▲ Sprinkle the cheese on top before serving.

QUICK PIZZA AND POTATO Serves 1 (500 calories)
1 × 200 g (7 oz) potato
1 × 225 g (8 oz) can tomatoes
100 g (4 oz) mushrooms, sliced
½ green pepper, cored, seeded and thinly sliced
salt
freshly ground black pepper
½ teaspoon mixed herbs
1 wholemeal pitta bread
40 g (1½ oz) fat-reduced Cheddar cheese, grated

▲ Bake the potato at 200°C, 400°F, Gas Mark 6 for 1 hour or until
soft when squeezed gently.
▲ About 20 minutes before the potato is cooked, place the
tomatoes and their juice in a saucepan with the mushrooms,
pepper, seasoning and herbs. Boil uncovered for 10 minutes until
the liquid has reduced.
▲ Spoon the tomato mixture on to the pitta bread, sprinkle with
the cheese and grill until the cheese has melted and is golden brown.
▲ Serve the pizza with the potato.

FRUIT MEALS

DRIED FRUIT SUNDAE Serves 1 (150 calories)
50 g (2 oz) vanilla ice cream
1 level tablespoon sultanas or raisins
2 cocktail cherries, chopped
2 dried apricots, chopped

▲ Mix the ice cream with the fruit and serve immediately.

GRAPE AND APRICOT YOGURT Serves 1 (200 calories)
175 g (6 oz) fresh apricots, stoned and finely chopped
1 × 150 g (5 oz) carton low-fat natural yogurt
1 egg white
75 g (3 oz) black grapes, halved and seeded

▲ Stir the apricots into the yogurt.
▲ Whisk the egg white until stiff and fold into the yogurt.
▲ Layer the yogurt mixture and grapes in an individual glass
serving dish, finishing with a layer of grapes.

HONEY BANANA SPLIT Serves 1 (200 calories)
1 medium banana, peeled and halved lengthways
50 g (2 oz) vanilla ice cream
1½ level teaspoons honey

▲ Place the banana in a serving dish. Top with the ice cream and
drizzle over the honey.
▲ Serve immediately.

APPLE, GRAPES AND CHEESE Serves 1 (300 calories)
1 medium eating apple
40 g (1½ oz) Lymeswold, Cheddar, Double Gloucester or Caerphilly cheese
100 g (4 oz) green grapes

▲ Serve the apple with the cheese and grapes.

THE <u>HOUSEWIFE'S</u> DIET

This diet is ideal if you are at home during the day. Breakfasts are simple, and because you probably won't want to bother with cooking much for lunch, we have kept these quick and easy, too. In the evening you may well want to eat with other members of the family, so we have devised recipes that serve two – no-one will notice that they are low-calorie meals. If there are more than two people in your family you can easily increase the amount accordingly and serve non-dieters extra vegetables.

It is always best to cook when you are not hungry; this way you will be less tempted to nibble away at that bit of leftover cheese or half-a-handful of dried fruit. If you are intending to cook a casserole for the evening meal, get it all prepared after you have eaten lunch. You could even part-cook it in the afternoon and just finish it off later on. Don't leave fresh vegetables soaking in cold water, though, or they will lose some of their vitamin value.

One of the problems of being at home is that it is very easy to slip into the kitchen and nibble away at whatever is available. We have included two snacks in this diet that you can eat at any time during the day. Your three meals and two snacks total 1,250 calories, a total at which everyone will lose weight. If, however, you are nearing target weight you may have to cut your calories down to 1,000 to achieve a speedy weight loss; you can do this by not eating your snack allowance. If you find it easy to miss breakfast, but long for something in the evening, save your breakfast meal and eat it later.

If you thought you'd never stick to a diet plan because of the problems of fitting it in with the family's needs, this is the diet that will succeed for you.

Diet Rules

1. Choose one menu each day. You can repeat menus if you wish but make sure you choose at least five different menus during a fortnight.
2. Do not swap meals between menus; if you do not like one day's choice, miss it out entirely.

3. Each day you are allowed 300 ml (½ pint) skimmed milk for use in drinks. This is in addition to any milk given in the menus.
4. You can drink as much as you wish of water, tea and coffee with milk from your allowance and artificial sweeteners if liked. You can also drink unlimited soft drinks with the low-calorie label.
5. Each day's allowance adds up to 1,250 calories. If you wish to reduce calories to 1,000, don't eat the snacks – they add up to 250 calories in total.
6. Breakfast and lunches serve one, but the evening meal serves two. If you are eating alone you can either halve quantities or, where appropriate, freeze or refrigerate a portion for another day. If you are serving more than two people, quantities can be increased accordingly. You can serve non-dieting members of the family extra vegetables if you wish.

DAY 1

BREAKFAST

BRAN CEREAL AND DRIED APRICOTS
4 dried apricots
25 g (1 oz) all bran
75 ml (3 fl oz) skimmed milk

▲ Chop the apricots, add to the cereal and serve with the milk.

LUNCH

CHEESE AND TOMATO SANDWICH; FRUIT
2 × 25 g (1 oz) slices wholemeal bread
2 teaspoons low-fat spread
1 tomato
25 g (1 oz) Edam cheese, grated
1 medium pear or peach

▲ Spread the 2 slices of bread with low-fat spread.
▲ Slice the tomato and arrange on one slice of bread. Top with the grated cheese and the remaining slice of bread.
▲ Follow with fruit.

EVENING MEAL (Serves 2)

STEAK AND KIDNEY CASSEROLE; FRUIT

225 g (8 oz) lean stewing steak
100 g (4 oz) pigs' or lambs' kidneys
1 level tablespoon plain flour
salt
freshly ground black pepper
100 g (4 oz) mushrooms
100 g (4 oz) carrots, peeled and sliced
1 small onion, peeled and chopped
250 ml (8 fl oz) boiling water
1 beef stock cube, crumbled
1 teaspoon Worcestershire sauce
bouquet garni
2 × 175 g (6 oz) potatoes
225 g (8 oz) fresh or frozen French beans
2 mandarin oranges, tangerines or satsumas

▲ Discard all visible fat from the beef and cut into bite-sized pieces.
▲ Core the kidneys and cut into small pieces.
▲ Season the flour with salt and pepper, toss the meat in the flour and place in a casserole dish with any excess flour.
▲ Quarter the mushrooms if large; leave whole if small. Add all the vegetables to the meat.
▲ Stir the crumbled stock cube into the boiling water with the Worcestershire sauce. Pour over the meat and vegetables and add the bouquet garni.
▲ Cover and cook at 150°C, 300°F, Gas Mark 2 for 1½ hours. Increase the oven temperature to 180°C, 350°F, Gas Mark 4, place the potato at the top of the oven and cook for a further 1½ hours or until the potato is soft when squeezed gently.
▲ Cook the French beans in boiling salted water. Drain and serve with the baked potato and casserole.
▲ Follow with the fruit.

SNACK 1

YOGURT AND FRUIT

1 *small banana*
1 × 150 *g* (5.3 *oz*) *carton low-fat natural yogurt*
25 *g* (1 *oz*) *black grapes, halved and deseeded*

▲ Peel and slice the banana and mix into the yogurt with the halved grapes.

SNACK 2

DRINKING CHOCOLATE

150 *ml* (¼ *pint*) *skimmed milk*
2 *rounded teaspoons drinking chocolate*
artificial sweetener (optional)

▲ Heat the milk and make up the drinking chocolate. Sweeten with an artificial sweetener, if liked.

——————————DAY 2——————————

BREAKFAST

BOILED EGG AND BREAD

1 *egg, size 3*
1 × 25 *g* (1 *oz*) *slice wholemeal bread*
1 *level teaspoon low-fat spread*

▲ Boil the egg.
▲ Spread the low-fat spread on the slice of bread and serve with the egg.

LUNCH

BAKED BEANS ON TOAST; FRUIT

1 × 150 *g* (5.3 *oz*) *can baked beans with tomato sauce*
1 × 25 *g* (1 *oz*) *slice wholemeal bread*
1 *apple, pear or peach*

▲ Place the baked beans in a saucepan and heat through.
▲ Toast the bread and serve topped with the baked beans.
▲ Follow with fruit.

EVENING MEAL (Serves 2)

CHICKEN CURRY
2 chicken leg joints, 225 g (8 oz) each
1 small onion, peeled and chopped
1 bay leaf
½ chicken stock cube
300 ml (½ pint) water
1½ level teaspoons butter or margarine
1 level teaspoon curry powder, mild or hot
4 level teaspoons plain flour
15 g (½ oz) skimmed milk powder
1 level tablespoon sultanas
175 g (6 oz) fresh or frozen peas
salt
freshly ground black pepper
75 g (3 oz) long-grain brown rice
2 medium-sized oranges

▲ Skin the chicken joints, then cut each one in half. Place in a saucepan with the onion, bay leaf, stock cube and water. Cover the pan, bring to the boil, then simmer for 30 minutes.
▲ Remove the chicken and keep warm. Strain 150 ml (¼ pint) of the stock into a measuring jug; discard the rest. Discard the bay leaf.
▲ Boil the rice, and while it is cooking, make the curry sauce: melt the butter or margarine, then stir in the curry powder and cook over a low heat for 1 minute. Remove from the heat, stir in the flour and cook for a few minutes.
▲ Whisk the skimmed milk powder into the reserved stock, then add to the curry mixture, whisking constantly. Bring back to the boil, simmer for 1-2 minutes and add the sultanas.
▲ Boil the peas for 5 minutes, then drain and add a few to the sauce. Season to taste with salt and pepper.
▲ Pour the sauce over the chicken joints and serve with the remaining peas and strained rice.
▲ Follow with the fruit.

SNACK 1

CURRANT BUN
1 × 40 g (1½ oz) *currant bun*

SNACK 2

APRICOT AND BRANFLAKE MUNCH
2 *dried apricots*
1 *level tablespoon sultanas or raisins*
25 g (1 oz) *branflakes*

▲ Chop the dried apricots and mix with the sultanas or raisins and the cereal.

─────────────────**DAY 3**─────────────────

BREAKFAST

TOAST AND JAM OR MARMALADE
2 × 25 g (1 oz) *slices wholemeal bread*
2 *level teaspoons low-fat spread*
2 *level teaspoons jam or marmalade*

▲ Toast the bread, spread each slice with the low-fat spread and jam or marmalade.

LUNCH

TOMATO OMELETTE; FRUIT
2 *eggs, size 3*
1 *tablespoon water*
salt and freshly ground black pepper
1 *level teaspoon butter or margarine*
2 *tomatoes, sliced*
1 *medium orange or apple*

▲ Lightly beat the eggs with the water and seasoning.
▲ Melt the butter or margarine in a small omelette pan and brush

all over the surface. Pour in the eggs and just before the omelette begins to set, add the sliced tomatoes.

▲ Cook until the omelette is set, then serve folded in half.

▲ Follow with fruit.

EVENING MEAL (Serves 2)

CIDERED PORK CASSEROLE

225 g (8 oz) pork fillet/tenderloin, all visible fat discarded
1 level tablespoon plain flour
½ red or green pepper, cored, seeded and sliced
1 leek or onion, chopped
175 g (6 oz) carrots, sliced
100 g (4 oz) button mushrooms, halved if large
250 ml (8 fl oz) dry cider
bay leaf
salt
freshly ground black pepper
2 × 175 g (6 oz) potatoes
2 level teaspoons cornflour
225 g (8 oz) cauliflower

▲ Cut the pork fillet into bite-sized pieces.

▲ Season the flour with salt and pepper, toss the pork in the flour and place in a casserole dish with any excess flour. Add all the vegetables to the casserole with the cider, bay leaf and seasoning.

▲ Cover and cook at 150°C, 300°F, Gas Mark 2 for 1½ hours. Increase the oven temperature to 180°C, 350°F, Gas Mark 4, place the potatoes at the top of the oven and cook for 1½ hours or until soft when squeezed gently.

▲ Blend the cornflour with cold water and add to the casserole half an hour before the end of the cooking time.

▲ Boil the cauliflower and serve with the casserole and potatoes.

SNACK 1
CHEESE, CELERY AND FRUIT MUNCH
1 medium apple
a little lemon juice
25 g (1 oz) Edam cheese, cut into cubes
2 sticks celery, chopped
1 level teaspoon sultanas or raisins

▲ Core and dice the apple and sprinkle with a little lemon juice.
▲ Mix all the ingredients together and serve in a bowl.

SNACK 2
ALL BRAN
25 g (1 oz) all bran
5 tablespoons skimmed milk

▲ Serve the all bran with the milk.

——————————————DAY 4——————————————

BREAKFAST
GRAPEFRUIT AND CEREAL
½ medium grapefruit
1 level teaspoon sugar (optional)
25 g (1 oz) all bran
1 level tablespoon sultanas or raisins
75 ml (3 fl oz) skimmed milk

▲ Prepare the grapefruit and sprinkle with the sugar, if using.
▲ Follow with the cereal mixed with the sultanas or raisins and served with the milk.

LUNCH
PRAWN SANDWICH; FRUIT
2 × 25 g (1 oz) slices wholemeal bread
lettuce, shredded
50 g (2 oz) peeled prawns
1 level tablespoon low-calorie seafood dressing
salt
freshly ground black pepper
1 medium pear or peach

▲ Place the shredded lettuce on one slice of bread.
▲ Mix the prawns, dressing and seasoning together. Spread the mixture on the remaining slice of bread and make a sandwich.
▲ Follow with fruit.

EVENING MEAL (Serves 2)
GRILLED LAMB CHOP AND MUSHROOM SAUCE
2 × 150 g (5 oz) lamb chump chops
225 g (8 oz) potatoes, weighed peeled, chopped
225 g (8 oz) carrots, sliced
100 g (4 oz) mushrooms, finely chopped
300 ml (½ pint) skimmed milk
2 level tablespoons cornflour
salt
freshly ground black pepper
175 g (6 oz) fresh or frozen peas
2 medium apples

▲ Grill the lamb chops well.
▲ Boil the carrots and potatoes in boiling, salted water.
▲ Whilst the chops and vegetables are cooking, make the mushroom sauce. Blend a little skimmed milk with the cornflour, then pour the remainder of the milk into a saucepan and heat. Stir the blended cornflour into the hot milk.
▲ Add the mushrooms and seasoning, then bring to the boil, simmer for 2 minutes, stirring constantly. Cook the peas.
▲ Serve the grilled chop with the mushroom sauce and strained vegetables. Follow with the fruit.

SNACK 1

TOAST AND HONEY
1 × 25 g (1 oz) slice wholemeal bread
1 level teaspoon honey

▲ Toast the bread and spread with the honey.

SNACK 2

BANANA AND ICE CREAM
1 small banana
50 g (2 oz) vanilla ice cream

▲ Peel and slice the banana and serve with the ice cream.

───────────────**DAY 5**───────────────

BREAKFAST

POACHED EGG ON TOAST
1 egg, size 3
1 × 40 g (1½ oz) slice wholemeal bread
2 level teaspoons ketchup

▲ Poach the egg and toast the bread.
▲ Serve the egg on the toast, accompanied by the ketchup.

LUNCH

CORNED BEEF SANDWICH
2 × 25 g (1 oz) slices wholemeal bread
2 level teaspoons low-fat spread
40 g (1½ oz) slice corned beef
mustard (optional)

▲ Spread the bread with the low-fat spread.
▲ Place the corned beef on one slice of bread, spread with a little mustard if liked, and top with the remaining slice of bread.

EVENING MEAL (Serves 2)

CHEESE-STUFFED TROUT

2 fresh or frozen trout, 175 g (6 oz) each
½ small onion, finely chopped
65 g (2½ oz) Edam cheese, grated
1 small lemon
25 g (1 oz) fresh wholemeal breadrumbs
2 level tablespoons chopped parsley
salt
freshly ground black pepper
175 g (6 oz) potatoes, weighed peeled
175 g (6 oz) fresh or frozen peas
100 g (4 oz) frozen or canned sweetcorn

▲ Wash the fish thoroughly.
▲ Cut 2 slices from the centre of the lemon and set aside. Finely grate the rind from the remaining lemon and squeeze out the juice.
▲ Mix together the onion, cheese, rind and half of the lemon juice, breadcrumbs and parsley. Season with salt and pepper and stuff into the trout cavities.
▲ Lay the trout side by side in an ovenproof dish and pour over the remaining lemon juice. Cover with a lid or foil and bake at 170°C, 325°F, Gas Mark 3 for 30 minutes.
▲ Cook the vegetables, drain and serve with the trout garnished with the lemon slices.

SNACK 1

CHEESE AND BISCUITS

2 cream crackers
25 g (1 oz) Brie, Edam or Camembert

SNACK 2

CRUMPET AND JAM
1 × 40 g (1½ oz) crumpet
1 level teaspoon low-fat spread
1 level teaspoon jam

▲ Toast the crumpet and spread with the low-fat spread and the jam.

—————————————————**DAY 6**—————————————————

BREAKFAST

BRAN CEREAL AND FRUIT
1 small banana
25 g (1 oz) all bran
1 level tablespoon sultanas or raisins
120 ml (4 fl oz) skimmed milk

▲ Peel and slice the banana and mix with the cereal and sultanas or raisins.
▲ Serve with the milk.

LUNCH

FISH FINGERS AND BAKED BEANS; FRUIT
2 fish fingers
1 × 150 g (5.3 oz) can baked beans with tomato sauce
1 medium pear or peach

▲ Grill the fish fingers without adding any fat.
▲ Heat the baked beans and serve with the fish fingers.
▲ Follow with the fruit.

EVENING MEAL (Serves 2)

MIXED GRILL
225 g (8 oz) *lamb's liver, sliced*
2 *lamb's kidneys, halved and cored*
1 *teaspoon oil*
2 *rashers streaky bacon*
4 *tomatoes, halved*
225 g (8 oz) *mushrooms*
2 × 40 g (1½ oz) *slices wholemeal bread*

▲ Wash and dry the liver. Brush the liver and kidney halves with oil and place on a grill rack with the bacon.
▲ Grill until cooked on one side, then turn over and add the tomato halves. Continue to grill until the liver and kidneys are cooked, the bacon is crisp and tomatoes are soft.
▲ Poach the mushrooms in a little stock or water.
▲ Serve the mixed grill with the drained mushrooms and wholemeal bread.

SNACK 1

CRISPBREAD WITH COTTAGE CHEESE AND PICKLE
1 *bran or high-fibre crispbread*
2 *level tablespoons cottage cheese with chives*
1 *level teaspoon sweet pickle*

▲ Top the crispbread with the cottage cheese and pickle.

SNACK 2

YOGURT MUESLI
3 *dried apricots*
150 g (5.3 oz) *low-fat natural yogurt*
2 *level tablespoons muesli*

▲ Chop the apricots and mix into the yogurt with the muesli.

————————————**DAY 7**————————————

BREAKFAST
TOAST WITH JAM OR MARMALADE
2 × 25 g (1 oz) slices wholemeal bread
1 level tablespoon low-fat spread
1 level tablespoon jam or marmalade

▲ Toast the bread and spread with the low-fat spread and jam or marmalade.

LUNCH
TUNA SALAD; FRUIT
1 × 100 g (3½ oz) can tuna in brine, drained
lettuce, shredded
¼ cucumber, diced
2 tomatoes, sliced
1 carrot, grated
1 level tablespoon low-calorie salad dressing
1 × 25 g (1 oz) slice wholemeal bread
1 level teaspoon low-fat spread
1 medium apple, pear or peach

▲ Serve the tuna with the lettuce, cucumber, tomatoes, carrot and low-calorie salad dressing.
▲ Spread the slice of bread with the low-fat spread and serve with the salad.
▲ Follow with fruit.

EVENING MEAL (Serves 1)
ROAST CHICKEN
150 g (5 oz) roast chicken
100 g (4 oz) potatoes
100 g (4 oz) carrots
100 g (4 oz) French beans
2 level tablespoons gravy (thick), made without fat
2 level tablespoons bread sauce

▲ Cook the chicken.
▲ Boil the potatoes, carrots and French beans.
▲ Serve the chicken with the vegetables, gravy and bread sauce.

SNACK 1
1 glass (120 ml (4 fl oz)) dry or medium white wine
50 g (2 oz) vanilla ice cream

▲ Serve the ice cream and wine separately (add to a meal if you wish).

SNACK 2
See Snack 2 on Day 1 (page 88).

THE LOW-FAT DIET

A glance at any calorie chart will show you that fats are by far the highest calorie foods of all. If you cut all the obvious fats out of your menus, you would undoubtedly greatly reduce your calorie intake. However, some fats are less obvious than those such as butter, margarine, lard and cooking oils. Fat also lurks in peanuts, pâté, cheese, even avocado pears. In order to reduce fat intake sufficiently to shed weight and to comply with modern health recommendations, it is necessary to ration the invisible fats as well as the more obvious ones.

In 1979 Slimming Magazine experts devised and tested a method by which all foods were given a simple unit count relating to their fat content. They called this the Dieting Revolution. To ration fats sufficiently to shed surplus weight all you have to do is keep to a fat count of 10 units a day. There are many fat-free foods that you can eat in ample quantities without all the weighing and measuring that is necessary on a calorie-controlled diet. The medical profession and leading nutritionists throughout the world now recommend a reduction in fat intake for better health.

On the low-fat diet you will also automatically be eating a healthy amount of high-fibre foods. This is not a no-fat diet. It is necesary for you to eat a little fat, but, if you wish, you may safely reduce the number of fat units you eat each day to 7.

At the start of the diet we give you a list of 0-fat unit foods that can be eaten in unlimited amounts. Add these to meals, or eat them as between-meals snacks. These foods play an important rôle in a healthy diet for their vitamin, bulk and fibre content and you should include items from this list each day.

Do not cook or serve fat-free vegetables with butter, margarine or fat of any sort. It doesn't matter if vegetables are fresh, frozen or canned as long as they don't come in a sauce, but don't include any pre-cooked vegetable products (for example, potato waffles or fritters) unless they are given in a menu.

Salads should be served plain or with a little oil-free French dressing unless another dressing is allowed for in your meal.

Fruits that have been frozen without added sugar or fruits canned in natural juice may be substituted for fresh fruit if you wish.

Dried fruits contain no fat but are high in calories and should only be eaten when included in a recipe.

Fruit canned in syrup should be avoided because of its high sugar content.

Fresh fruits may be eaten raw, baked or stewed but shouldn't be sweetened with sugar. Use artificial calorie-free sweetener with stewed fruit if necessary.

Fresh skimmed milk or reconstituted low-fat powdered milk contains no fat units. However, we recommend that you restrict yourself to 300 ml (½ pint) a day for use in drinks. Skimmed milk used on cereals in the recipes is extra to this allowance. If you wish to use other sorts of milk see the chart at the back of the book for fat units.

The simplicity of this low-fat diet makes it an easy and highly successful way to lose weight. Try it.

Diet Rules

1. Choose meals and snacks totalling up to 10 fat units a day.

2. Choose as many items as you wish from the 0-fat unit lists to eat either with meals or between meals.

3. You may drink unlimited tea and coffee, either black or with skimmed milk. Use artificial sweeteners only. You may also drink low-calorie soft drinks in unlimited amounts.

4. Vary the foods you eat each day to ensure you get all the nutrients you need.

5. If you wish to speed up your weight loss, reduce your fat units to 7 a day (no less). You may also limit fruit to 2 pieces a day and help yourself to no more than 225 g (8 oz) in total of any of the following vegetables: peas, sweetcorn, broad beans, sweet potato, yams, potatoes and plantain. These vegetables are higher in calories and could slow your weight loss if eaten in large quantities. Continue to eat any of the other vegetables in whatever quantity you wish.

0-FAT UNITS
FREE VEGETABLES
Without butter, dressings or sauces

Asparagus	Cucumber	Peppers
Aubergine	Endive	Plantain
Beansprouts	Fennel	Potatoes
Broad beans	French beans	Pumpkin
Butter beans	Globe artichoke	Radishes
Beetroot	Jerusalem artichoke	Runner beans
Broccoli	Leeks	Seakale
Brussels sprouts	Lentils	Spinach
Cabbage	Lettuce	Spring onions
Carrots	Marrow	Swede
Celeriac	Mouli	Sweetcorn
Celery	Mushrooms	Sweet potato
Chicory	Okra	Tomatoes
Chinese leaves	Onions	Turnips
Courgettes	Parsnips	Yams
Cress	Peas	

0-FAT UNITS
FREE FRUIT
Fresh or canned in natural juice or frozen without added sugar.
Dried fruits only when included in a meal.

Apples	Grapefruit	Paw Paw
Apricots	Grapes	Peaches
Bananas	Guava	Pears
Bilberries	Kiwi fruit	Pineapple
Blackberries	Loganberries	Plums
Blackcurrants	Mandarins	Raspberries
Cherries	Mango	Rhubarb
Clementines	Melon (all types)	Satsumas
Damsons	Nectarines	Strawberries
Figs	Oranges	Tangerines
Gooseberries	Passion fruit	Watermelon

SNACKS
½-FAT UNIT
Biscuits (1 biscuit)
Chocolate biscuit finger
Fig roll
Garibaldi
Ginger snap/nut
Malted biscuit
Morning coffee
Rich tea

Yogurt
Any low-fat fruit or low-fat natural yogurt

1-FAT UNIT
Biscuits (1 biscuit)
Shortcake
Bourbon cream
Custard cream
Digestive

Yogurts
Low-fat hazelnut

1½-FAT UNITS
Biscuits (1 biscuit)
Large chocolate digestive
Shortbread
Chocolate-coated orange cream
Chocolate chip cookie

2-FAT UNITS
Cakes & muffins
Chocolate mini roll
1 × 60 g (2¼ oz) muffin, toasted and spread with 2 level teaspoons low-fat spread
1 × 50 g (2 oz) teacake, split and toasted, filled with 1 level teaspoon jam or honey
1 × 50 g (2 oz) large slice malt bread, topped with 1 level teaspoon low-fat spread and 1 level teaspoon honey

——————————— **½-FAT UNIT MEALS** ————————

LENTIL AND VEGETABLE SOUP WITH BREAD ROLL
25 g (1 oz) red lentils
1 × 225 g (8 oz) can tomatoes
1 small onion, chopped
25 g (1 oz) carrot, chopped
½ level teaspoon curry powder
salt and freshly ground black pepper
1 × 45 g (1¾ oz) wholemeal roll

▲ Place the lentils in a small pan.
▲ Break up the tomatoes and add to the pan with their juice, the onion, carrot and curry powder. Bring to the boil and simmer, covered, for 45-50 minutes or until the lentils are tender.
▲ Season and serve with the bread roll.

TOAST AND YEAST EXTRACT; FRUIT
2 small slices wholemeal bread, total weight 50 g (2 oz)
2 level teaspoons yeast extract
1 piece of fruit

▲ Toast the bread and spread with the yeast extract. Follow with a piece of fruit from the 'free fruit' list.

POACHED FISH AND VEGETABLES
200 g (7 oz) cod, coley or haddock fillet
free vegetables
wedge of lemon

▲ Steam or poach the fish in water for about 15 minutes.
▲ Serve with boiled vegetables of your choice and the lemon.

——————————— **1-FAT UNIT MEALS** ————————

WHEAT CEREAL WITH RAISINS
2 wheat breakfast biscuits
1 level tablespoon raisins
120 ml (4 fl oz) skimmed milk

▲ Serve the wheat breakfast biscuits with the raisins and milk.

ALL BRAN AND BANANA
25 g (1 oz) all bran
1 small banana, chopped
1 level tablespoon wheatgerm
1 × 150 g (5 oz) carton low-fat natural yogurt
1-2 tablespoons skimmed milk

▲ Put the cereal in a bowl.
▲ Mix the banana, wheatgerm, yogurt and milk together. Pour over the cereal and serve.

POTATO WITH RICH KIDNEY SAUCE
1 potato, 225 g (8 oz), raw weight
50 g (2 oz) onion, chopped finely
25 g (1 oz) mushrooms, sliced
¼ beef stock cube, crumbled
120 ml (4 fl oz) boiling water
¼ level teaspoon thyme
2 lambs' kidneys, cored and chopped
1 level teaspoon cornflour
salt
freshly ground black pepper

▲ Scrub and prick the potato, and bake at 200°C, 400°F, Gas Mark 6 for about 1 hour or until soft when squeezed gently.
▲ About 15-20 minutes before the end of the cooking time, place the onion and mushrooms in a pan. Dissolve the stock cube into the boiling water and add to the pan with the thyme. Bring to the boil and simmer, covered, for 10 minutes, stirring frequently to prevent sticking.
▲ Add the kidneys to the pan and simmer gently, covered, for 5 minutes until cooked. If necessary add a little water to prevent sticking.
▲ Blend the cornflour with a little cold water until smooth and stir into the mixture. Season.
▲ Split the potato lengthways and pour over the kidney mixture.

'PRESTO' PASTA
50 g (2 oz) wholewheat pasta
50 g (2 oz) cottage cheese
15 g (½ oz) ham, chopped
50 g (2 oz) canned sweetcorn
garlic salt
freshly ground black pepper

▲ Cook the pasta in boiling water according to the packet instructions.
▲ When tender, drain thoroughly, then return to the pan with the cheese, ham, sweetcorn, garlic salt and pepper.
▲ Stir over a low heat for 1 minute until heated through and serve immediately.

BAKED BEANS ON TOAST
1 × 150 g (5.3 oz) can baked beans in tomato sauce
2 × 25 g (1 oz) slices wholemeal bread

▲ Heat the beans and serve on toasted bread.

—————————1 ½-FAT UNIT MEALS—————————

HAZELNUT YOGURT; TOAST
1 × 150 g (5 oz) carton low-fat hazelnut yogurt
1 × 40 g (1½ oz) slice wholemeal bread
1 level teaspoon yeast extract

▲ Serve the hazelnut yogurt.
▲ Follow with toasted bread spread with yeast extract.

CHEESE AND PICKLE ROLL
1 × 45 g (1¾ oz) wholemeal bread roll
25 g (1 oz) curd cheese
1 level tablespoon sweet pickle

▲ Split the roll and fill with the curd cheese and sweet pickle.

RICE AND CHEESE-STUFFED PEPPER SHELLS

1 large red or green pepper
25 g (1 oz) white long-grain rice
15 g (½ oz) Edam cheese, grated
2 level tablespoons canned sweetcorn, drained
2 level teaspoons chopped parsley
15 g (½ oz) mushrooms, finely chopped
pinch of cayenne pepper
salt
freshly ground black pepper

▲ Cut the pepper in half lengthways and remove the stalk, pith and seeds. Boil for 3-4 minutes, then drain and rinse under cold water.
▲ Boil the rice in water for 12-15 minutes, or until tender.
▲ Mix the hot rice with the remaining ingredients.
▲ Pile the mixture into the pepper shells. Place the peppers in an ovenproof dish and pour enough water in the dish to come half an inch up the sides of the pepper shells. Bake, uncovered, at 180°C, 350°F, Gas Mark 4, for 30 minutes. Serve hot.

KIDNEY RISOTTO WITH SALAD

1 small onion, chopped
50 g (2 oz) red pepper, cored, seeded and chopped
50 g (2 oz) white long-grain rice
50 g (2 oz) mushrooms, sliced
¼ stock cube, crumbled
150 ml (¼ pint) boiling water
salt
freshly ground black pepper
50 g (2 oz) frozen or canned sweetcorn
175 g (6 oz) lambs' kidneys, cored and halved, fat discarded
salad made with free vegetables

▲ Place the onion, pepper, rice and mushrooms in a pan. Dissolve the stock cube in the boiling water and add to the pan with the seasoning. Bring to the boil, add the sweetcorn and stir once.
▲ Reduce the heat, cover the pan and simmer for 15-20 minutes, stirring occasionally. If necessary add water to prevent sticking.
▲ Grill the kidneys without added fat for 6-10 minutes.
▲ Chop the kidneys and stir into the rice. Serve with a salad.

CELERY CHEESE-STUFFED POTATO WITH SALAD

1 potato, 225 g (8 oz) raw weight
1 tablespoon skimmed milk
15 g (½ oz) low-fat Cheddar cheese, grated
50 g (2 oz) cottage cheese
25 g (1 oz) celery, grated or finely chopped
salt
freshly ground black pepper
free vegetables

▲ Scrub and prick the potato and bake at 200°C, 400°F, Gas Mark 6, for about 1 hour or until soft when squeezed gently. Cut in half lengthways, scoop out the flesh and mash with the milk.
▲ Mix the cheeses and celery, stir into the potato flesh and season.
▲ Pile back into the potato cases and reheat for 10-15 minutes.
▲ Serve with a salad made from the 'free vegetables' list.

PORRIDGE AND SULTANAS

25 g (1 oz) porridge oats
1 level tablespoon sultanas
150 ml (¼ pint) skimmed milk

▲ Mix the oats, sultanas and milk in a pan, and bring to the boil, stirring thoroughly. Cook for 2-3 minutes and serve at once.

————————2-FAT UNIT MEALS————————

FISH IN PRAWN SAUCE WITH RICE AND SALAD

25 g (1 oz) brown rice
100 g (4 oz) haddock, cod or coley, fresh or frozen
1 level teaspoon tomato purée
25 g (1 oz) onion, chopped
1 level teaspoon mango chutney
120 ml (4 fl oz) dry white wine
skimmed milk
2 level teaspoons cornflour
50 g (2 oz) fresh prawns, rinsed and drained
salt
freshly ground black pepper
free vegetables

▲ Boil the rice for about 25 minutes until tender.
▲ While it is cooking, put the fish in a baking dish. Mix the tomato purée, onion and chutney with the wine and pour over the fish.
▲ Cover loosely with foil and bake at 180°C, 350°F, Gas Mark 4, for 20-25 minutes. Lift out the fish and keep warm.
▲ Strain the cooking liquid into a measuring jug and make up to 150 ml (¼ pint) with the skimmed milk. Pour into a pan, blend in the cornflour and bring to the boil, stirring.
▲ Add the prawns and simmer for 1-2 minutes.
▲ Season and serve with the boiled rice and a salad made from the 'free vegetables' list.

LEMON CHICKEN WITH JACKET POTATO AND SALAD

1 × 200 g (7 oz) potato
225 g (8 oz) chicken leg joint, skin removed
1 level teaspoon grated lemon rind
1 tablespoon lemon juice
1 small onion, chopped
25 g (1 oz) celery, chopped
¼ level teaspoon thyme
½ chicken stock cube, crumbled
150 ml (¼ pint) boiling water
salt
freshly ground black pepper
1½ level teaspoons cornflour
free vegetables

▲ Scrub and prick the potato and bake at 200°C, 400°F, Gas Mark 6 for about 1 hour or until soft when squeezed gently.
▲ Place the chicken in an ovenproof dish and add the lemon rind, juice, onion, celery and thyme. Dissolve the stock cube in the water and pour over the chicken.
▲ Cover and cook alongside the potato for 50 minutes-1 hour.
▲ Transfer the chicken to a heated dish and strain the stock into a measuring jug. Make up to 150 ml (¼ pint) with water if necessary.
▲ Blend in the cornflour, bring to the boil, stirring, and simmer for 1-2 minutes.
▲ Season and pour over the chicken.
▲ Serve with the jacket potato and a salad made from the 'free vegetables' list.

BEEFBURGER WITH SALAD
50 g (2 oz) beefburger, fresh or frozen
1 × 65 g (2½ oz) wholemeal muffin
½ level teaspoon mustard or 1 level tablespoon tomato ketchup
free vegetables

▲ Grill the beefburger well.
▲ Split and lightly toast the inside of the muffin. Top one half of the muffin with the beefburger and mustard or tomato ketchup, then replace the other half.
▲ Serve with salad vegetables from the 'free vegetables' list.

——————2½-FAT UNIT MEALS——————

BANANA AND HAZELNUT BREAKFAST
1 banana, sliced
15 g (½ oz) hazelnuts, chopped
1 level teaspoon clear honey
1 crispbread, crumbled
150 g (5 oz) low-fat natural yogurt

▲ Stir the banana, hazelnuts, honey and crispbread into the yogurt.

PARSLEY HAM STEAK AND VEGETABLES
100 g (4 oz) ham steak
150 ml (¼ pint) skimmed milk
2 level teaspoons cornflour
2 level teaspoons chopped parsley
15 g (½ oz) Gouda cheese, grated
¼ level teaspoon grated nutmeg
salt
freshly ground black pepper
free vegetables

▲ Grill the ham for 8-10 minutes, turning once. Discard any fat.
▲ Blend the milk and cornflour together in a pan, bring to the boil and simmer for 1-2 minutes, stirring constantly. Remove from the heat and stir in the parsley, cheese, nutmeg and seasoning.
▲ Serve the sauce over the ham steak with boiled vegetables from the 'free vegetables' list.

TUNA PIZZA WITH SALAD

1 × 225 g (8 oz) can tomatoes, drained
¼ level teaspoon mixed herbs
1 level teaspoon tomato ketchup
salt
freshly ground black pepper
1 wholemeal pitta bread
1 × 100 g (3½ oz) can tuna in brine, drained and flaked
1 level teaspoon capers, chopped
25 g (1 oz) fat-reduced cheese, grated
15 g (½ oz) mushrooms, sliced

▲ Discard the tomato juice and place the drained tomatoes in a
pan with the herbs, tomato ketchup and seasoning.
▲ Break up the tomatoes, bring to the boil and simmer uncovered
vigorously for 5-10 minutes, stirring frequently, until the mixture is
reduced and thick and pulpy.
▲ Warm the pitta bread under the grill for a few minutes on either
side, but do not brown.
▲ Spread the tomato mixture on the pitta bread. Spread the tuna
fish on the pitta bread with the capers.
▲ Sprinkle over the cheese and mushrooms, and grill for 5-7
minutes until heated through and bubbling.

POACHED EGG AND CRUMPET

1 egg, size 3
1 crumpet

▲ Poach the egg until just set, about 2-3 minutes.
▲ Toast the crumpet and serve the egg on the crumpet.

HERRING ROES ON TOAST

100 g (4 oz) soft herring roes
50 ml (2 fl oz) skimmed milk
2 × 25 g (1 oz) slices wholemeal bread

▲ Wash the herring roes and poach in the milk for about 5 minutes
until firm.
▲ Toast the bread and serve the drained roes on top.

——————3-FAT UNIT MEALS——————

APRICOT AND YOGURT CRUNCH

3 dried apricots, chopped
1 × 150 g (5 oz) carton low-fat natural yogurt
15 g (½ oz) porridge oats
2 level teaspoons soft brown sugar
15 g (½ oz) hazelnuts, chopped

▲ Stir the apricots into the yogurt.
▲ Mix the porridge oats, sugar and hazelnuts together and sprinkle on top of the yogurt mixture.
▲ Place under a hot grill until the topping is brown.

WAFFLES WITH HONEY OR JAM

2 waffles
2 level teaspoons honey or jam

▲ Grill the waffles and top with 1 level teaspoon of honey or jam.

CHICKEN WARMER WITH BREAD ROLL

1 small onion, chopped
50 g (2 oz) celery, chopped
50 g (2 oz) carrots, chopped
½ chicken stock cube, crumbled
450 ml (¾ pint) boiling water
1 level teaspoon tomato purée
50 g (2 oz) frozen or canned sweetcorn
15 g (½ oz) pearl barley or brown lentils
2 chicken drumsticks, 90 g (3½ oz) each, skin removed
salt
freshly ground black pepper
1 × 45 g (1¾ oz) wholemeal roll

▲ Place the onion, celery and carrots in a pan. Dissolve the stock cube in the water and add to the pan with the tomato purée, sweetcorn, pearl barley or lentils.
▲ Bring to the boil, add the chicken and seasoning and simmer, covered, for 50 minutes-1 hour, stirring occasionally to prevent sticking. Serve with the bread roll.

————————3½-FAT UNIT MEALS————————

CHEESY STUFFED TOMATOES WITH WHOLEMEAL BREAD

2 large tomatoes
1 crispbread, crushed
25 g (1 oz) fat-reduced Cheddar-type cheese, grated
¼ level teaspoon basil
salt
freshly ground black pepper
2 × 25 g (1 oz) slices wholemeal bread
2 level teaspoons low-fat spread

▲ Slice the top off each tomato and scoop out the pulp and seeds from each. Mix the tomato pulp and seeds with the crispbread, cheese, basil and seasoning.
▲ Pack into the tomato shells, allowing the mixture to stand proud of the top. Place the tops of the tomato at an angle on each.
▲ Stand in an ovenproof dish and bake uncovered at 180°C, 350°F, Gas Mark 4, for 20 minutes.
▲ Serve with the slices of wholemeal bread spread with the low-fat spread.

CURRIED CHICKEN PITTA POCKET

1 wholemeal pitta bread
75 g (3 oz) cooked chicken, skin removed, chopped
2 level teaspoons low-calorie mayonnaise
2 level tablespoons low-fat natural yogurt
¼ level teaspoon curry powder
1 level tablespoon sultanas
salt
freshly ground black pepper
shredded lettuce

▲ Cut the wholemeal pitta bread in half. Carefully slip a knife between the 2 layers to make a pocket, making sure you do not split the sides of the bread.
▲ Mix the chicken with the mayonnaise, yogurt, curry powder, sultanas and seasoning.
▲ Line each pitta pocket with lettuce and spoon the chicken mixture into each.

HAM, CHEESE AND PINEAPPLE FLUFF WITH VEGETABLES

½ level teaspoon low-fat spread
1 egg, size 3, separated
25 g (1 oz) ham, fat discarded, lean chopped
50 g (2 oz) cottage cheese with pineapple
salt
freshly ground black pepper
free vegetables

▲ Lightly grease a small ovenproof dish with the low-fat spread.
▲ Add the ham and cheese to the egg yolk, season and mix well.
▲ Whisk the egg white until stiff but not dry. With a metal spoon, fold lightly into the yolk mixture and pour into the ovenproof dish.
▲ Bake at 190°C, 375°F, Gas Mark 5 for 20 minutes until fluffy and golden brown.
▲ Serve with boiled vegetables from the 'free vegetables' list.

EGG AND BACON MUFFIN

1 rasher streaky bacon
1 egg, size 3
1 tablespoon skimmed milk
1 × 60 g (2¼ oz) wholemeal muffin

▲ Grill the bacon until crisp, then break into small pieces.
▲ Beat the egg and milk together, pour into a non-stick pan and cook over a low heat, stirring constantly until just beginning to set.
▲ Add the bacon and continue cooking until the eggs are scrambled.
▲ While the eggs are cooking, split and toast the muffin. Put the egg on one half of the muffin and top with the other half.

————————4-FAT UNIT MEALS————————

EASTERN STYLE BEEF AND BEANS WITH RICE

150 g (5 oz) ground or very lean minced beef
1 × 225 g (7.9 oz) can baked beans
2 level tablespoons sultanas
½ level teaspoon curry powder
½ beef stock cube, crumbled
150 ml (¼ pint) boiling water

1 *small onion, chopped*
1 *level teaspoon tomato purée*
salt
freshly ground black pepper
40 *g* (1½ *oz*) *brown rice*

▲ Brown the meat in a non-stick pan and drain off all the fat.
▲ Mix the beans with the sultanas and curry powder.
▲ Dissolve the stock cube in the water and add to the pan with the onion, tomato purée and beans.
▲ Bring to the boil, season, cover the pan and simmer gently for 20-30 minutes. Stir occasionally and add a little water to prevent sticking if necessary.
▲ Meanwhile boil the rice until tender.
▲ Serve the beef and bean mixture with the boiled rice.

PIQUANT PLAICE WITH CUCUMBER SAUCE AND SALAD

1 *crispbread, crumbled*
25 *g* (1 *oz*) *curd cheese*
½ *level teaspoon lemon rind*
1 *teaspoon lemon juice*
salt
freshly ground black pepper
100 *g* (4 *oz*) *plaice fillet*
½ *level teaspoon low-fat spread*
2 *level tablespoons low-fat natural yogurt*
1 *level tablespoon low-calorie mayonnaise*
50 *g* (2 *oz*) *cucumber, chopped*
free vegetables

▲ Mix the crispbread, cheese, lemon rind and juice and seasoning.
▲ Split the plaice fillet lengthways. Put half the mixture on each piece of fish skin-side up and roll up.
▲ Place the fish in an ovenproof dish, greased with low-fat spread. Cover loosely with foil and bake at 180°C, 350°F, Gas Mark 4, for 20-25 minutes.
▲ When cooked, mix the yogurt, mayonnaise and cucumber in a pan. Season. Heat gently and pour over the fish.
▲ Serve with a salad made with vegetables from the 'free vegetables' list.

BACON, EGG AND BEANS

1 *streaky bacon rasher*
1 × 25 g (1 oz) *slice wholemeal bread*
1 *egg, size 3*
100 g (4 oz) *baked beans in tomato sauce*

▲ Grill the bacon until crisp.
▲ Toast the bread alongside the bacon.
▲ Poach the egg until just set, about 2-3 minutes.
▲ Heat the beans in a small pan.
▲ Serve the egg on the toast with the bacon and beans.

CHEESE AND SARDINE TOASTS

50 g (2 oz) *sardines in tomato sauce, drained*
salt
freshly ground black pepper
1 *teaspoon lemon juice*
15 g (½ oz) *Gouda cheese, grated*
1 × 60 g (2¼ oz) *wholemeal muffin*

▲ Mix the sardines together with the seasoning, lemon juice and cheese.
▲ Split and grill the muffin, then top each half with the sardine mixture.
▲ Return to the grill for 2-3 minutes until warmed through.

EGGS AND LEEK AU GRATIN WITH BOILED VEGETABLES

1 *egg, size 3, hardboiled and sliced*
50 g (2 oz) *leek, sliced*
1 *level tablespoon Parmesan cheese*
40 g (1½ oz) *fat-reduced Cheddar cheese, grated*
4 *level tablespoons wholemeal breadcrumbs*
2 *level teaspoons cornflour*
¼ *level teaspoon mustard powder*
120 ml (4 fl oz) *skimmed milk*
salt
freshly ground black pepper
cayenne pepper
free vegetables

▲ Place the leek in a pan with water, boil for 5 minutes, then drain.
▲ Mix the cheeses together and reserve 1 level tablespoon. Mix the remaining cheese mixture with the breadcrumbs.
▲ Put half of the mixture in the bottom of a small ovenproof dish. Top with half the leeks and sliced egg, then season.
▲ Mix the cornflour, mustard powder and milk together in a small pan. Bring to the boil and simmer for 1-2 minutes. Add the reserved cheese and season.
▲ Pour over the egg and top with the remaining leek, cheese and breadcrumb mixture.
▲ Sprinkle with a pinch or two of cayenne pepper. Bake at 220°C, 425°F, Gas Mark 7 for 20-25 minutes until bubbling and browned on top.
▲ Serve with free boiled vegetables, with no added fat.

CHEESE SALAD FRENCH STICK

50 g (2 oz) French bread
25 g (1 oz) Gouda cheese
1 tomato, sliced
lettuce, shredded

▲ Split the bread and fill with the cheese, tomato and lettuce.

CHINESE-STYLE PRAWNS

1 level teaspoon clear honey
1 teaspoon vinegar
2 teaspoons soy sauce
4 tablespoons juice from the pineapple
1 level teaspoon cornflour
2 teaspoons oil
50 g (2 oz) carrots, cut into matchstick strips
2 rings pineapple canned in natural juice, drained
100 g (4 oz) fresh or canned beansprouts
50 g (2 oz) sweetcorn
75 g (3 oz) fresh or frozen prawns

▲ Mix together the honey, vinegar, soy sauce, pineapple juice and cornflour.
▲ Cut each pineapple slice into 8 pieces. Heat the oil in a wok or frying pan, and add the carrot, pineapple, beansprouts and sweetcorn and stir-fry for 2 minutes.
▲ Stir the sauce mixture, add to the pan and bring to the boil, stirring constantly. Reduce the heat, add the prawns and simmer for 1-2 minutes. Serve immediately.

————4½-FAT UNIT MEALS————

WHEAT OR RICE SALAD WITH CORNED BEEF

25 g (1 oz) bulgar cracked wheat or long-grain brown rice
2 spring onions, chopped
1 tomato, chopped, seeds removed
50 g (2 oz) canned red kidney beans, drained and rinsed
50 g (2 oz) canned sweetcorn, drained and rinsed
25 g (1 oz) red pepper, cored, seeded and chopped
1 level tablespoon raisins
4 teaspoons oil-free French dressing
1 level teaspoon parsley, chopped
100 g (4 oz) corned beef

▲ Soak the bulgar cracked wheat in cold water for 30 minutes and drain well, or prepare according to packet instructions, if supplied.
▲ If using brown rice, cook in boiling water for 25-30 minutes or until tender. Drain and allow to cool.

▲ Mix the onions, tomato, kidney beans, sweetcorn, pepper and raisins together.
▲ Blend the dressing with the parsley, pour over the salad and toss thoroughly.
▲ Add the wheat or rice and mix together with the salad ingredients.
▲ Serve with the corned beef.

CHICKEN AND HAM SAVOURY

150 ml (¼ pint) skimmed milk
¼ level teaspoon grated nutmeg
¼ level teaspoon ground mace
1 level tablespoon cornflour
90 g (3½ oz) cooked chicken, skin removed, chopped
15 g (½ oz) cooked lean ham, fat discarded, chopped
salt
freshly ground black pepper
1 wheat breakfast biscuit, crumbled
25 g (1 oz) fat-reduced cheese, grated
cayenne pepper

▲ Blend the milk, spices and cornflour together until smooth. Pour into a pan and bring to the boil, stirring constantly.
▲ Add the chicken and ham, season, reduce the heat and simmer for 3-4 minutes, stirring occasionally.
▲ Pour the mixture into a small ovenproof dish. Top with the wheat biscuit and cheese mixed together and sprinkle with a pinch or two of cayenne pepper.
▲ Place under the grill for 2-3 minutes until bubbling and browned on top.
▲ Serve immediately.

CHEESY POTATO NEST

40 g (1½ oz) instant mashed potato
2 level teaspoons cornflour
150 ml (¼ pint) skimmed milk
25 g (1 oz) Edam cheese, grated
¼ level teaspoon grated nutmeg
salt and freshly ground black pepper
1 egg, size 3, hardboiled and sliced

▲ Make up the potato with water. Spoon the mashed potato into a small baking or pie dish, making a nest shape. Keep warm.
▲ Blend the cornflour with the milk until smooth. Pour into a pan and bring to the boil, stirring, then simmer for 1-2 minutes.
▲ Add half the cheese, nutmeg and seasoning. Remove from the heat and add the egg. Pour the mixture into the potato nest. Top with the remaining cheese and grill until golden brown.

CHEESE AND HONEY SCONE

1 × 50 g (2 oz) wholemeal scone
25 g (1 oz) curd cheese
2 teaspoons clear honey

▲ Split the scone and top each half with the cheese and honey.

SALMON AND PASTA BAKE WITH SALAD

25 g (1 oz) wholewheat pasta shapes
¼ level teaspoon low-fat spread
2 level teaspoons cornflour
120 ml (4 fl oz) skimmed milk
1 level teaspoon gherkins, finely chopped
1 level teaspoon capers, chopped
1 teaspoon lemon juice
1 × 90 g (3½ oz) can salmon, drained and flaked
salt
freshly ground black pepper
2 level tablespoons wholemeal breadcrumbs
15 g (½ oz) low-fat Cheddar cheese, grated
cayenne pepper
free vegetables

▲ Cook the pasta shapes until just tender and drain.

▲ Grease a small ovenproof dish with the low-fat spread and place the pasta in the bottom.

▲ Blend the cornflour with the milk in a small pan. Bring to the boil, stirring, and simmer for 1-2 minutes.

▲ Add the gherkins, capers, lemon juice and the drained and flaked salmon. Season to taste. Pour the mixture over the pasta.

▲ Mix the breadcrumbs and cheese together with one or two pinches of cayenne pepper.

▲ Sprinkle the breadcrumb mixture over the salmon mixture and bake at 180°C, 350°F, Gas Mark 4, for 20-25 minutes.

▲ Serve with a salad made from the 'free vegetables' list.

5-FAT UNIT MEALS

TURKEY SAUSAGES WITH VEGETABLE RICE

1 small onion, chopped
50 g (2 oz) carrot, diced
40 g (1½ oz) long-grain brown rice
1 × 225 g (8 oz) can tomatoes
¼ teaspoon Worcestershire sauce
50 g (2 oz) fresh or frozen peas
salt
freshly ground black pepper
2 turkey with pork sausages

▲ Put the onion, carrot and rice into a pan.

▲ Drain the tomatoes, pour the tomato juice into a measuring jug and make up to 150 ml (¼ pint) with water. Add to the rice and vegetables, cover and cook for 5 minutes.

▲ Add the tomatoes, Worcestershire sauce, peas and seasoning. Bring to the boil, stirring once.

▲ Reduce the heat and simmer, covered, for 25-30 minutes until all the liquid is absorbed and the rice is cooked. If the mixture sticks before the rice is cooked, add a little extra water.

▲ Meanwhile, grill the sausages well.

▲ Serve the vegetable rice with the sausages.

TOASTED CHEESE

40 g (1½ oz) Gouda cheese, grated
¼ level teaspoon mustard powder
salt
freshly ground black pepper
¼ teaspoon Worcestershire sauce
skimmed milk
2 × 25 g (1 oz) slices wholemeal bread

▲ Mix the cheese, mustard, salt, pepper and Worcestershire sauce together. Add enough skimmed milk to bind.
▲ Toast the bread on both sides, leaving one side less brown. Spread this side with the cheese mixture.
▲ Return to the grill and cook until golden and bubbling.
▲ Serve at once.

KIPPER AND ROLL

175 g (6 oz) kipper on the bone
1 × 45 g (1¾ oz) wholemeal roll
1 level teaspoon low-fat spread
free vegetables

▲ Grill the kipper gently without added fat for 4-5 minutes on each side.
▲ Split the bread roll and spread with the low-fat spread.
▲ Serve the kipper with the bread roll and boiled vegetables from the 'free vegetables' list.

FRENCH GARLIC BREAD

50 g (2 oz) French bread
25 g (1 oz) Boursin cheese
1 medium tomato, sliced

▲ Cut the bread lengthways and spread with the cheese. Place the tomato along the centre and put the two halves together.
▲ Wrap tightly in foil and bake at 220°C, 425°F, Gas Mark 7, for 20 minutes.
▲ Remove the foil and return to the oven for 3-4 minutes to crisp.

CHEESY PORK WITH CREAMED POTATO AND VEGETABLES

1 *crispbread, crumbled*
15 *g (½ oz) low-fat Cheddar cheese, grated*
¼ *level teaspoon dried sage*
1 *tablespoon skimmed milk*
salt
freshly ground black pepper
1 × 185 *g (6½ oz) pork chop, raw weight, fat removed*
150 *g (5 oz) potato, raw weight, mashed with*
3 *tablespoons skimmed milk*
free vegetables

▲ Mix the crispbread, cheese, sage, milk and seasoning together.
▲ Grill the pork chop for 15 minutes, turning once. Place the stuffing on top, and replace under the grill for 5 minutes.
▲ Meanwhile, boil the potato and mash with the milk.
▲ Serve with vegetables from the 'free vegetables' list.

———————5½-FAT UNIT MEALS———————

BEAN AND BEEFBURGER WAFFLES

2 *potato waffles*
2 *beefburgers, 50 g (2 oz) each*
1 × 225 *g (7.9 oz) can baked beans in tomato sauce*

▲ Grill the waffles and beefburgers. Heat the beans.
▲ Serve the beefburgers and beans on top of the waffles.

BACON AND SAUSAGE ROLL

1 *rasher streaky bacon*
½ *level teaspoon tomato ketchup*
1 *large pork sausage*
1 × 45 *g (1¾ oz) soft brown bread roll*

▲ Trim the rasher of visible fat and spread one side with the ketchup.
▲ Wrap the bacon, with the ketchup inside, around the sausage. Grill well for about 10-15 minutes, turning frequently.
▲ Split the roll and toast the inside lightly. Place the cooked bacon and sausage inside and serve immediately.

────────6-FAT UNIT MEALS────────

CHEESE AND TOMATO OMELETTE WITH SALAD

2 eggs, size 3
1 tablespoon water
salt
freshly ground black pepper
1 level teaspoon butter
¼ level teaspoon dried oregano or basil
1 tomato, chopped
15 g (½ oz) fat-reduced Cheddar-like cheese, grated
free vegetables

▲ Lightly beat the eggs, water, and seasoning together.
▲ Melt the fat in a non-stick omelette pan and brush all over the pan's surface.
▲ Add the egg mixture and cook until just set. Tilt the pan and lift the edges of the omelette while cooking so that the runny mixture goes underneath.
▲ Place the herbs, chopped tomato, cheese and seasoning along the centre of the cooked omelette and fold over.
▲ Serve with salad vegetables from the 'free vegetables' list.

BACON SCRAMBLE ON TOAST

1 rasher streaky bacon
2 eggs, size 3
2 tablespoons skimmed milk
salt
freshly ground black pepper
½ level teaspoonn low-fat spread
2 × 25 g (1 oz) slices wholemeal bread

▲ Grill the bacon until crisp, then crumble.
▲ Lightly beat the eggs and skimmed milk together and season with salt and pepper. Stir in the crumbled bacon.
▲ Melt the low-fat spread in a small non-stick pan, pour in the egg mixture and cook over a low heat, stirring until lightly set.
▲ Toast the bread and serve the eggs on the toast.

GAMMON WITH RAISIN SAUCE
1 *gammon rasher, 175 g (6 oz) raw weight*
1 *level tablespoon raisins*
1 *clove*
120 ml (4 fl oz) water
1 *level teaspoon brown sugar*
1 *level teaspoon cornflour*
1 *level teaspoon butter*
½ teaspoon lemon juice
seasoning
free vegetables

▲ Grill the gammon rasher for 3-4 minutes on each side.
▲ Put the raisins and clove in a pan with the water, bring to the boil and simmer uncovered for 10 minutes. Remove the clove and add the sugar.
▲ Blend the cornflour with a little water, add to the pan and stir until thickened. Add the butter, lemon juice and seasoning.
▲ Serve the sauce over the gammon with boiled vegetables from the 'free vegetables' list.

*T*HE <u>SOCIAL</u> DIET

If you frequently have to eat business lunches or enjoy dining out with friends, this is the ideal diet for you. You are allowed two restaurant meals a week as long as you are prepared to diet strictly for the remaining five days.

Your breakfast and lunch each day totals 400 calories, your milk allowance 100 calories and your snack 150 calories. On strict days you choose a low-calorie main meal at 350 calories which brings your daily calorie total to 1,000. On eating-out days, your restaurant meal comes to approximately 1,050 calories, bringing your day's total up to 1,700.

Over seven days this averages out to 1,200 calories a day, a calorie total on which everyone with over 1 stone to lose will shed weight quickly and on which all men will lose weight even if they have only a few pounds to go. Women with 1 stone or under to lose may find they have to be a bit stricter to get the pounds off at a reasonably fast rate. You can take your average daily calories down to 1,050 by not eating (or drinking) your snack or indulgence.

▲ When you choose one of the restaurant menus make sure that you choose only the items we list. If you nibble on a buttered bread roll before you start your meal, for example, it could cost you an extra 250 calories. The Social Diet allows you to dine out and still achieve a fast weight loss.

Diet Rules
1. Each day select one of the breakfast and light meal combinations. You may eat these meals at any time of the day. For instance, you may have the light meal at lunchtime or in the evening and if you do not wish to eat breakfast you can eat that meal later in the day.
2. For five days a week you must select your main meal from the 'Strict Days Main Meal' list. On the remaining two days choose a meal from the 'Eating Out' list. You can use your eating-out days for business lunches or for social dinners, depending on your lifestyle.
3. In addition to your 3 meals each day you may choose one item

from the Snacks and Indulgences list. This includes a choice of savoury and sweet snacks and some alcoholic drinks. If you wish, you can save up your snack allowance and spend it all on one evening, which is useful if there is a special celebration coming up. Alcoholic drinks contain few nutrients and can lower willpower, so it is best to restrict them to two days a week. For good nutrition choose a cereal snack or fruit on strict days.

4. You are allowed 300 ml (½ pint) skimmed milk to use in tea or coffee throughout the day. Milk included in menus is extra to this allowance. You may drink unlimited water, low-calorie squashes and fizzy drinks.

5. Although the menus are listed Day 1-14, you may eat them in any order and miss out any you don't like. However, you should not swap breakfasts or lunches from different days. For nutritional balance you should have at least four different menus each week.

6. If you don't eat your snack allowance each day your calorie total will go down to a strict 1,000.

————————DAY 1————————

BREAKFAST

TOAST AND MARMALADE

1 × 40 g (1½ oz) *slice wholemeal bread*
2 *level teaspoons low-fat spread*
2 *level teaspoons jam or marmalade.*

Toast the bread and spread with low-fat spread and jam or marmalade.

LIGHT MEAL

BACON ROLL

2 *rashers streaky bacon*
1 × 45 g (1¾ oz) *wholemeal roll*
1 *level tablespoon tomato ketchup*

▲ Grill the bacon until crisp. Split the roll and fill with the bacon and tomato ketchup.

————————————**DAY 2**————————————

BREAKFAST

YOGURT WITH MUESLI AND PEAR
1 *medium pear, cored and diced*
1 × 150 *g* (5.3 *oz*) *carton low-fat natural yogurt*
2 *level tablespoons muesli*

▲ Mix all the ingredients together and serve.

LIGHT MEAL

CRAB AND OLIVE TOASTS
2 × 25 *g* (1 *oz*) *slices wholemeal bread*
45 *g* (1¾ *oz*) *crabmeat*
2 *stuffed olives, sliced*
1 *tomato, sliced*

▲ Toast the bread and spread with the dressed crab.
▲ Top with the olives and tomatoes.

————————————**DAY 3**————————————

BREAKFAST

FLAKES AND BANANA
25 *g* (1 *oz*) *branflakes*
1 *small banana, peeled and sliced*
85 *ml* (3 *fl oz*) *skimmed milk*

▲ Serve the branflakes with the banana and milk.

LIGHT MEAL

KIDNEYS AND BAKED BEANS
2 *lamb's kidneys, halved and cored*
1 × 150 *g* (5.3 *oz*) *can baked beans in tomato sauce*
1 *high-fibre crispbread*

▲ Grill the kidneys.
▲ Heat the beans and serve with the kidneys and crispbread.

———————————**DAY 4**———————————

BREAKFAST

BOILED EGG AND CRISPBREADS
1 *egg, size 3*
2 *high-fibre crispbreads*
2 *level teaspoons low-fat spread*
1 *level teaspoon yeast extract*

▲ Boil the egg and serve with the crispbreads, spread with low-fat spread and yeast extract.

LIGHT MEAL

PRAWNS AND SOFT CHEESE SANDWICH
2 × 25 g (1 oz) *slices wholemeal bread*
50 g (2 oz) *low-fat soft cheese*
25 g (1 oz) *peeled prawns*
few slices of cucumber

▲ Spread the bread with the low-fat soft cheese and fill with prawns and cucumber.

———————————**DAY 5**———————————

BREAKFAST

BRANFLAKES WITH SULTANAS
25 g (1 oz) *branflakes*
1 *level tablespoon sultanas or raisins*
85 ml (3 fl oz) *skimmed milk*

▲ Mix the branflakes with the sultanas or raisins and serve with the skimmed milk.

LIGHT MEAL

BEEF SANDWICH; ORANGE

2 level teaspoons low-calorie salad dressing
½ level teaspoon mustard
2 × 25 g (1 oz) slices wholemeal bread
40 g (1½ oz) lean roast beef, visible fat discarded
1 small orange

▲ Mix the salad dressing with the mustard and spread on the bread. Fill with the beef.
▲ Eat the orange for dessert.

─────────────────**DAY 6**─────────────────

BREAKFAST

SAVOURY TOAST

1 × 40 g (1½ oz) slice wholemeal bread
1 level teaspoon yeast extract
25 g (1 oz) low-fat soft cheese

▲ Toast the bread and spread with the yeast extract and cheese.

LIGHT MEAL

BEAN SALAD

1 × 225 g (8 oz) can red kidney beans, drained
25 g (1 oz) garlic sausage, diced
1 spring onion, trimmed and chopped
1 stick celery, thinly sliced
3 olives, stoned and diced
2 tablespoons oil-free French dressing

▲ Mix all the ingredients together and serve.

---------------------**DAY 7**---------------------

BREAKFAST
See Day 1.

LIGHT MEAL

CHICKEN LIVERS AND MUSHROOMS WITH TOAST
50g (2 oz) button mushrooms, sliced
1 teaspoon oil
100 g (4 oz) chicken livers, trimmed and thickly sliced
1 × 25 g (1 oz) slice wholemeal bread

▲ Cook the mushrooms in the oil in a non-stick pan for 2-3 minutes. Add the chicken livers and cook until firm.
▲ Toast the bread and serve with the livers and mushrooms.

---------------------**DAY 8**---------------------

BREAKFAST

CEREAL AND BANANA
1 wheat breakfast biscuit
1 small banana, peeled and sliced
85 ml (3 fl oz) skimmed milk

▲ Serve the cereal with the banana and milk.

LIGHT MEAL

COTTAGE CHEESE AND HAM CRISPBREADS
1 × 113 g (4 oz) carton cottage cheese with chives or pineapple
25 g (1 oz) lean cooked ham, fat discarded and chopped
2 small gherkins, chopped
3 high-fibre crispbreads

▲ Mix the cottage cheese with the ham and gherkins and spread on the crispbreads.

─────────────DAY 9─────────────

BREAKFAST

SCRAMBLED EGG AND BACON

1 *rasher streaky bacon*
1 *egg, size 3*
1 *tablespoon skimmed milk*
salt
freshly ground black pepper
1 *high-fibre crispbread*

▲ Grill the bacon until crisp.
▲ Lightly beat the egg and milk together, season and cook in a non-stick pan until scrambled.
▲ Serve the egg and bacon with the crispbread.

LIGHT MEAL

CHEESY BEANS ON TOAST

1 × 40 g (1½ oz) *slice wholemeal bread*
1 × 150 g (5.3 oz) *can baked beans in tomato sauce*
15 g (½ oz) *fat-reduced Cheddar cheese, grated*

▲ Toast the bread.
▲ Heat the beans and place on the toast. Sprinkle the cheese on top and grill until melted.

─────────────DAY 10─────────────

BREAKFAST

TOAST AND HONEY

1 × 40 g (1½ oz) *slice wholemeal bread*
2 *level teaspoons low-fat spread*
2 *level teaspoons honey*

▲ Toast the bread and top with the low-fat spread and honey.

LIGHT MEAL
SMOKED TROUT SALAD
cucumber, sliced
celery, sliced
green or red pepper, sliced
carrot, grated
lettuce
1 tablespoon oil-free French dressing
1 × 150 g (5 oz) smoked trout
1 level teaspoon creamed horseradish or horseradish sauce
1 × 25 g (1 oz) slice wholemeal bread
1 level teaspoon low-fat spread

▲ Make a salad with the vegetables and sprinkle with the oil-free French dressing.
▲ Serve with the trout, horseradish, bread and low-fat spread.

——————————————**DAY 11**——————————————

BREAKFAST
BOILED EGG AND CRISPBREADS
1 egg, size 3
2 high-fibre crispbreads
2 level teaspoons low-fat spread

▲ Boil the egg and serve with the crispbreads and low-fat spread.

LIGHT MEAL

MUSHROOMS ON TOAST; FRUIT

100 g (4 oz) button mushrooms
120 ml (4 fl oz) water
¼ chicken stock cube, crumbled
3 level tablespoons skimmed milk powder
2 level teaspoons cornflour
1 × 40 g (1½ oz) slice wholemeal bread
1 medium pear or 1 small orange

▲ Put the mushrooms, 85 ml (3 fl oz) water and the crumbled stock cube in a pan, cover and poach for 4 minutes.
▲ Blend the remaining water with the powdered skimmed milk and cornflour until smooth. Stir into the pan and simmer for 1 minute, stirring constantly.
▲ Toast the bread and serve the mushrooms on top.
▲ Follow with the fruit.

——————————DAY 12——————————

BREAKFAST

SHREDDED WHEAT AND DRIED APRICOTS

1 shredded wheat breakfast biscuit
3 dried apricots, chopped
85 ml (3 fl oz) skimmed milk

▲ Serve the shredded wheat breakfast biscuit with the apricots and milk.

LIGHT MEAL

LIVER SAUSAGE AND TOMATO CRISPBREADS

2 high-fibre crispbreads
50 g (2 oz) liver sausage, sliced
2 tomatoes, sliced

▲ Top the crispbreads with the liver sausage and tomato slices.

─────────DAY 13─────────

BREAKFAST

YOGURT WITH FRUIT
1 × 150 g (5.3 oz) carton low-fat natural yogurt
1 small orange, peeled and segmented
1 level tablespoon raisins
2 level teaspoons wheatgerm

▲ Mix the yogurt with the orange, raisins and wheatgerm.

LIGHT MEAL

HAM AND TOMATO ROLL; FRUIT
1 × 45 g (1¾ oz) wholemeal roll
2 level teaspoons low-fat spread
25 g (1 oz) lean cooked ham, fat discarded
1 tomato, sliced
1 small orange or 1 medium pear

▲ Split the roll and spread with low-fat spread. Fill with the ham and tomato.
▲ Eat the fruit for dessert.

─────────DAY 14─────────

BREAKFAST

BRANFLAKES AND SULTANA
25 g (1 oz) branflakes
1 level tablespoon raisins or sultanas
85 ml (3 fl oz) skimmed milk

▲ Serve the branflakes with the raisins or sultanas and serve with the skimmed milk.

LIGHT MEAL

CHICKEN LIVER SPREAD ON TOAST

50 g (2 oz) *chicken livers, trimmed and cut into small pieces*
¼ *stock cube, crumbled*
water
2 level teaspoons tomato ketchup
few drops of Worcestershire sauce
50 g (2 oz) *cottage cheese with chives*
salt
freshly ground black pepper
1 × 40 g (1½ oz) *slice wholemeal bread*
1 *tomato, sliced*

▲ Place the chicken livers in a small pan with the crumbled stock cube and enough water to just cover. Cover and simmer for 5 minutes. Drain off any excess water.

▲ Turn into a basin and add the tomato ketchup, Worcestershire sauce and cottage cheese. Season, then mash with a fork.

▲ Toast the bread. Spread with the liver mixture. Top with the tomato slices and grill until hot.

LOW-CALORIE MAIN MEALS

Choose any one of these meals each 'strict' day.

TROUT AND ALMONDS

100 g (4 oz) potatoes, weighed peeled
100 g (4 oz) fresh or frozen French beans
1 × 175 g (6 oz) trout
¼ teaspoon oil
1 level tablespoon flaked almonds
wedge of lemon

▲ Boil the vegetables.
▲ Brush the trout with the oil and grill, turning once.
▲ Sprinkle the almonds on to a piece of foil and grill until golden –
watch carefully as they burn easily.
▲ Sprinkle the trout with the almonds and serve with the lemon
and vegetables.

CAULIFLOWER IN BLUE CHEESE SAUCE; FRUIT

225 g (8 oz) fresh or frozen cauliflower
1 level teaspoon cornflour
150 ml (¼ pint) skimmed milk
50 g (2 oz) Danish Blue cheese, grated
salt
freshly ground black pepper
1 medium peach or kiwi fruit

▲ Boil the cauliflower until just tender. Drain and keep warm.
▲ Blend the cornflour with a little milk until smooth.
▲ Heat the rest of the milk to boiling point and then pour on to the
cornflour, stirring. Return to the pan and simmer for 1 minute,
stirring constantly.
▲ Stir in the cheese and season. Pour over the cauliflower.
▲ Eat the fruit for dessert.

LIVER AND BACON
1 × 175 g (6 oz) potato
75 g (3 oz) lamb's liver
1 rasher streaky bacon
75 g (3 oz) button mushrooms

▲   Bake the potato in its jacket at 200°C, 400°F, Gas Mark 6 for 45 minutes or until soft when squeezed gently.
▲   Grill the liver without added fat and grill the bacon until crisp.
▲   Poach the mushrooms in a little salted water or stock for 5 minutes.
▲   Drain and serve with the liver, bacon and potato.

KIDNEY, SAUSAGE AND BAKED BEANS
2 lamb's kidneys, halved and cored
2 pork or beef chipolata sausages
75 g (3 oz) button mushrooms
1 × 150 g (5.3 oz) can baked beans in tomato sauce

▲ Grill the kidneys lightly without added fat and grill the sausages thoroughly.
▲   Poach the mushrooms in a little salted water or stock for 5 minutes.
▲   Heat the beans and serve with the kidneys, sausages and drained mushrooms.

PORK STIR-FRY
1 level teaspoon honey
2 teaspoons soy sauce
1 teaspoon vinegar
2 teaspoons oil
50 g (2 oz) carrots, cut into matchsticks
100 g (4 oz) lean pork fillet or tenderloin, trimmed of fat and cut into small pieces
50 g (2 oz) red or green pepper, cored, seeded and sliced
1 spring onion, trimmed and sliced
1 ring pineapple, canned in natural juice, drained and chopped
75 g (3 oz) bean sprouts

▲ Mix together the honey, soy sauce and vinegar.
▲ Heat the oil in a non-stick wok or frying pan, add the carrots and stir-fry for 1 minute.
▲ Add the pork and stir-fry for a further 4 minutes.
▲ Add the pepper and spring onion and stir-fry for 2 minutes.
▲ Add the bean sprouts and cook for 1 minute.
▲ Add the soy sauce mixture and stir until well mixed.
▲ Serve hot.

GRILLED STEAK; ICE CREAM
100 g (4 oz) *fresh or frozen broccoli*
100 g (4 oz) *button mushrooms*
100 g (4 oz) *fillet or rump steak*
1 *tomato*
50 g (2 oz) *vanilla ice cream*

▲ Boil the broccoli.
▲ Poach the mushrooms in a little stock or water.
▲ Grill the steak until done to your liking and grill the tomato.
▲ Serve the steak with the broccoli, mushrooms and tomato.
▲ Follow with the ice cream.

GRILLED FISH AND VEGETABLES; FRUIT
100 g (4 oz) *fresh or frozen peas*
100 g (4 oz) *fresh or frozen broccoli*
175 g (6 oz) *plaice, sole or cod fillet*
½ *teaspoon oil*
1 *wedge of lemon*
1 *medium banana or* 1 *large orange*

▲ Boil the peas and broccoli.
▲ Brush the fish with the oil and grill, turning once, until it flakes easily.
▲ Serve with the lemon and vegetables.
▲ Eat the fruit for dessert.

EATING-OUT MAIN MEALS

On an 'Eating Out' day choose any one of the menus listed.

INDIAN MEAL
Starter
2 poppadoms

Main Course
Tandoori Chicken
1 Chapati OR 4 rounded tablespoons plain boiled rice OR 3
   rounded tablespoons pilau rice
Yogurt Relish
Tomato Sambal
2 rounded teaspoons Cucumber Raita
1 rounded teaspoon mango chutney

Drinks
2 × 300 ml (½ pint) glasses beer or lager OR 2 glasses dry or
medium red or white wine OR unlimited unsweetened tea or coffee
with milk if you wish.

Eating-Out Tips
Avoid Indian starters for they are all high in calories. A couple of
poppadoms will give you something to nibble if companions are
ordering a first course, or you could eat the poppadoms with your
main course.
   Tandoori Chicken is the safest main course to choose in an
Indian restaurant. The skin is normally removed from the chicken
before cooking, which saves a considerable number of calories and
the chicken is then baked Tandoori-style. Many other Indian dishes
are fried which make them very high in calories.

FRENCH MEAL
Starter
Mushrooms à la Grecque
OR Consommé
OR Melon

Main Course
Kidneys Turbigo
OR Sauté de Veau Marengo (Veal Marengo)
OR Steak Tartare
OR Grilled Sole
Boiled potatoes or rice
Plus one portion of any of the following:
Broccoli, Brussels sprouts, Cabbage, Carrots, French beans,
Jerusalem artichokes, Cauliflower (not in cheese sauce) or Leeks
(not in sauce).

Dessert (*no cream*)
Fruit Mousse
OR Pears in Red Wine
OR Bombe
OR Ice Cream
OR Fresh Fruit Salad

Drinks
Coffee – black or with milk, not cream
2 glasses dry or medium white or red wine

Eating-Out Tips
The French love to serve dishes made with rich sauces and these are
all high in calories. Avoid also pâtés and creamy soups which are
probably much higher in calories than you imagine. Ask for
vegetables without added butter or a sauce topping. If the waiter
presents a dish of chocolates with the coffee, either ask the people
you are dining with to eat them up quickly or ask the waiter to take
the plate away before your willpower weakens.

ITALIAN MEAL
Starter
Parma Ham with Melon
OR Stracciatella Soup plus 3 bread sticks

Main Course
Calves' Liver with Sage
OR Veal Marsala
OR Veal Escalope with Ham and Sage

2 portions of any of the following vegetables:
Broccoli, Brussels sprouts, Cabbage, Carrots, Courgettes,
Cauliflower, Peas, Mushrooms or French beans
OR Spaghetti or Rigatoni Napoletana (with tomato sauce) without
additional vegetables

Dessert (*no cream*)
Zabaglione
OR Fruit Salad
OR Strawberries with sugar
OR Ice Cream

Drinks
Coffee – black or with milk
2 glasses dry or medium red or white wine

Eating-Out Tips
Pasta dishes are usually too high in calories for a dieting meal. This
is because sauces are high in fat unless you choose pasta covered
with Napoletana tomato sauce. But if pasta is your passion you
could probably afford a starter-size portion of another pasta dish
served as your main course.

FISH RESTAURANT
Starter
Oysters (12)
OR Smoked Salmon
OR Turtle Soup

Main Course
Grilled Fish (Halibut, Lobster, Salmon, Sole or Turbot)
OR Poached Halibut, Salmon or Turbot (served without Hollandaise Sauce)
OR Trout and Almonds
OR Crab, Lobster or Prawn Salad without dressing

1 portion of boiled potatoes or 1 jacket-baked potato
Plus one of any of the following vegetables:
Broccoli, Carrots, French beans, Peas, Courgettes or Leeks

Drinks
Coffee – black or with milk
2 glasses dry or medium red or white wine

Eating-Out Tips
Avoid fish that is covered in a creamy or cheese sauce. A grilled sole costs about 300 calories but sole in a rich sauce could amount to as much as 570 calories. You can have a portion of potatoes with your main course but choose boiled or baked, not fried. Ask for vegetables to be served without added butter.

BRITISH RESTAURANT
Starter
Consommé or Game Consommé
OR Oysters (12)
OR Grapefruit with 1 teaspoon sugar

Main Course
Roast Lamb with Mint Sauce
OR Grilled Trout
OR Roast Beef

1 jacket-baked potato or 2 roast potatoes or 1 portion boiled potatoes
1 portion of the following vegetables:
Brussels sprouts, Cabbage, Carrots, Cauliflower, Peas, French beans, Runner beans, Leeks, Swede, Turnips or Parsnip.

Pudding
Fruit Pie (no cream, custard or ice cream)
OR Bread and Butter Pudding
OR Castle Pudding and Jam Sauce
OR Custard Tart

Drinks
Coffee – black or with milk
2 glasses dry or medium red or white wine

Eating-Out Tips
You can afford to eat a Yorkshire pudding with your beef main
course as long as you are willing to give up your potato portion. Cut
off all the fat from the meat and leave it on the side of your plate.
This menu allows you a portion of a traditional British pud – don't
add any extra cream, custard or ice cream, though.

GREEK MEAL
Starter
Hummus or Tzatziki with 1 piece of pitta bread

Main Course
Dolmades with Tomato Salad or Cabbage Salad

Drinks
Coffee – black or with milk
2 glasses dry or medium red or white wine

Eating-Out Tips
The Greeks like to cover most of their dishes in olive oil which
makes them out of bounds for a dieter. Choose a pitta bread with
hummus or tzatziki for a starter. We've allowed for a whole pitta
spread reasonably thickly – don't finish off any extra hummus or
tzatziki. Salads will always come with an oily dressing, but we've
allowed for this in our calculations. Greek desserts are so high in
calories that they could never be included in a 3-course meal for a
dieter. An average portion of Baklava would cost 475 calories and an
average portion of Galaktoboureko would cost all of 600.

CHINESE MEAL
Starter
Any Chinese soup, such as Crab and Sweetcorn

Main Course
4 rounded tablespoons Chicken and Mushrooms
4 rounded tablespoons Prawn Chop Suey
3 rounded tablespoons Beef in Oyster Sauce
4 rounded tablespoons boiled rice

Sweet
Lychees

Drinks
Chinese tea
2 glasses medium or dry red or white wine
OR two 300 ml (½ pint) glasses lager or beer

Eating-Out Tips
It's traditional in Chinese restaurants to share dishes with the
people you are dining with, which makes it easy to help yourself to
just a little of each. You'll have to persuade everyone to order the
three we recommend, though, and at all costs talk them out of
ordering battered and fried dishes such as Sweet and Sour Pork,
Butterfly Prawns in Batter and Spring Rolls.

STEAK BAR
Starter
Melon (plain or cocktail)
OR Grapefruit (plain or cocktail)

Main Course
225 g (8 oz) Steak (fillet, rump or sirloin) cooked to your liking
OR 3 Lamb cutlets
OR Gammon and pineapple

Jacket baked potato
Peas or French beans

Sweet
Ice Cream or Sorbet (without sauce or nuts)

Drinks
Coffee – black or with milk
2 glasses dry or medium red or white wine

Eating-Out Tips
Cut all fat off your meat as eating this would cost more calories than we have allowed. Do not have any butter or sour cream on your potato and stay clear of chips. Also try to avoid nibbling away at a roll and butter before your meal arrives. If you feel your willpower weakening, ask for the roll and butter to be taken away.

INDULGENCES AND SNACKS

Choose just one of any of the following each day:

Alcoholic Drinks
2 × 120 ml (4 fl oz) glasses dry or medium white wine
3 pub measures (25 ml) whisky, gin, brandy, rum or vodka
2 × 50 ml schooners cream sherry
2 × 50 ml schooners dry sherry

Fruit
3 medium apples
3 medium pears
2 medium bananas
2 large oranges
250 g (9 oz) grapes

Desserts and Yogurt
75 g (3 oz) vanilla ice cream
1 individual carton low-fat fruit yogurt
1 individual carton natural low-fat yogurt mixed with 2 level
   tablespoons muesli

Cereals
Branflakes and Raisins
25 g (1 oz) branflakes
1 level tablespoon raisins or sultanas
120 ml (4 fl oz) skimmed milk

▲ Serve the branflakes with the raisins or sultanas and milk.

All Bran
40 g (1½ oz) all bran
120 ml (4 fl oz) skimmed milk

▲ Serve the all bran with the milk.

Cereal and Banana
1 wheat breakfast biscuit
1 small banana, peeled and sliced
85 ml (3 fl oz) skimmed milk

▲ Serve the breakfast biscuit with the banana and milk.

Cornflakes or Crispy Rice Cereal
25 g (1 oz) cornflakes or crispy rice cereal
1 level teaspoon sugar
120 ml (4 fl oz) skimmed milk

▲ Serve the cereal with the sugar and milk.

Porridge
25 g (1 oz) instant porridge oats
150 ml (¼ pint) skimmed milk

▲ Heat the milk and mix with the porridge oats.

Biscuits
2 large digestives
6 chocolate finger biscuits
6 rich tea fingers
3 fig rolls

Bread Snacks
Toast and Marmalade or Jam
1 × 40 g (1½ oz) slice wholemeal bread
2 level teaspoons low-fat spread
2 level teaspoons jam or marmalade

▲ Toast the bread and top with low-fat spread and marmalade.

Bread and Peanut Butter
1 × 40 g (1½ oz) slice wholemeal bread
2 level teaspoons peanut butter

▲ Spread the bread with peanut butter.

Cheese Spread Sandwich
2 × 25 g (1 oz) slices wholemeal bread
1 × 15 g (½ oz) triangle cheese spread

▲ Make a sandwich with the bread and cheese spread.

Currant Bun
1 × 45 g (1¾ oz) currant bun

Salad Roll
1 × 45 g (1¾ oz) wholemeal roll
1 level tablespoon low-calorie salad cream
1 small tomato
lettuce
few slices of cucumber

▲ Split the roll and fill with the low-calorie salad cream and vegetables.

Cheese on Toast
1 × 25 g (1 oz) slice wholemeal bread
35 g (1¼ oz) fat-reduced Cheddar cheese, grated

▲ Toast the bread on one side only. Place the grated cheese on the other side and grill until melted.

Savoury Snacks
1 × 25 g (1 oz) packet potato crisps, any flavour
25 g (1 oz) dry roasted or roasted, salted cashew nuts or peanuts
1 × 25 g (1 oz) packet prawn cocktail snacks
1 × 25 g (1 oz) packet cheese flavoured corn snacks

THE <u>GOOD COOK'S</u> DIET

Follow this diet for good eating, good health – and a swift goodbye to every surplus pound!

Low-fat . . . low sugar . . . low salt . . . high-fibre: That's how the world's top nutritionists would like to see you eating. And that doesn't mean that meals have to be boring. This diet uses tasty foods that can help a body towards better health – which includes, of course, a trim shape.

We use low-fat milk, cheese and yogurts which cut fats but still supply lots of valuable nutrients.

Salads and green vegetables add colour, interest, texture and because they are so low in calories you can afford to eat plenty. To make the most of their vitamin C content, buy vegetables fresh and serve them fresh.

We've used wholegrain breads, pastas and brown rice because unrefined products offer more vitamins and minerals than white refined versions – they also add valuable fibre to your diet. Breakfast cereals, again, are of the high bran sort.

Root vegetables come high on the list of 'eat more of' foods because they have plenty of low-calorie filling power along with varying amounts of vitamin C and useful amounts of minerals.

The true health benefits of humble beans and pulses have only recently been given their proper due – they are now seen as a useful source of protein and fibre and provide valuable minerals.

All the meats and fish we've used are low in fat. Cockles and mussels are especially high in iron, even when they come in jars, and canned small fish such as pilchards and sardines are good sources of calcium. Liver and kidney are the best sources of iron and contain lots of other vitamins.

If you fancy something sweet, then choose fresh or dried fruit.

What daily calorie allowance should you choose?

A woman with less than a stone to lose will see the pounds disappearing swiftly and safely on 1,000 calories a day.

If you have between 1 stone and 3 stones to lose, then you'll find you can afford to eat an extra 250 calories a day – and still lose weight. If you have 3 stones to lose you can eat up to 1,500 calories a day. Men can add 250 calories to these totals.

The following menus all total 1,000 calories a day. If you wish to add extra calories, choose any extra fruit or vegetables from the chart at the back of this book.

Diet Rules

FOR BREAKFAST (or an anytime snack each day)
You are allowed 150 ml (¼ pint) skimmed milk with one of the following breakfast cereals:
40 g (1½ oz) *branflakes*
40 g (1½ oz) *toasted farmhouse bran cereal*
40 g (1½ oz) *bran muesli with 50 g (2 oz) raspberries*
40 g (1½ oz) *all bran with 40 g (1½ oz) green grapes*
40 g (1½ oz) *St Michael Bran Cereal with fruit and nuts with 40 g (1½ oz) green grapes*

EVERY DAY
You are allowed 300 ml (½ pint) skimmed milk for use in tea and coffee, plus 2 choices of fruit from the following list:
1 *medium apple*
1 *medium orange*
1 *medium pear*
1 *medium peach*
1 *small banana*
100 g (4 oz) *fresh cherries*
200 g (7 oz) *fresh strawberries*

EVERY DAY
You are allowed unlimited black coffee, lemon tea (use low-calorie sweeteners only), water and drinks sold specially for slimmers.

EVERY DAY
Choose one of the menus that follow. You can follow the days in any order, but do not swap meals from one day to the next.
If you do not like any of the menus, then miss it out and repeat a favourite.

————DAY 1————

LIGHT MEAL

PROVENÇAL BEAN SALAD

25 g (1 oz) wholemeal pasta
2 tablespoons oil-free French dressing
2 teaspoons low-calorie salad dressing
½ clove garlic, crushed (optional)
100 g (4 oz) courgettes, sliced
3 tomatoes, chopped
100 g (4 oz) cooked cannellini or butter beans

▲ Cook the pasta in boiling water, rinse in cold water and drain.
▲ Mix the dressings with the crushed garlic, if using, and stir into the prepared vegetables with the beans and pasta.

MAIN MEAL

INDIAN FISH KEBABS

100 g (4 oz) monkfish or firm white fish, cut into small cubes
1 teaspoon lemon juice
¼ teaspoon ground cumin
pinch of chilli powder
½ teaspoon garam masala or curry powder
4 level tablespoons low-fat natural yogurt
50 g (2 oz) mushrooms
40 g (1½ oz) brown rice
100 g (4 oz) broccoli
1 peach

▲ Place the fish in a small bowl and sprinkle with the lemon juice.
▲ Mix the spices with the yogurt and pour over the fish. Stir well to mix thoroughly. Cover and refrigerate for at least 1 hour.
▲ Thread the fish cubes and mushrooms on to 2 skewers. Grill under a moderate heat, turning frequently, and basting with the yogurt mixture.
▲ Serve with the cooked rice and boiled or steamed broccoli.
▲ Follow with the peach.

————————**DAY 2**————————

LIGHT MEAL

CALIFORNIAN COTTAGE CHEESE SALAD

1 small banana, peeled and sliced
lettuce
1 peach, sliced
50 g (2 oz) strawberries, sliced
50 g (2 oz) black grapes, halved
1 × 100 g (4 oz) carton cottage cheese

▲ Dip the banana slices in lemon juice if not serving immediately.
▲ Cover a plate with lettuce. Spoon the cottage cheese on to the lettuce and arrange the prepared fruit around it.

MAIN MEAL

PAPRIKA CHICKEN AND BAKED POTATO

1 × 225 g (8 oz) chicken leg joint
½ red pepper, sliced
1 small onion, sliced
150 ml (¼ pint) tomato juice
2 level teaspoons paprika
¼ level teaspoon sugar
1 bay leaf
150 g (5 oz) potato
2 tablespoons low-fat natural yogurt

▲ Discard the skin and fat from the chicken joint.
▲ Place the pepper in a casserole dish with the onion and chicken.
▲ Mix together the tomato juice, paprika and sugar. Add to the casserole with the bay leaf and cover.
▲ Place the casserole and potato in the oven and cook at 190°C, 375°F. Gas Mark 5, for 1 hour.
▲ Stir the yogurt into the casserole and cook uncovered for a further 10 minutes.

DAY 3

LIGHT MEAL

VEGETABLE SOUFFLÉ

50 g (2 oz) cooked potato
50 g (2 oz) cooked Brussels sprouts
1 tablespoon skimmed milk
1 egg, size 3, separated
25 g (1 oz) reduced-fat hard cheese, grated
freshly ground black pepper
pinch of dry mustard powder
mixed salad of lettuce, cucumber, peppers, radishes, watercress and 1 tomato
1 tablespoon oil-free French dressing

▲ Place the potato and sprouts in a bowl with the skimmed milk and mash together thoroughly.
▲ Beat the egg yolk into the vegetable mixture, stir in the grated cheese and seasonings.
▲ Whisk the egg white until stiff and fold into the vegetable mixture. Spoon into a lightly greased ovenproof dish and bake at 220°C, 425°F, Gas Mark 7, for 30 minutes.
▲ Serve immediately with the mixed salad.

MAIN MEAL

BEAN PAELLA

40 g (1½ oz) brown rice
pinch of turmeric
275 ml (10 fl oz) water
100 g (4 oz) aubergine, cubed
salt
1 small onion, chopped
1 carrot, chopped
½ clove garlic, crushed
1 stick celery, sliced
½ green pepper, sliced
25 g (1 oz) mushrooms, sliced
175 g (6 oz) tomatoes, chopped
pinch of ground coriander
175 g (6 oz) cooked red kidney beans

▲ Cook the rice with the turmeric and water for 15 minutes.
▲ Sprinkle the aubergine cubes with salt and leave to stand for 10 minutes. Rinse in cold water and drain.
▲ Add all the prepared vegetables, the tomatoes, coriander and the beans to the rice and continue cooking for 15 minutes or until all the liquid is absorbed.
▲ Serve immediately.

————————DAY 4————————

LIGHT MEAL

SWEETCORN SOUP WITH WHOLEMEAL BREAD
½ *medium onion, chopped*
1 *carrot, chopped*
175 *g (6 oz) sweetcorn*
225 *ml (8 fl oz) water*
squeeze of lemon juice
15 *g (½ oz) watercress*
2 *level teaspoons low-fat natural yogurt*
1 × 25 *g (1 oz) slice wholemeal bread*

▲ Place the onion and carrot in a saucepan with the sweetcorn, water and lemon juice. Cover, bring to the boil and simmer for 25 minutes. Add the watercress and purée in a blender.
▲ Stir in the yogurt and re-heat gently without boiling.
▲ Serve with the wholemeal bread.

MAIN MEAL

CHICKEN LIVER RISOTTO
40 *g (1½ oz) brown rice*
100 *g (4 oz) chicken livers, roughly chopped*
50 *g (2 oz) mushrooms, chopped*
¼ *chicken stock cube, crumbled*
1 *level tablespoon tomato purée*
275 *ml (10 fl oz) boiling water*
50 *g (2 oz) peas*
dash of Worcestershire sauce

▲ Place the rice in a small pan. Add the chicken livers and mushrooms with the stock cube, tomato purée and water.
▲ Bring to the boil, cover and simmer for 25 minutes, stirring occasionally. Add extra water if necessary, to prevent sticking.
▲ Add the peas, bring back to the boil and simmer for 5 minutes.
▲ Add a dash of Worcestershire sauce before serving.

―――――――――――――**DAY 5**―――――――――――――

LIGHT MEAL

MEXICAN MARINATED FISH
100 g (4 oz) fresh fillet of any firm white fish
2 spring onions, thinly sliced
juice of 1 lime
2 tablespoons unsweetened orange juice
1 teaspoon oil
1 level tablespoon tomato ketchup
dash of Worcestershire sauce
pinch of dried oregano
pinch of chilli powder
freshly ground black pepper
1 large tomato, deseeded and chopped
½ wholemeal pitta bread

▲ Discard any skin from the fish; cut the flesh into small cubes.
▲ Place the fish and spring onions in a non-metallic dish. Add the lime and orange juice. Stir well, cover and refrigerate for 3 hours.
▲ One hour before serving stir in the oil, ketchup, Worcestershire sauce, oregano, chilli powder and pepper.
▲ Stir the chopped tomato into the fish. Serve with the pitta bread.

MAIN MEAL

LENTIL LASAGNE
25 g (1 oz) wholemeal lasagne
1 small onion, chopped
50 g (2 oz) mushrooms, sliced
2 sticks celery, sliced
1 × 225 g (8 oz) can tomatoes

25 g (1 oz) red lentils
75 ml (3 fl oz) water
pinch of mixed herbs
1 clove garlic, crushed
1 level teaspoon cornflour
1 small carton low-fat natural yogurt
1 level tablespoon Parmesan cheese
mixed green salad

▲ Cook the lasagne in boiling water, then drain on paper towels.
▲ Place the onion, mushrooms and celery in a small pan with the tomatoes, lentils, water, herbs and garlic. Bring to the boil, cover and simmer for 30 minutes, or until the lentils are very tender.
▲ Place half of the lentil mixture in a small ovenproof dish and cover with half of the lasagne. Repeat the layers.
▲ Mix the cornflour with a little cold water. Stir into the yogurt with half the Parmesan cheese. Spread the mixture over the lasagne.
▲ Sprinkle the remaining Parmesan on top and cook at 200°C, 400°F, Gas Mark 6 for 35-40 minutes. Serve with the green salad.

---DAY 6---

LIGHT MEAL
BEAN-STUFFED ONION WITH KIWI FRUIT AND GRAPE SALAD
1 × 175 g (6 oz) onion, peeled
1 × 150 g (5.3 oz) can baked beans in tomato sauce
1 level tablespoon chutney
100 g (4 oz) broccoli
1 kiwi fruit, peeled and diced
40 g (1½ oz) black grapes, halved
1 tablespoon unsweetened orange juice

▲ Place the onion in a saucepan, cover with water and bring to the boil. Cover and simmer for 20 minutes.
▲ Drain the onion and allow to cool. Remove the centre of the onion, leaving 3 layers as an outside wall.
▲ Roughly chop the centre of the onion, and stir into the beans with the chutney.
▲ Place the onion shell in an ovenproof dish, spoon the bean

mixture into the centre of the onion and around the side. Add 1 tablespoon of water to the dish.

▲ Cover and bake at 200°C, 400°F, Gas Mark 6 for 30 minutes.

▲ Serve with boiled or steamed broccoli.

▲ Mix the kiwi fruit and grapes together, sprinkle with the orange juice and serve as a dessert.

MAIN MEAL

SPAGHETTI WITH SEAFOOD SAUCE

50 g (2 oz) wholewheat spaghetti
½ medium onion, chopped
1 × 225 g (8 oz) can tomatoes
½ clove garlic, crushed
pinch of dried rosemary
1 × 150 g (5 oz) jar cockles, drained or 65 g (2½ oz) fresh cockles (cooked and
    shelled weight)
50 g (2 oz) peeled prawns
50 g (2 oz) canned sweetcorn

▲ Cook the spaghetti in boiling water.

▲ Place the onion in a small pan with the tomatoes, crushed garlic and herbs. Bring to the boil and simmer gently, uncovered, for 12 minutes.

▲ Add the drained cockles, prawns and sweetcorn. Heat the mixture through. Toss the drained spaghetti in the seafood sauce.

---------------------DAY 7---------------------

LIGHT MEAL

CHICKEN LIVER PÂTÉ WITH CRISPBREADS

½ level teaspoon oil
100 g (4 oz) chicken livers
1 teaspoon brandy
pinch of allspice
3 bran crispbreads
lettuce
cucumber, sliced

▲ Heat the oil in a non-stick frying pan, add the chicken livers and cook until tender.

▲ Mash the chicken livers with a fork. Add the brandy and allspice, then mix well.

▲ Chill the pâté for at least 30 minutes and serve with the crispbreads, lettuce and cucumber.

MAIN MEAL
STIR-FRIED CHICKEN

25 g (1 oz) brown rice
1 egg, size 3
1 teaspoon water
2 teaspoons oil
2 spring onions, thinly sliced
50 g (2 oz) red or green pepper, diced
50 g (2 oz) button mushrooms, thinly sliced
½ clove garlic, crushed
50 g (2 oz) cooked chicken, skin removed, sliced
50 g (2 oz) bean sprouts
1 teaspoon soy sauce
½ level teaspoon of vinegar

▲ Boil the rice until tender, then drain.

▲ Lightly beat the egg and water together. Brush the surface of a small non-stick omelette pan with a little oil and heat. Pour in the egg and make an omelette. Slide the omelette on to a plate and cut into strips.

▲ Heat the remaining oil in a non-stick wok or large frying pan. Add the spring onions, pepper, mushrooms and garlic. Stir-fry for 3 minutes. Add the rice, chicken, bean sprouts, soy sauce and vinegar. Stir-fry for 2 minutes.

▲ Stir in the omelette strips and serve.

CHAPTER 3

TURNING OVER A NEW LEAF

ARE SOME BAD HABITS STOPPING _YOU_ SLIMMING?

1. How quickly do you eat? Get out your kitchen timer tomorrow and just jot down how long it takes you to eat every meal and snack.
a. Breakfast..............
b. Midday meal..............
c. Evening meal..............
d. Snack 1..............
e. Snack 2..............

2. How often do you shop for food?
a. Every day ☐
b. Several times a week ☐
c. Once a week ☐
d. Once a fortnight ☐

3. The next time you go shopping, jot down here the time of day and if you had a meal before you went.
Time left for shopping..............
Time returned..............
Did you eat before you left? Yes/No

4. Did you eat anything while you were on your shopping trip? If so, what?

....

5. Do you buy certain sweet foods or savoury treats for the family rather than yourself? Write down here everything

you buy for them. Then tick the ones you sometimes
indulge in yourself.

....
....
....

6. Why do you eat snacks? During the next few days every
time you eat a snack, ask yourself if you are eating it
because you are really hungry and write down what snack
you ate and why you ate it.

Snack	**Why you ate**
a.	....
b.	....
c.	....
d.	....

7. Where were you when you ate the above snacks? Write
down the time of day, where you were and exactly what
you were doing. (For example 4 p.m., in kitchen, preparing
casserole.)
a. ....
b. ....
c. ....
d. ....

8. How often do you bake cakes and pastries for the family
or friends?
a. Once a week ☐
b. Once a fortnight ☐
c. Once a month ☐
d. Rarely ☐

9. Your family loves chips and insist on a fry-up at least
twice a week. Do you:
a. Refuse to cook them saying if you have to suffer then
everyone else must? ☐
b. Measure out enough potatoes for reasonable-sized
portions for the family and a small portion for yourself? ☐
c. Feel put out that they can eat chips without getting fat
and make yourself an extra large portion too? ☐

10. Three or four days prior to your period, do you:
   a. Go absolutely berserk and eat everything you can get your hands on? ☐
   b. Remember it's a dangerous time of the month and plan to include a few comforting foods in your diet to help you through these days? ☐
   c. Resign yourself to taking a diet holiday and promise yourself faithfully that you'll be super-strict in a week's time to make up for your lapse? ☐

11. You've had a trying and depressing day: temptation all round and nobody has noticed that you've lost a few pounds. You decide to have a drink to cheer yourself up. Do you:
   a. Have a small can of lager, or a single measure of spirit with a low-calorie mixer and sip it slowly so it lasts ages? ☐
   b. Telephone a friend to catch up on all the news and forget about the drink? ☐
   c. Pour yourself your favourite drink and have one, then another . . . well, who wants to diet anyway? ☐

12. You can't sleep and you know there's some leftover cheesecake in the fridge. Do you:
   a. Switch the light on and read for a while to make yourself sleepy? ☐
   b. Creep stealthily to the kitchen and finish up the cheesecake saying you'll start your diet properly tomorrow? ☐
   c. Make your way to the kitchen, trip over the cat, wake up the whole house and deny you were anywhere near the fridge? ☐

13. If the coffee trolley comes round at work full of delicious pastries and cakes, do you:
   a. Rush out of the room screaming, 'It's not fair!'? ☐
   b. Take a low-calorie snack to work with you so that you don't feel 'deprived'? ☐
   c. Give into temptation, saying, 'Well, just this once won't hurt. I'll make up for it later.'? ☐

14. TV is boring, the children in bed and your husband is out. Do you:
  a. Find some knitting and keep your fingers occupied before they stray to food temptation? ☐
  b. Go in search of sweets the children have hidden from greedy mummy? ☐
  c. Decide you'll cheer yourself up and open a packet of peanuts? ☐

15. A friend brings you a box of chocolates and you put them in the cupboard for later. Do you:
  a. Think you'll have just one as soon as she has gone and end up eating the lot? ☐
  b. As soon as she has gone, give the box to that nice old lady next door? ☐
  c. Tip the box into the dustbin and cover it with tea leaves? ☐

16. Your weakness is biscuits – especially the chocolate-covered variety. Do you:
  a. Buy a packet of family favourites, resolving to allow yourself just one a day, but once the packet is open you scoff the lot? ☐
  b. Ban all biscuits for ever and decide never to buy them again? ☐
  c. Buy one individually-wrapped chocolate biscuit a day to satisfy the craving? ☐

Check your answers to question 1.
DON'T EAT QUICKLY: Eating very slowly, savouring every mouthful, is one of the surest ways of keeping to your diet and avoiding overeating. Did you grab breakfast on the wing, eat a quick bar of chocolate instead of lunch? If you're in the habit of eating while you rush from one place to another or while getting on with the chores, try to break this habit now.

ENJOY YOUR FOOD: When you are trying to control your weight it is vitally important that every calorie you eat gives you maximum psychological and sensuous pleasure. There is a great deal of evidence to show that when you are fully aware of what you are eating, and enjoying the flavours and textures of your foods, you are satisfied with a smaller quantity.

Check your answer to question 2.

KEEP SHOPPING TO A MINIMUM: If you are in the habit of shopping for food every day, sit down and try to plan how you can cut this down to every other day — shopping just once a week would be even safer. Before you go shopping make a very careful list of what you want to buy and make sure you keep to it.

Check your answers to questions 3 and 4.

DON'T SHOP WHEN YOU ARE HUNGRY: This is the time when you are most vulnerable to those fatal impulse buys (and equally fatal impulse eats). If you ate something while you were on your shopping trip, was it because you felt hungry, or was it because you came face to face with some particularly tempting food? The next time you go shopping, could you avoid some of that temptation?

CHANGE THE FOOD, CHANGE THE SHOP: Unless you are immune to the willpower-melting scent of freshly-made bread and the sight of luscious cakes it's probably best to keep away from bakery shops and buy ready-wrapped bread from the supermarket instead. Did you buy a chocolate bar when you were in the newsagent buying a magazine? If so, could you arrange to have the magazine delivered to your home instead, or send the children or a friend to collect it for you?

DON'T PLACE TEMPTING GOODIES AT THE TOP OF YOUR SHOPPING BASKET: If you place tempting bags of nuts or packets of biscuits at the top of your shopping basket where you can get at them easily, they may not get as far as your kitchen. If you must buy these items, always bury them at the bottom of the basket and save battling with your willpower.

Check your answer to question 5.

DON'T BUY YOUR DOWNFALL FOODS FOR THE FAMILY: If you have honestly answered this question, you've probably discovered that at least some of those chocolate bars or biscuits or pies you buy for the family got eaten by yourself as well. It's also unrealistic to buy one of your favourite downfall foods with the idea that you'll just have a little and save the rest for another day. The experience of thousands of slimmers has proved the rule that what you buy, you will certainly eat. And probably now.

Check your answers to question 6.

KEEP SNACK-EATING UNDER CONTROL: Regular snacking is often what keeps people overweight. So try to discover why you really want to eat at certain times. You may well find that you have a couple of biscuits with a cup of coffee largely because it has become a habit; or that you ate a piece of cheesecake because you felt bored and fed up. Work at breaking snack-eating habits that you don't really get a great deal of satisfaction out of.

Check your answers to question 7.

DELAY SNACK EATING: This technique can work particularly well in helping you to cope with the compelling, rather than the absent-minded, urge to eat between meals. Look at the clock and promise yourself that you will not eat for another 15 minutes. A lot can happen in 15 minutes – you may get absorbed in a task that takes your mind away from food. But if, after 15 minutes, you still want your snack, go ahead and eat it. The technique is successful if it at least reduces the total number of snacks that you eat in a week. It also increases your awareness of snack-eating habits.

STOP BEING SOCIABLE: Don't eat snacks or meals for any other reason except that you really want to eat that particular food at that particular time. Never eat just to be sociable.

KEEP BUSY: Don't allow yourself to go through lengthy periods of boredom when you are dieting. If you are bored, you will eat. Boredom is the most food-inducing mood of all – so work out ways of finding things to do to keep you busy and interested.

BAN NIBBLES: Don't keep cheese or any other food you love to nibble in large quantities in the kitchen. It's safest to buy just as much as is needed for your day's dieting meals, and no more, so that you won't be tempted.

DISPOSE OF LEFTOVERS: Don't keep leftover portions of puddings, flans, quiches, and so on, in the fridge just to save wasting them. You will most likely end up eating them in addition to your diet meals. If you can't get another (slim) member of the family to eat them up, feed them to the dog or the birds.

IDENTIFY DANGER ZONES: You may be tempted to eat snacks when you are in particular areas, or when you are doing particular chores. You will see from your answers to question 7 if certain times of the day are hardest for you to be in control. Once you have this information you are in a much stronger position to plan some strategies to change and control your snack eating.

Check your answer to question 8.
BAKE AS LITTLE AS POSSIBLE: Home-made cakes and bread are very much more tempting than shop-bought varieties, so don't bake unless you really have to. You may tell yourself that you won't indulge or you'll have just a little, but you'll probably be tempted by those wonderful aromas even before the family has had time to sample them.

Check your answer to question 9.
SOMETIMES A LITTLE IS BETTER THAN NOTHING: If your family insists on eating some of your most tempting foods while you are dieting (it may be worth asking them to help you by not doing so) then your best plan is probably to allow yourself a small portion. Resentment can lead to your eating *their* leftovers secretly when you are alone in the kitchen. As long as you count the calories for a small portion of, say, chips into your daily total, then no serious harm will be done to your diet.

Check your answer to question 10.
BANK SOME CALORIES FOR PMT TIMES: You may find you have pre-menstrual cravings for certain foods, and that all your dieting willpower suddenly deserts you at this time of the month. Eating little and often (not going foodless for more than two or three hours) can help you by making cravings more manageable. A low-calorie nibble should do the trick between main meals. One of the most helpful things you can do when you are slimming is to 'bank' some calories for these trying days. By eating less before PMT, or planning to be extra-strict when PMT is over, you can afford to indulge a bit – and if eating a few favourite high-calorie foods at this time helps ease your tension, why not?

Check your answer to question 11.
DON'T DRINK UNLESS YOU CAN STOP: The problem with alcohol is that it has a nasty habit of dissolving willpower entirely. Using alcohol to 'cheer you up' makes dieting difficult, too, because in the end alcohol acts as a depressant on the nervous system and can make you feel worse than you did to begin with. If you enjoy the occasional drink then there is no reason why you shouldn't include your tipple in your calorie allowance. But find another cheer-up ploy, such as reading a magazine or phoning a friend.

Check your answer to question 12.
DECIDE ON INSOMNIA TACTICS: If once in a while you can't sleep and
decide to finish up some tempting goody whose siren call you can
hear all the way from the kitchen, then your best plan is to eat it and
undo the damage tomorrow. But if you frequently lie tossing and
turning and dreaming of food, then avoidance tactics are necessary.
Get up and do something else – take a hot bath or switch on the
light and read for a while. If you are really craving for a particular
food, it will help if you work out how you can include some of that
food in tomorrow's calorie allowance. If you know that you can have
a tempting food tomorrow, its importance today somehow
diminishes a little.

Check your answer to question 13.
PLAN FOR DAILY TEMPTATION: If the coffee trolley comes round at
work every morning, you know you will have to deal with that daily
temptation. Your first step is to find out the calories for the foods
you find most difficult to resist. Ask yourself if all you really want is
a break from work, and if just a cup of tea or coffee will satisfy. If

having a snack at this time is really important to you, see if you can allow for it in your calorie budget. Maybe you could have a very low-calorie breakfast or very low-calorie lunch so that you have calories to spare. If there is nothing on the trolley that is reasonable enough in calories, take your own mid-morning snack to work.

Check your answer to question 14.

KEEP HANDS OCCUPIED: Idle fingers often stray into biscuit tins and sweet packets. Keep your hands busy with knitting, sewing, turning the pages of magazines. Or give yourself a manicure. It's impossible to dip into a bag of nuts when your nails are sticky.

Check your answers to questions 15 and 16.

ARE YOU A CHOCOHOLIC?: If you have never indulged in a chocolate binge, you're a very unusual person. Sometimes chocolate cravings are so strong and so persistent they call for special measures. See 'Binge Beaters' on pages 305 to 307 for ideas on how to fight off a powerful craving.

> ### SLICING THE PROBLEM DOWN
> While dieting, I used to buy a chocolate bar every day, slice it up into as many tiny pieces as possible and have one – just one – every time I got a pang. Knowing that the rest was there if I wanted it helped enormously and once the bar was gone, that was it for the day. Although the longings didn't disappear, I gradually found that they certainly became less frequent. Now I can honestly say that I no longer feel the need.

> ### SEWN-UP
> Take up embroidery to keep busy – preferably in a pale colour that even a trace of stray chocolate would ruin.

THE CALORIE CUTTER'S GUIDE

You can cut many everyday calories quite painlessly if you check this guide before you eat. And when you have reached your target weight, these tips will help to keep you there.

Aubergines. A whole 200 g (7 oz) aubergine costs just 28 calories raw, but calories soar to 405 for a whole aubergine sliced and fried. Boil or bake aubergines without fat and they'll keep their nice low calorie figure.

Bacon. Grill rashers of bacon until crisp so that most of the fat runs off and can be discarded. A 35 g (1¼ oz) back bacon rasher will reduce from 150 calories to 80 calories; a 20 g (¾ oz) streaky bacon rasher will crisp down from 85 calories to 50 calories.

Bean sprouts. Use lightly boiled bean sprouts (7 calories per 25 g (1 oz)) instead of rice (35 calories per boiled 25 g (1 oz)) with kebabs and curries. Or mix half rice with half bean sprouts. Bean sprouts have a lovely crunchy texture and make a good, very low-calorie mixer with savoury meals.

Beefburgers. Grill beefburgers really well to remove as much fat as possible. A frozen 50 g (2 oz) beefburger will reduce from about 150 calories to 115 calories when cooked in this way. Grill on a wire rack so that the fat drips into a pan below.

Biscuits. If you haven't banned the biscuit tin completely, fill it with semi-sweet varieties rather than chocolate digestives or shortcakes which contain more fat and sugar, and are, therefore, higher in calories.

Bread. If you switch from white to wholemeal bread you will gain more fibre, extra nutrients and be eating fewer calories. If you normally buy a large loaf, try switching to one with smaller slices. Often you may well find you are perfectly satisfied with a sandwich made from a small loaf, and you could save about 20 calories on each bread slice.

Breakfast cereals. Choose the lighter types of cereals – puffed wheat, cornflakes, bran flakes, etc. – so that 25 g (1 oz) gives a generous bowlful. Sugary cereals aren't necessarily higher in calories than the unsweetened sort, so choose to suit your taste and avoid adding extra sugar. If you work at retraining a sweet tooth you'll probably find that you will come to prefer less sweet cereals.

Butter. A scraping of butter can cost as many calories as the bread slice you spread it on. Margarine has exactly the same number of calories – 210 per 25 g (1 oz) – as butter. Halve calories by using a low-fat spread. If you use a moist filling for a sandwich you may not need a spread at all. Another lower-calorie alternative is cheese spread at around 80 calories per 25 g (1 oz) or try spreading bread and crispbreads with yeast extract at 10 calories for a 5 ml teaspoon.

Cabbage. If you like to see a pile of food on your plate, fill it up with cabbage. At just 6 calories per 25 g (1 oz) raw and 4 calories boiled, any cabbage is an excellent low-calorie fill-up food. White and red cabbage can be served raw in salads as well as lightly boiled with a hot dish. Ounce for ounce cabbage is not as high in fibre as beans and pulses, but because of its low calorie content you can afford to eat much more. A 50 g (2 oz) portion of cooked red kidney beans will cost you 50 calories and give you 4.6 grams fibre. A 275 g (10 oz) portion of lightly boiled cabbage will cost you 40 calories and give you about 6.3 grams fibre (each variety differs a little).

Cakes. If you cannot resist cakes, choose something light and airy such as sponge, or something fatless such as a meringue. As manufacturers whisk as much air into their products as possible, you will often find that bought cakes are lower in calories than those you bake at home.

Casseroles. Many recipes for rich casseroles say you must pre-fry meat and vegetables before adding any liquid. This is not necessary; you can simply put the chopped vegetables and meat straight into the stock and cook until tender. If your recipe calls for flour to be stirred in after pre-frying, leave out this stage and thicken your casserole at the end of cooking time by adding a little cornflour mixed with water. If you haven't managed to cut off all the fat from the meat (see meat and poultry) wait until the casserole cools, skim any fat from the surface, then reheat quickly.

Cheese. If you find natural cottage cheese rather bland with a salad, choose one of the flavoured varieties or add a little higher calorie cheese that has more flavour. Low-fat versions of Cheddar and Cheshire cheese are now available, and you will save about 40 calories per 25 g (1 oz) by changing to one of these. If you swap from cream cheese to skimmed milk soft cheese you will save a whole 100 calories every time you spread 25 g (1 oz) on your crispbreads. Make a portion of hard cheese look more by serving it grated rather than sliced, and make a little go a long way in a salad by mixing grated cheese with grated carrot.

Chips. If you love chips and want to include them in your daily calorie allowance, save calories by serving oven or grill chips. These average 45 calories for 25 g (1 oz) (weighed uncooked) while the same amount of average thickness home-fries will cost 70 calories. Frozen chips also have the advantage that you can take from the packet exactly the number you intend to eat. When you make home-made chips you have to guess how many potatoes will make the amount you want. And if you make too many, are you really going to throw away the remainder?

Coleslaw. Most shop-bought coleslaw products are covered in mayonnaise and are therefore very high in calories. Look out for coleslaws labelled 'low-calorie' or make your own with thinly sliced white cabbage, grated carrot, a little finely chopped onion and mix with a low-calorie salad dressing.

Cream. If you exchange double cream for half cream you'll save 92 calories with every 25 g (1 oz). Ask yourself if you really do need cream anyway to top fruit, such as strawberries. If you never really crave cream, your best plan is to cut it from your diet entirely. Use natural low-fat yogurt instead of cream in soups and casseroles.

Custard. Save calories by making custard with skimmed milk and halve the amount of sugar manufacturers recommend you use. If you don't mind using an artificial sweetener, add liquid sweetener instead of sugar after the custard has thickened.

Desserts. Fresh fruit makes the lowest calorie and healthiest sort of dessert. But if this does not satisfy your pudding yearnings, the next best choices are sorbet, water ice, jelly or ice cream (but not home-made with double cream).

Eggs. One of the most fattening ways to eat eggs is scrambled. A couple of buttery scrambled eggs on a slice of buttered toast can soon take you up to around 400 calories. There's no need to forgo scrambled eggs if you love them, though. Scramble 2 eggs (size 3) with 30 ml (2 tablespoons) skimmed milk in a non-stick pan and place them on a large, thin slice of unbuttered toast and the count comes down to 245. The egg white is much lower in calories than the yolk. The yolk of a size 3 egg costs 65 calories, while its white costs 15 calories.

Fish. Choose white fish such as cod, plaice, haddock, sole and coley rather than the oilier herring or mackerel and you'll save calories. But remember that if you grill white fish, a knob of butter on top is likely to increase its count considerably. White fish is best steamed, casseroled or baked with a low-calorie topping. It also remains nicely moist when cooked in a microwave oven. If you eat tinned fish, such as tuna, choose the sort canned in brine rather than oil.

Fish cakes and fish fingers. Grill frozen, crumbed fish products without any fat – you'll find they cook just as well without. Never fry fish cakes unless you want to add about 80 calories to each patty. Fish fingers are a little less absorbent, but even they can soak up about 10 calories each finger when fried – and you'd probably eat four or five fish fingers for a meal.

Fried bread. If you are yearning for a slice of fried bread with your egg, spread a bread slice with just a little fat and fry it on one side only in a non-stick pan. It will then cost you no more than a slice of buttered bread (about 95 calories for a small slice). A slice of bread fried in the normal way will cost at least 160 calories.

Fruit, canned. Choose fruits canned in natural juice or low-calorie syrup. Fruit canned in sugary syrup can be very costly calorie-wise. A 275 g (10 oz) can of strawberries in syrup can amount to as much as 325 calories, while strawberries canned in natural juice cost 140 calories for the same quantity.

Fruit, dried. Dried fruit is high in fibre, but don't nibble it without counting the cost. Fresh fruit is low in calories because it contains a high percentage of water. When the water is dried out, you are left with the same calories for far less volume and weight. Sometimes sugar is added to dried fruit, too.

Fruit, stewed. Instead of stewing fruit with sugar, save calories by adding liquid sweetener to the fruit after cooking.

Fruit fools. Use yogurt and sweetener in place of custard or cream to stir into the puréed fruit.

Fruit juices. Mix soda water – half and half – with your fruit juice. Not only is it more refreshing but you get twice the amount for the same number of calories. Don't ever drink a fruit juice without counting the calorie cost, even if it is unsweetened. Just a small glass of orange juice can cost you 45 calories.

Grapefruit. If you are accustomed to eating lots of sugar you'll probably find grapefruit too tart to eat on its own. Sprinkle with a powdered or granulated artificial sweetener, or allow yourself half the amount of sugar you usually sprinkle on and gradually cut down until you can do without. Grapefruits vary enormously in sweetness, so try to pick ones that are naturally sweet and you will find it easier to give up sugar.

Gravy. Always make gravy with a gravy powder mixed with water, never use the juices from the roasting pan. A tablespoon of fatty gravy will cost you 30 calories, while a fatless thick gravy will come down to 10 calories and a thin gravy to 5 calories for the same quantity.

Ham. Always choose the leanest slices of ham you can find and remove any visible fat before you eat. Don't just count calories by the slice – thin, vacuum-packed slices weigh much less than slices carved straight from a joint.

Jams and Preserves. Just a teaspoon or two of jam or preserve with your toast at breakfast isn't going to do you any harm, and won't cost many calories – 15 calories for a 5 ml level teaspoon. But most preserves are high in sugar and have little nutritional value. Swap to low-sugar jam and you'll save calories and your teeth will benefit. Check labels on products sold specially for diabetics, though, as these may not be any lower in calories than ordinary jam.

Meat. Choose lean meat whenever possible and pick a cooking method which rids the meat of most fat. Grill chops, beefburgers, sausages and bacon well. Always pre-fry minced beef without added fat and drain off the fatty juices before adding other ingredients. When using fatty meat such as lamb or oxtail in casseroles, cool the cooked casserole, skim off fat from the surface and then quickly reheat. When choosing cold meats for salads, avoid fatty meats, particularly salami and pâtés and instead go for the really lean meats such as chicken, turkey and lean boiled ham.

Melon. Serve a slice of melon sprinkled with a little ground ginger rather than sugar as a very low-calorie starter.

Milk. Choose skimmed milk or reconstituted low-fat powdered skimmed milk instead of whole milk and you will halve your milk calories (per 600 ml (1 pint): gold top 445 calories; homogenized or silver top 380; skimmed 200). Skimmed milk may taste a little thin at first, but most people who use it regularly find they come to prefer it. If you find the transition a little difficult, swap first to a semi-skimmed milk which will bring your calories down to 300 per 600 ml (1 pint). If you use skimmed milk in sauces, custards and desserts you probably won't notice much difference and the calorie saving is very worthwhile.

Mushrooms. Raw mushrooms are saintly at just 4 calories per 25 g (1 oz), but once they meet the demon fat they shoot up in calories. Button mushrooms fried whole cost at least 40 calories per 25 g (1 oz) and flat mushrooms sliced and fried amount to as much as 75 calories per 25 g (1 oz). Mushrooms poached in water or a little fatless stock remain a very low-calorie vegetable. Try them sliced raw in salad – they're delicious.

Onions. The don't-fry recommendation applies to onions, too. Raw they are 7 calories per 25 g (1 oz), sliced and fried they soar to 45 calories. If a recipe calls for chopped onions to be pre-fried, poach them in a little liquid until softened instead.

Parmesan cheese. Try Parmesan instead of ordinary cheese when you want to sprinkle cheese on a cooked dish or soup. Although Parmesan is high in calories, it has a strong flavour so a little goes a long way.

Parsnips. Boil parsnips for minimum calories – just 16 calories per 25 g (1 oz) weighed boiled. But if you must roast them, leave them whole or cut into large chunks so that the minimum amount of surface comes into contact with the fat. You'll still need to count 30 calories for each 25 g (1 oz) of roast parsnip, though.

Pasta. Both wholemeal and white pasta are reasonable in calories – 33 per 25 g (1 oz) when boiled. What can really tip the dieting scales is the sauce you serve with your pasta. Make a macaroni cheese using skimmed milk and a low-fat cheese to cut down its calories. Pre-fry minced beef for a Bolognese sauce, drain off any fat that cooks out, then add your other ingredients.

Pastry. If you must make pies, roll the pastry as thinly as possible and only put pastry on top of the pie.

Pickles. Pickles of all sorts can cheer up a bland-tasting meal. But choose with care. Pickled onions at 5 calories each or gherkins at 5 calories per 25 g (1 oz) can be eaten pretty freely, but sweet pickles, at 40 calories per 15 ml tablespoon, need to be measured more carefully.

Potatoes. Potatoes have received an unfairly fat public image in past years, but dieters are no longer asked to cut them out. But be careful how you serve potatoes. Mashed with butter and whole milk, an average 150 g (5 oz) portion will cost you about 200 calories, while potatoes mashed with skimmed milk will cost about

140 calories. A 200 g (7 oz) jacket-baked potato served with a knob of butter will cost 275 calories, while served plain it comes down to 170 calories. Try topping a baked potato with low-fat yogurt which adds just 10 calories per 15 ml tablespoon, or cottage cheese which adds 15 calories. If you indulge in the occasional roast potato, always cook them in large chunks. Small chunks of potato absorb more fat than large ones and will cost you about 20 calories more for each 50 g (2 oz) portion. Roast potatoes are not cheap calorie-wise, though, and even a large chunk will cost a hefty 80 calories for 50 g (2 oz).

Poultry. Always remove the skin from chicken or turkey before you eat, as it can make a big difference to your calorie intake. A 225 g (8 oz) chicken leg costs 410 calories when raw. Grill and eat it with the skin and calories will come down to 250. But grill it and discard the skin before eating and you'll be consuming just 165 calories. When you grill a chicken joint you lose some calories when the fat just under the skin melts and drips into your grill pan. But if you put a chicken or turkey portion into a casserole, remove the skin first or all those fatty calories will go straight into the sauce.

Rice. Brown rice will give you more dietary fibre than white and is slightly lower in calories at 99 per 25 g (1 oz) raw compared with 102 calories for white. Rice absorbs lots of water during cooking which means that if you weigh your boiled rice, calories come down to 33 per 25 g (1 oz) for brown and 35 calories for white. Fry rice, though, and it will absorb lots of fatty calories. A 15 ml spoon (level tablespoon) of plain boiled rice will cost you 20 calories, while a tablespoon of fried rice costs 35 calories.

Salads. Not everything marked salad is safe for a slimmer. Avoid any salad product that comes covered in high-calorie mayonnaise. If you like to buy one of those useful little cartons of salad for a light meal, look for a low-calorie label. If you are making your own salads at home, indulge as much as you like in lettuce, tomatoes, celery, watercress, button mushrooms, cucumber, red or green peppers, spring onions, mustard and cress, grated raw carrot, white cabbage, chicory and radishes. They are all so low in calories it is hardly worth counting. A mixed green salad without dressing will cost you about 25 calories.

Salad dressings. The dressing you pour over your salad can treble (even quadruple) its calorie cost. Mayonnaise can cost as much as 120 calories for just 15 ml (1 level tablespoon). But you can buy a low-calorie mayonnaise which costs 45 calories a level tablespoon and a low-calorie dressing that comes down to 25 calories for the same amount. Even lower in calories is oil-free French dressing at just 2 calories per 15 ml (1 tablespoon).

If you have any difficulty buying a low-calorie dressing, try making your own. This Apple and Garlic Dressing makes four 15 ml tablespoons at 5 calories each: crush ½ clove garlic and mix with 45 ml (3 tablespoons) apple juice and 15 ml (1 tablespoon) red wine vinegar. Leave the mixture for 30 minutes, then strain the dressing, discarding the garlic.

Sauces. Watch out for creamy and buttery sauces when you are eating out. They can turn low-calorie innocents such as white fish or poultry into high-calorie monsters. When making a white sauce at home, use cornflour and skimmed milk rather than butter, flour and whole milk.

Sausages. Grill beef, pork or turkey sausages well, so that as much fat as possible runs out. The longer the sausages are cooked, the more calories they lose. Delicatessen sausages vary enormously in calories depending on their fat content. It is not always obvious which are the best buys, so always check the calorie chart at the back of this book before choosing.

Sponge cakes. Halve the calories in a sponge cake by making a whisked, fat-free sponge rather than a fat-containing Victoria sandwich. Recipe for the former: whisk 3 eggs with 75 g (3 oz) caster sugar until thick and creamy. Lightly fold in 75 g (3 oz) sieved plain flour and turn into two sandwich tins. This gives you one of the lowest calorie cakes you can eat.

Starters. Starters can help take the edge off your appetite so that you don't feel the need to gobble down the main course. But always choose a very low-calorie dish, such as grapefruit, melon, tomato juice or consommé so that you have plenty of calories left for what follows. When eating out, avoid thick or creamy soups, pâté, mixed hors d'œuvres or avocado pear.

Sugar. Save calories by replacing sugar with artificial sweetener. Each 5 ml (1 level teaspoon) of sugar costs 17 calories; an artificial sweetener will cost no calories at all. Use tablet sweeteners for drinks and liquid sweeteners for stewed fruit and cooked dishes. It is always best to add sweetener after cooking if possible. There are also granulated sweeteners available that can be used to bake specially devised cake recipes. Sweeteners lack sugar's caramelizing qualities and you can't simply substitute sweetener for sugar in your usual recipes.

Sweets. The lowest calorie sweets you can buy are those that are free of fat, such as wine gums, boiled sweets and mints. If you really must eat something sweet, choose these rather than toffees and chocolates.

Toast. Always wait for toast to cool before 'buttering'; this way the bread absorbs less. Use low-fat spread instead of butter or margarine.

Water. Always quench your thirst with water first, before turning to any calorie-supplying drink. It will often do the job better, and you will certainly be consuming fewer calories.

Yogurt. Always choose low-fat yogurts as they are lower in calories than whole milk yogurts. If you like fruit yogurts, either choose one that is specially made for slimmers or mix up your own, using low-fat natural yogurt and fresh fruit. Most fruit yogurts have a lot of sugar added and you can easily save about 50 calories by mixing your own. Stir natural low-fat yogurt into soups and casseroles instead of using cream.

*E*ATING OUT

SAVE UP SOME CALORIES FOR EATING OUT: It is your total calorie intake for the week that counts, so if you eat just 750 calories for three days you could save up an extra 750 calories for an eating out occasion and still average 1,000 calories a day.

PLAN AHEAD: If you know the restaurant where you will be eating, it is a good idea to try to plan your choice in advance. You can then order without looking at the menu, and avoid being wooed into choosing a higher-calorie item by mouthwatering meal descriptions.

DON'T BE A SAINT: Don't go to a restaurant expecting to be too saintly. When faced with a tempting array of all your favourite dishes it is extremely difficult not to indulge. Allow yourself one dish you really crave as a special treat, and try to keep accompaniments and any other courses as low-calorie as possible.

TAKE THE EDGE OFF HUNGER: Often, the most difficult time in a restaurant is the few minutes before you place your order. If you are feeling very hungry, all good intentions of ordering just a little can disappear. Try not to arrive at the restaurant absolutely starving. Eat an apple or pear before you leave home – that will cost you about 40 calories but could save you hundreds of restaurant calories later.

ORDER A COURSE AT A TIME: Refuse to consider ordering a dessert until after you have eaten your main course. You may well find that you can resist a sweet entirely once hunger pangs have stopped influencing your judgment.

CHOOSE À LA CARTE: When you pay the same regardless of how little you eat, it is very tempting to want to get your money's worth. Therefore, a restaurant which offers an à la carte menu is a better choice than one which only does a set menu. A carvery, where you can eat as much as you like for a set price, can also be an unsuitable place for a slimmer to eat.

BE IMPOLITE: Don't eat just to keep someone company. Save all your meal calories for food which will give you pleasure. If you can easily miss a starter you will have more calories to spend on the main course or dessert.

GO FAST: One of the advantages of eating in a fast food restaurant is that you can more or less guarantee that portions are always strictly controlled and that you will get the same dishes in whatever branch of the chain you eat in. You will also get served quickly, which means there is less time for your willpower to weaken before your meal arrives.

WHAT TO CHOOSE AND WHAT TO AVOID

———————————————STARTERS———————————————

An artichoke (plain) costs just 10 calories, but it is when you dip those delicious leaves into butter or vinaigrette dressing that calories start to soar. You will probably be served with 25 g (1 oz) butter (210 calories) or 2 tablespoons vinaigrette (150 calories). The more of this you manage to leave on the plate, the more calories you will save.

Asparagus is an excellent starter choice as each spear amounts to just 5 calories, but the accompanying butter or mayonnaise can add a lot of calories. To keep your starter as low-calorie as possible allow most of the butter or dressing to drip off your asparagus before you eat it. That way an average portion will cost between 150 and 200 calories.

Avocados are naturally high in fat and an average half will cost you 235 calories before you add any dressing. Vinaigrette dressing will cost you a little less than a prawn cocktail topping, but both are extravagant in terms of calories. Count about 310 calories for an avocado in vinaigrette and 400 calories for avocado with prawns.

Consommé is always low-calorie. Even in a restaurant that laces it with sherry you're unlikely to pay much more than 50 calories per portion. Careful, though – if you munch a roll (145 calories) spread with butter (about 105 calories) you could undo all the good work. Two breadsticks at 15 calories each keep your total under 100 calories.

A whole corn on the cob scores about 155 calories, but the butter dressing will double this figure. If you eat your sweetcorn sprinkled with black pepper, and say no to butter, you can keep this starter's calories fairly low.

Grapefruit is the perfect starter choice for a slimmer. A plain half costs about 20 calories and the half glacé cherry it's usually topped with costs just 5 calories more. However, sprinkling a rounded teaspoon of sugar over the grapefruit will add an extra 35 calories. Many restaurants now offer a low-calorie sweetener with coffee, so it is worth asking for this if you can't eat your grapefruit unsweetened.

Melon is always a very safe starter choice. Sprinkle on half a level teaspoon of ginger and you won't be adding any calories worth counting. Melons vary in sweetness and if you must have sugar add 35 calories for each rounded teaspoon. An average melon serving costs just 30 calories.

Smoked salmon costs 40 calories per 25 g (1 oz) and it is unlikely that you will be served with more than 50 g (2 oz) as a starter. But add a sparsely buttered slice of brown bread and you will add an extra 120 calories.

Sweetened juice is often served as a starter. Whether you choose orange, grapefruit or pineapple a small glass will cost you 50-60 calories. Cut calories by ordering tomato juice. Whether it is offered plain or as a tomato juice cocktail, a small glass will cost you 25 calories, a large glass about 50 calories.

MAIN COURSES

Chicken, turkey or duck as a main course can lose quite a few calories if you don't eat the skin.

Crab, lobster or prawn salads are usually low-calorie restaurant choices, but make sure they don't come smothered in mayonnaise. A whole crab should not cost more than 100 calories, but just 1 level tablespoon of mayonnaise would cost about 120 calories. A plain mixed salad without dressing won't add more than 30 calories to your meal total.

Fish in a rich cheese sauce should be avoided as the sauce adds more calories than if the fish is coated in crumbs and fried. Scallops crumbled and fried will cost about 400 calories a portion, but when they come in sauce as Scallops Mornay they can cost as much as 700 calories a portion.

Grilled fish is always a good main course dish as long as it is plain. But it is often grilled brushed with fat and arrives swimming in butter. Ask the waiter to serve your fish without the butter accompaniment and you will cut lots of calories.

Hamburger bars, despite their poor image, can supply a nutritious meal for a reasonable number of calories. A burger made from minced beef can be just as nutritious as an expensive steak and a small burger in a bun is unlikely to cost you more than 250 calories.

Pasta dishes can be ordered as a starter or a main course. A Spaghetti Bolognese served as a small starter portion will cost about 400 calories. Served as a main course you are likely to get your plate piled up with 720 spaghetti and sauce calories.

DESSERTS

Cheese and biscuits can be a far worse choice in terms of calories than a pudding. Two biscuits topped with butter and a chunk of Cheddar can cost 250 calories. If you prefer to choose cheese and biscuits to end a meal, select Brie or Camembert. Not only are these lower in calories than most hard cheeses but a little will spread a long way. With a soft cheese you shouldn't need to put butter on your crackers, either. Two water biscuits with 25 g (1 oz) Brie or Camembert will cost 150 calories.

A chocolate mint or a piece of Turkish Delight to finish off your meal will probably cost you less than any pudding on the menu. Count about 35 calories for each chocolate or sweet.

Fruit salad on its own is never high in calories, but sugar or syrup bases add calories to the otherwise innocent fruit. At home you can mix fresh fruit with apple juice, but restaurants will usually cover it in syrup, partly to stop it going brown, but also to please the average customer's sweet tooth. Count about 130 calories for an average restaurant portion of fruit salad served without cream.

Ice cream is always a reasonably low-calorie dessert. Flavours vary little in terms of calories, although if ice cream contains nuts, toffee pieces or chocolate chips it will cost you slightly more than the average 150 calories for two small scoops and a wafer.

Fresh raspberries or strawberries make a lovely dessert and cost just 30 calories a portion if you eat them plain. If you add sugar, though, allow 35 calories for a rounded teaspoon. And if you can't say no to cream allow 200 calories per portion. If you choose ice cream instead of cream you'll add about 75 calories to your fruit.

A sorbet is merely iced water with flavouring and a little sugar, so it is a safe dessert choice whichever restaurant you eat in. You will probably be served two small scoops which come to 100 calories. If you ask for just one scoop you can cut calories by half and make this a very low-calorie choice.

Wine costs calories, so don't forget to count drink calories into your total. An average half bottle of wine will cost about 250 calories. If you drink mineral water instead of wine, it won't cost you any calories at all.

Menu COUNTDOWN

Even when you are slim, there is no point in wasting calories by eating something that will give you no more pleasure than a lower-calorie alternative. If you eat out quite often it pays to get to know your best meal choices. To help you, here's a calorie chart of some of the most popular restaurant meals. Exact calories for each dish will vary a little from restaurant to restaurant because of different recipes and portion sizes. But you can use this list as a comparison between the alternatives to guide you to the lowest calorie eats when you are out.

STARTERS
Under 100 calories
Consommé

Fruit and Tomato Juice

Grapefruit, fresh, half

Grapefruit Cocktail

Oysters with Lemon

Smoked Salmon (without bread and butter)

101-200 calories
Asparagus with Butter

Corn on the Cob without Butter

Minestrone Soup

Mushrooms à la Grecque

Parma Ham with Fresh Figs

Parma Ham with Melon

Potted Shrimps (without bread and butter)

Prawn Cocktail (without bread and butter)

Prawn and Tomato Soup

Smoked Eel (without bread and butter)

Smoked Trout with Horseradish Sauce

Stuffed Vine Leaves

201-300 calories
Artichoke with Butter

Cream of Tomato Soup

Cream of Watercress Soup

Egg Florentine

Lobster or Crab Bisque

Mixed Fish Salad

Samosas

Smoked Mackerel (without bread and butter)

Spring Roll

301-400 calories
Avocado with Prawns

Avocado Vinaigrette

Cannelloni

Corn on the Cob with Butter

Cream of Mushroom Soup

Hummus with Pitta Bread

301-400 calories
Lasagne Verdi
Pâté with Toast
Ravioli
Scallops Mornay
Scallops Parisienne
Spaghetti Bolognese
Whitebait

401 calories and over
Bhajias
Chinese Spare Ribs
Fried Scampi with Tartare Sauce
Mixed Hors d'oeuvre
Taramasalata with Pitta Bread

MAIN COURSE DISHES
Under 300 calories
Beef or Ham Salad (no dressing)
Braised Kidneys
Cottage Cheese and Fruit Salad
(no dressing)
Crab, Lobster or Prawn Salad
(no dressing)
Fillet Steak, well grilled, 175 g
(6 oz) raw weight
Grilled Gammon and Pineapple
Grilled Halibut
Grilled Lobster
Grilled Trout
Grilled Turbot
Ham Salad (no dressing)
Herb Omelette or Plain
Omelette
Lobster Salad (no dressing or
seafood sauce)
Poached Halibut (no
Hollandaise sauce)
Prawn Salad (no dressing or
seafood sauce)

Under 300 calories
Rump or Sirloin Steak, well or
medium grilled, 175 g (6 oz) raw
weight
Trout au Bleu

301-400 calories
Calves' Liver with Sage
Cheese Salad (no dressing)
Fillet Steak, rare grilled, 175 g
(6 oz) raw weight
Fillet Steak, medium or well
grilled, 225 g (8 oz) raw weight
Grilled Dover Sole
Grilled Salmon
Ham Omelette
Kidneys Turbigo
Lamb Kebabs
Mixed Fish Salad
Poached Salmon (no
Hollandaise sauce)
Roast Beef, Yorkshire pudding
and gravy
Roast Chicken and trimmings
and gravy
Roast Lamb, mint sauce and
gravy
Roast Pheasant and trimmings
(excluding game chips)
Roast Pork, apple sauce and
gravy
Rump or Sirloin Steak, rare
grilled 175 g (6 oz) raw weight
Rump or Sirloin Steak, well or
medium grilled, 225 g (8 oz) raw
weight
Salmon Salad (no dressing or
mayonnaise)
Skate with Black Butter
Steak Tartare

301-400 calories
Tandoori Chicken
Trout with Almonds
Trout Meunière
Veal Marsala

401-500 calories
Beef Stroganoff
Carbonnade of Beef
Cheese Omelette
Chilli con Carne
Cod or Haddock Mornay
Fillet Steak, rare grilled, 225 g
(8 oz) raw weight
Escalope of Veal, fried in
Breadcrumbs
King Prawn Curry
Liver and Bacon
Plaice fried in Breadcrumbs
Rump or Sirloin Steak, rare
grilled, 225 g (8 oz) raw weight
Scampi Provençale
Sole Meunière
Trout with Almonds
Turbot with Shrimp or Prawn
Sauce
Vegetable Curry

501-600 calories
Beef Olives
Beef in Red Wine
Cannelloni
Escalope of Veal Holstein
Fried Scampi with Tartare Sauce
Goujons of Plaice with Tartare
Sauce
Meat Madras
Mixed Grill
Poached Halibut with
Hollandaise Sauce

501-600 calories
Poached Salmon with
Hollandaise Sauce
Poached Turbot with
Hollandaise Sauce
Salmon Mayonnaise
Sole Bercy
Sole Bonne Femme
Sole Portuguaise
Sole Véronique
Veal Cordon Bleu

601-700 calories
Beef Wellington
Chicken Chasseur
Chicken Marengo
Chicken Véronique
Coq au Vin
Lasagne
Lobster Thermidor
Paella
Steak and Kidney Pie
Steak and Kidney Pudding
Steak Diane
Tournedos Rossini

Over 700 calories
Chicken Korma
Chicken Maryland
Chicken Pie
Duck in Cherry Sauce
Duck in Orange Sauce
Fritto Misto
Moussaka
Pizza
Spaghetti Bolognese
Veal Escalope Milanese

DESERTS
Under 100 calories
Canned Lychees

Fresh Fruit

Fresh Pineapple and Kirsch (no cream)

Fresh Raspberries with sugar

Fresh Strawberries with sugar

Sorbet

101-200 calories
Cassata

Crème Caramel

Fresh Fruit Salad (no cream)

Ice Cream with Wafer

Orange in Caramel

Pancakes with Lemon and Sugar

Peaches Cardinal

Peach Melba (Ice Cream Sundae with Peach and Raspberry Sauce)

Pears in Red Wine

Zabaglione with Sponge Finger

201-300 calories
Bread and Butter Pudding

Chocolate Mousse

Coupe Jacques (Ice Cream Sundae with Fruit Salad and Cream)

Fruit Flan

Grand Marnier Soufflé (hot)

Ice Cream Sundae with Sauce and Nuts

Lemon Soufflé (cold) or Lemon Mousse

Pears Belle Hélène (Ice Cream Sundae with Pear and Chocolate Sauce)

Summer Pudding

301-400 calories
Apple Strudel

Black Forest Gâteau

Crêpe Suzette

Meringue Gâteau with Fruit and Cream

Raspberries with Sugar and Cream

Sponge Gâteau with Fruit and Cream

Strawberries with Sugar and Cream

Syllabub

401-500 calories
Cheesecake

Chocolate Soufflé (hot)

Jam Roly Poly (no custard)

Lemon Meringue Pie

Orange Soufflé (cold)

Orange Mousse

Rum Baba

Savarin

Spotted Dick (no custard)

Over 500 calories
Apple Pie and Cream or Custard or Ice Cream

Chocolate Meringue Gâteau

Chocolate Profiteroles

Chocolate Sponge Pudding with Chocolate Sauce

Christmas Pudding with Brandy Butter or Cream

Jam Roly Poly and Custard

Mille Feuille

Spotted Dick and Custard

Treacle Tart and Custard

Trifle

LOW AND HIGH-CALORIE MENUS

Here are examples of low and high-calorie restaurant menus which demonstrate the calorie saving you can achieve by choosing certain dishes and avoiding others.

INDIAN RESTAURANT
Low-calorie menu
Starter
1 small samosa   140 calories

Main Course
Tandoori Chicken   315 calories
Green Salad   30 calories
1 poppadom   75 calories

                                   Total   560 calories

High-calorie menu
Starter
1 large onion bhajia   245 calories

Main Course
Chicken Korma, without rice   870 calories
Pilau Rice   470 calories
Naan bread   295 calories

                                   Total   1,875 calories

FRENCH RESTAURANT
Low-calorie menu
Starter
Consommé   50 calories

Main Course

Truite au Bleu (poached trout)	180 calories
Potatoes, new boiled	160 calories
French beans	60 calories

Dessert

Pêches Melba	160 calories
	————
Total	610 calories
	————

High-calorie menu
Starter

Coquilles St Jacques Mornay (scallops in cheese sauce)	350 calories

Main Course

Poulet Grille Diable (grilled chicken in savoury breadcrumbs with a tangy sauce)	820 calories
Potatoes, sauté	200 calories
Petits Pois à la Française	120 calories

Dessert

Charlotte de Pommes (apple charlotte)	690 calories
	————
Total	2,130 calories
	————

ITALIAN RESTAURANT
Low-calorie menu
Starter

Melone (melon)	30 calories

Main Course

Saltimbocca alla Romana (slices of veal, cooked with ham and sage)	300 calories
Potatoes, new boiled	160 calories
Broccoli	50 calories

Desserts

Zabaglione	110 calories
Total	650 calories

High-calorie menu
Starter

Lasagne al Forno (pasta with meat and white sauce)	500 calories

Main Course

Fritto Misto (mixed meat and vegetable, fried)	1,100 calories
Salad with oily dressing	100 calories

Dessert

Bongo Bongo/Profiteroles (small choux buns filled with cream)	600 calories
Total	2,300 calories

FISH RESTAURANT
Low-calorie menu
Starter

Turtle Soup with Sherry	60 calories

Main Course

Prawn Salad (no dressing)	150 calories
Total	210 calories

High-calorie menu
Starter

Smoked Mackerel Pâté with toast (no butter)	500 calories

Main Course

Scallops Mornay	700 calories
Total	1,200 calories

TRADITIONAL BRITISH RESTAURANT
Low-calorie menu
Starter

½ fresh grapefruit or tomato juice   25 calories

Main Course

Crab Salad (no dressing or salad)   130 calories

Dessert

Summer Pudding   200 calories

                                    Total   355 calories

High-calorie menu
Starter

Kipper Pâté with toast   500 calories

Main Course

Cornish Pasty with Chips   1,000 calories

Dessert

Crème Brûlée   700 calories

                                    Total   2,200 calories

GREEK TAVERNA
Low-calorie menu
Starter

Avgolemono (clear chicken soup with rice, eggs and
lemon)   120 calories

Main Course

Dolmades (stuffed vine leaves)   350 calories
Domatosalata (tomato salad)   150 calories

                                    Total   620 calories

High-calorie menu
Starter

Taramasalata with Pitta Bread (smoked roe pâté)	660 calories

Main Course

Kleftiko (lamb sprinkled with wine and herbs)	670 calories
Chips, 1 portion	250 calories
Honatiki (Greek salad with Feta cheese)	180 calories

Dessert

Baklava	475 calories
Total	2,235 calories

CHINESE RESTAURANT
Low-calorie menu
Starter

Crab and Sweetcorn Soup	140 calories

Main Course

Prawn Chop Suey	310 calories
5 tablespoons plain boiled rice	100 calories
Total	550 calories

High-calorie menu
Starter

Barbecue Spare Ribs	495 calories

Main Course

Sweet and Sour Pork	860 calories
Fried rice, serving	555 calories
Spring roll	240 calories
Total	2,150 calories

STEAK BAR
Low-calorie menu
Starter

Melon Cocktail	50 calories

Main Course

150 g (5 oz) Rump Steak, well grilled	215 calories
Peas	30 calories
French beans	40 calories

Dessert

Ice Cream		120 calories
	Total	455 calories

High-calorie menu
Starter

Pâté with toast and butter	575 calories

Main Course

275 g (10 oz) Rump Steak, rare	515 calories
Chips	350 calories
Peas	30 calories
Bread roll and butter	200 calories

Dessert

Apple Pie and Cream		450 calories
	Total	2,120 calories

CARVERY
Low-calorie menu
Starter

Fruit Juice	60 calories

Main Course

2 slices turkey, no skin	160 calories
2 medium boiled potatoes	115 calories
4 rounded tablespoons cabbage	40 calories

Dessert

Sorbet with wafer, 2 scoops	100 calories
Total	475 calories

High-calorie menu
Starter

Avocado with Prawns	400 calories

Main Course

2 slices beef, lean and fat	320 calories
Yorkshire Pudding	120 calories
1 level teaspoon mustard	10 calories
2 medium chunks roast potatoes	150 calories
4 rounded tablespoons broad beans	100 calories

Dessert

Chocolate Profiteroles	600 calories
Total	1,700 calories

HEALTH FOOD RESTAURANT
Low-calorie menu

Chilli Beans	240 calories
Celery, apple, raisin and yogurt salad	140 calories

Dessert

Low-fat natural yogurt	100 calories
Total	480 calories

High-calorie menu

Cheese and Onion Quiche	550 calories
Celery, apple, walnut and mayonnaise salad	420 calories

Dessert

Apricot Slice or Date Slice	500 calories
Total	1,470 calories

FISH AND CHIP SHOP
Low-calorie menu

Scampi in Batter	240 calories
Mushy Peas	140 calories
Total	360 calories

High-calorie menu

Plaice in Batter	650 calories
Chips, large portion	580 calories
Total	1,230 calories

10 STRATEGIES TO GET <u>YOU</u> SLIM

1 Select a diet that's realistic.
2 Chart all your usual food choices.
3 Savour every single mouthful.
4 Make food a pleasure.
5 Plan for temptation!
6 Protect your willpower.
7 Plan your menus in advance.
8 Keep yourself busy – have other things to do besides eat.
9 Watch out for PMT time.
10 Understand your problem.

Do you regard yourself as a failed slimmer or a hopeless case? Maybe you're always going to stick to a diet this time – and always, somehow, break your resolve and hate yourself for it? These ten strategies will help you learn to control your weight.

1: Select a diet that's realistic
Choose a diet that fits into your lifestyle and makes nutritional sense. But, for heaven's sake, make sure that you include, either in the diet or in your calorie calculations, at least a once-a-week allowance of the foods you really love most. That way, you can look forward to them and enjoy them, without feeling guilty at all, and this is going to make it much easier for you to stick to your weight loss promises.

2: Chart all your usual food choices
We often eat when we're not hungry. In fact, one of the very last reasons people in our western society eat food is because they're hungry! It's also vitally important for an overweight person to realize that most of us have eating habits of which we are quite unaware. Become aware of your exact eating pattern. Keep a day-to-day diary of every bite you eat and drop you drink . . . and keep the record for at least one week.

WRITE IT DOWN: Write down all the items you swallow: what quantity, what time you eat them, and how long it takes you to eat them. Make a note of how hungry you are. Say whether you are sitting or standing at the time; and what else you are doing. State the mood you are in.

CHART YOUR PROGRESS: Rule out a chart like the one on the right and carry it everywhere with you so that you can make your records there and then. Don't worry if it turns out to be a 'shameful' fact sheet. The object isn't to construct a stick to whack you with! It's to make you find out a lot of useful information about yourself to use in the future.

KNOW YOUR WEAKNESSES: If you've been honest, these daily records will have teased out all the forces that are influencing your eating pattern. You'll see which moods trigger off a breakdown of control, which times of day are hardest for you to be in control. Are there particular people who influence your eating behaviour, or particular occasions? Your record will show you. Once you have this kind of information, you are aware; and so you're in a much stronger position to plan some strategies to change and control some of the eating habits that have been helping you stay overweight.

On the right is a specimen record chart that you can use as a guide to make your own intake diary.

Column 1: Record starting and finishing times of each meal or snack. A lapse of 15 minutes since the last bite calls for a brand new chart entry.
Column 2: Record your physical stance: sitting, standing, etc.
Column 3: If eating in company, name the person(s). This will help to identify who, if anyone, influences your eating behaviour to any degree. Note any associated activity. This means anything you are doing at the same time as eating, like watching TV, talking, reading.
Column 4: Record your mood before eating: content, tense, depressed, angry, happy, bored, tired, rushed, 'neutral'?
Column 5: How hungry were you? Use the figures 1 to 5 to express your degree of hunger. Not hungry=1, Very hungry=5.
Column 6: Note what food(s) you ate and how much. Estimate weight, portion size, and so on.
Column 7: Note the number of calories per item eaten.

TIME START END	PHYSICAL POSITION	WHERE AND WITH WHOM	MOOD	HOW HUNGRY ON SCALE (1-5)	FOOD AND AMOUNT	CALORIES
10 - 10:30	Sitting	With neighbour in sitting room	Relaxed	1	4 Digestive biscuits	260
12 - 12:15	Standing	Alone in Kitchen	Bored	1	½ oz Cheddar 1 Slice bread	60 65
4:30 - 5:00	Standing	Kitchen	Rushed	2	2 Slices toast 1 oz butter	130 210

3: Savour every single mouthful

Mindless eating is one of your worst enemies. Whether you go on a strict diet, or simply cut down on the amount of food you eat, from now on make an effort to enjoy and savour every mouthful. Your food record will show whether you're in the habit of eating while you rush about from one place to another or while getting on with the chores. Try to break this habit and concentrate on your food, and you may well find that you eat less.

4: Make food a pleasure

Lay your tray or table attractively. Sit down to eat. Eat slowly. Put your knife and fork down between bites. Have a cup of a favourite low-calorie beverage with your meal if you like, and sip it slowly. Savour your snacks in the same way. Sit down with your biscuit and your cup of coffee. If you've counted a cream cake in with your calories, sit down and enjoy every little bite.

EAT SLOWLY: There's simply no point in gulping food down or eating it fast, when you can get so much more pleasure from savouring your food slowly. And if you can learn to do this, there's a bonus. By eliminating mindless eating, you can effortlessly cut your calorie intake quite considerably. You'll probably be very surprised at the calorie saving you can achieve this way.

5: Plan for temptation!

There's a natural human tendency to consume food if it's to hand. It's a habit we've probably inherited from our primeval ancestors in ancient times when it was important for man to eat food whenever it was available, because this was the way to survive in periods of famine. Unfortunately, there's a little of that prehistoric creature still in us!

BE PREPARED: Certainly, there is no human being who can resist the temptation to eat delicious foods and unnecessary calories every day of every month of every year. There will be birthdays, parties, celebrations, dinners out. Somebody will open a box of chocolates, somebody else will serve a luscious cake. You're going to be tempted – and, when these occasions happen, you'd be superhuman if you could always say no. So, as far as you can, plan for them.

DECIDE ON A PLAN OF ACTION: Some slimmers prefer to cut down on calorie intake a day or two beforehand, in order to put some calories 'in the bank' to spend at the special occasion. Others find it easier to cut down on calories afterwards. Choose the method that suits you.

DON'T LOSE HEART: There will be times when, regardless of the best-laid plans, you're going to have an unexpected encounter with real temptation; and you'll lose control. This is no reason to call yourself a failure, a greedy glutton, or any other hateful self-castigating name. Don't feel guilty and don't let your momentary lapse upset your long-term diet plans. Just remember that you are human. Say to yourself: 'All right, I'm going to give in to temptation, but I'm going to make it a deliberate act. I'm going to sit down and pay attention to this food. I'm going to eat it slowly and relish every single bite.'

TRY TO FIGHT TEMPTATION: We're not for a moment suggesting you should automatically fall by the wayside every time a temptation comes your way. If you did that, your next diet might fade fast. Say no as often as you possibly can. But don't be too surprised when you can't resist temptation because there will certainly be times when it does happen.

6: Protect your willpower

Willpower is a very fragile thing: if you test it repeatedly, it finally breaks. Knowing this, aim to reduce the number of times when you have to use willpower.

DON'T BUY SWEETS FOR THE FAMILY: You'll have a much easier time if you don't have nuts and sweets in the sitting room 'for the others to eat'. It will be easier if you don't allow any of your downfall foods into the house at all. You needn't buy them for anybody else, not even if you have children. Very young children won't miss sweets and cakes, and don't need them. Older children can be given the money to buy their own – and asked not to eat them in front of you or leave them around where you'll find them.

HIDE THE FOOD: Make it more difficult for yourself to get at food. If you see leftover pie every time you open the fridge door, or your glance falls on jars full of currants and glacé cherries whenever you look at the shelves, you're making it hard for yourself. Keep leftovers well wrapped, preferably in boxes with lids on; put foods like currants in opaque containers behind closed doors. You could even stick your weight loss chart on the fridge door as a constant reminder.

AVOID SOCIAL NIBBLES! If you can, keep your distance from foods when you're out socially. At parties and celebrations where there are buffets and bowls of nuts and crisps around, it isn't difficult to place yourself a good few paces away from the food. If you stand right next to it, the likelihood of your eating a lot is near enough 100 per cent!

7: Plan your menus in advance

You're going to be far less susceptible to random temptations if you plan what you're going to serve and eat in advance.

START MAKING LISTS: Food manufacturers know just how to entice you to buy more than you want or need. Make very careful shopping lists and write down exactly what you are going to buy and stick rigidly to your list.

THINK ABOUT LUNCH: If you go out to work, it helps to plan what you're going to have for lunch; and it's even better if you can take your lunch with you and thus save yourself from being tempted by high-calorie foods in the canteen or snack bar.

8: Keep yourself busy – have other things to do besides eat

Many an idle snack is eaten out of boredom, and a lot of uncontrolled eating is triggered off by a blue mood. This is quite understandable. Food can be tranquillizing – temporarily. But if you're trying to control your weight, it's best not to deal with negative moods and frustrations by taking in extra calories. The good feeling lasts a very short time, and the guilty feelings last long enough to wreck many a diet.

KEEP YOUR MIND OFF FOOD: There are two kinds of activities: work and fun. Make out two lists. The first list should be of chores you'd like to get done. This one usually includes items like cleaning the silver, sewing on buttons, clearing out a drawer and so on. The second list is the fun list and this one includes pleasurable activities such as doing a crossword, knitting, reading a book, having a scented bath, arranging flowers, and so on.

TIME YOUR ACTIVITIES: Sort out the different activities under time headings. Five-minute chores or pastimes, then ten-minute ones, twenty minutes, half an hour, and so on. Next time you feel an impulse to eat unnecessarily, pick up one of your lists and do one of the chores or fun things first. If, when you've cleaned the silver or done some knitting or whatever, you still feel an overwhelming urge to eat, have a little of the food you crave. Sit down and savour it. Know what you're doing.

ENJOY THE SENSE OF ACHIEVEMENT: The ploy of diverting your attention from food while you get on and do something else usually works very well. Doing a chore may not sound a very attractive alternative to a chunky cheese sandwich, but the nice thing is the glow of virtue and achievement you get when it's done. Recreational pursuits are pleasurable in themselves; and while you're having a bath or talking to a friend on the telephone or taking a walk you have no desire to eat.

MAKE SURE YOU CAN START STRAIGHTAWAY: Whatever you choose to do must be easy to start on. It's easy to pick up some knitting, for example. But if you fancy dressmaking and go to get the machine out only to find it buried beneath a load of clutter in the cupboard under the stairs you may be tempted to leave it there and go back to the kitchen. Making your lists isn't quite enough. You have to make sure that all the things you enjoy doing are ready to start on the minute you have an 'uncontrollable' urge to eat.
(See page 305 for more 'binge-beaters'.)

9: Watch out for PMT time
To be successful at anything, you have to know yourself; and this goes for dieting, too. Keep track of your pre-menstrual food behaviour, and make a note of any special cravings.

KEEP A DIARY: Fill out a food record diary covering PMT time for two or three months. Then, in future, when you wake up in the morning in a frame of mind to blow your diet, you can say to yourself, 'I know what the problem is. I always feel like this and get these cravings at PMT time.'

LEARN TO COPE: Now you are aware, you can begin to deal with these extra-tough days. It may be best to stay out of certain restaurants and snack bars. It's best not to go out to do a mammoth shopping trip in a supermarket, but to have necessary foods in the house beforehand. But don't expect to be a saint. It's a very good idea to allow yourself a controlled amount of foods you really crave.

10: Understand your problem

All these strategies are geared towards making you aware of the forces that are at work when you are putting food into your mouth.

KNOW WHY YOU EAT: Each time you eat, ask yourself: 'Why at this particular moment am I sitting/standing here with this particular food and about to eat it?'

Sometimes you'll find the answer is really good; you are hungry, you're truly enjoying the food. Sometimes you'll find that the reasons for eating are unreasonable and irrational. And this is when you put the food away, and find something more rewarding to do.

DON'T BE TOO HARD ON YOURSELF: From now on don't ever call yourself a fat, greedy pig or use words like 'weak willpower' . . . 'hopeless' . . . or 'stupid'.

You are none of these things. You are a worthwhile human being who – with the aid of these strategies – can conquer your weight problem. No matter how hard it seems, every diet can be made easier to stick to by following these ten rules.

CHAPTER 4

KEEP MOVING

ARE <u>YOU</u> GETTING ENOUGH EXERCISE?

1. Do you attend an exercise class? YES/NO

2. If yes, how often? ....

3. Do you play any sports? YES/NO

4. If so, how often? ....

5. Write down approximately how many hours a week you spend doing the following:
a. Sleeping ....
b. Sitting, watching television, sewing, knitting, washing dishes
....

c. Playing snooker or card games, cleaning out cupboards, cooking, driving a car, dusting, ironing, dressmaking, vacuuming ....

d. Bedmaking, mopping floors, cleaning windows, home decorating, polishing, shopping, washing clothes by hand, playing table tennis, doing yoga ....

e. Weeding the garden, playing golf, scrubbing the floors, playing tennis or volley ball, walking at a comfortable pace..........
....

f. Playing badminton, cycling, ballroom dancing, digging the garden, horse riding, ice skating, gentle swimming.........................

g. Jogging, playing netball, walking upstairs, brisk walking...........
....

h. Athletics training, playing basketball, country dancing, judo
....

i. Circuit training, strenuously cycling, mountaineering, running uphill, skipping, playing squash...

6. Write down the activities and tasks that make you feel really tired...
....

7. Write down any regular trips you do on foot each day and approximately how long each journey takes.
....
....

8. How many times last week did you ask the children to fetch and carry for you, or your husband to get something from the garage or garden, etc? ....
....

9. Are you afraid of being made a fool of if you can't play a game well? YES/NO

KINDLY KICK

❝*The sun was shining, the sea was blue – but being 2st overweight, I felt more than a bit nervous of appearing in my swimming costume. 'Don't worry,' said my six-year-old son, kindly. 'I've been looking round, Mummy, and you aren't quite the fattest lady on the beach.*❞

THE <u>BIG</u> BURN

BURNING UP: Even if you are doing nothing but lying in bed worrying about your weight, you are burning calories. Ms Average is expending about one calorie per minute on basic body maintenance; that is, keeping her heart beating, blood circulating, and so on; this is her Basal Metabolic Rate or BMR. Once you start moving your body in any way, you burn extra calories.

The chart on pages 214 to 221 shows how many calories per 15 minutes various activities are likely to burn. The calorie figures are based on the average expenditure by a woman of average weight. An average man will use up a half calorie a minute more on light exercise and one calorie more on strenuous sports.

REMEMBER YOUR BMR: When you are totting up the calorie total of your day's hours (or minutes!) of activity, remember that you have to subtract the average calorie per minute which your body would be burning, even if you were totally inert in that nice new leotard!

Remember, too, that one calorie per minute is an average BMR. Many people will have a slower metabolic rate: they are likely to be the ones who find it harder to stay slim. And, of course, lean people are often the ones who tend to have a higher-than-average BMR.

BODY WEIGHT: When it comes to burning up extra calories in physical activity, overweight people have an advantage. In walking, or in any exercise that involves moving the whole body from place to place, overweight people burn up more calories per minute than slim people do. The heavier the body, the more energy (in the form of calories) is needed to move it.

NEVER OVER-ESTIMATE! Even average normal-weight people show differences in the way they tackle various tasks and exercises; some put far more energy into them than others do. It is fairly safe to say that, no matter what weight you are, if you go about your daily activities in an unhurried way your calorie expenditure will be about average as shown in these charts.

BURN-UP RATE: Other factors can affect the rate at which you burn up calories. Walking up a steep gradient on uneven ground against a strong wind, for instance, will mean you'll burn more calories than the average-per-fifteen minutes figure given: figures can only be well-educated estimates.

Calories USED PER 15 MINUTES

Look at your answers to the questionnaire and see if you are spending most of your time during the week on activities that are burning up few calories. Make a resolution that you will go through those activity categories again in a month's time and make sure you are spending more time on those listed in groups F to I in Question 5.

Archery
A pleasant pastime, but really an arms-only activity plus leisurely walking . . .   **45**

Athletics
Can be extremely strenuous for short periods of time.
During training, count . . .   **105**

Badminton
Playing with average effort means running about a lot . . **75**

Basketball
Lots of very fast running, jumping and stretching . . .   **105**

Bedmaking
Real bends and stretches with sheets and blankets . . .   **45**
With a duvet . . .   **30**

Bends and Stretches
On-the-spot exercises such as touching your toes, kneebends, and so on . . .   **45**

Billiards or Snooker
A game that is mostly arm movement. Alas,
concentration does not burn calories . . .   **30**

Bowls
A leisurely sport with little speed, but some bending . . .   **45**

Canoeing
Paddling down the river at 3 km (2 miles) an hour . . .   **45**
Racing along at about 6 km (4 miles) an hour . . .   **90**

Card Games
Sitting and puzzling uses few calories and you only add
the occasional flick of the wrists . . .   **under 30**

Circuit Training
Climbing gymnasium bars, jumping over the
vaulting-horse and other equipment,
all very strenuous exercise . . .   **150**

Cleaning
Cupboards and drawers, mostly arm movement . . .   **under 30**
Floors, with mop or broom and some walking . . .   **45**
Windows, if lots of bending and stretching is involved . . . **45**

Climbing
Rock climbing and hill walking are very strenuous
activities and enthusiasts keep going for many hours.
Walking up sloping terrain . . .   **90**
Tackling arduous rock faces . . .   **up to 180**

Cooking
Does not involve much strenuous physical effort and
consists mostly of arm movement . . .   **30**

Cricket
If you are fielding . . .   **under 30**
If you are batting or bowling, the calorie output should rise . . .   **60**

Croquet
Another leisurely game that does not demand strenuous
activity . . .   **45**

Cross-Country Running
Marathon events can last for three or four hours so lots
of calories are consumed . . .   **105**

Cycling
At a pleasant, easy pace along the straight . . .   **75**
Strenuous, enthusiastic style . . .   **150**

Dancing
Traditional ballroom, fairly stately in style . . .   **75**
Strenuous dancing; Scottish, country,
square and disco . . .   **105**

Darts
You probably burn up more calories walking to and
from your throwing position on the
mat than actually throwing the darts . . .   **under 30**

Driving a Car
Through normal traffic . . .   **30**

Dusting
Just flicking the duster over surfaces, even though you
are moving the ornaments, is mostly arm movement. So
not a big calorie-burner . . .   **30**

Fishing
Sitting on the river bank . . .   **under 30**
Scrambling in and out of boats and rowing to the fishing
spot . . .   **45**

Gardening
Heavy work, like digging . . .   **75**
Lighter work, like weeding . . .   **60**

Golf
Some walking and effort required, so expect to chalk up
an average calorie expenditure of . . .   **60**

Gymnastics
The kind that demand you bend, stretch, jump and so on
with your whole body . . .   **75**

Hockey
If you stand about a lot, do not count
this as a calorie-burner of much value.
If you play a reasonably vigorous game,
expect an average . . .   **75**

Home Decorating
Lots of arm movement and clambering up ladders . . .   **45**

Horse Riding
If you just sit on the horse while it walks
along, the horse, not you, is getting
the exercise; but if you trot, canter
or gallop, you are doing better in the
calorie-burning stakes . . .   **75**

Ice-Skating
At an average pace which can be
kept up for quite a while . . .   **75**

Ironing
Alas, one of those tiring jobs that
does not use up many calories
because the movement is mostly
in the arms . . .   **under 30**

Jogging
At a comfortably steady pace that
can be maintained for quite a long
time . . .   **90**

Judo
When you actually come to grips with your opponent, a
very strenuous sport . . .   **105**

Knitting
Requires almost no energy, however fast your
needles click . . .   **under 30**

Mountaineering
Not an activity anyone could tackle
without being very fit. Very hard
exercise for long
periods . . .   **up to 180**

Music
Playing an instrument (except
drums) or conducting an
orchestra . . .   **30-45**
Playing the drums . . .   **60**

Netball
Calorie expenditure varies a lot
depending on how much you put
into it. However, a reasonably fast
game can burn up calories
speedily . . .   **90**

Polishing
Furniture polishing can be a
vigorous activity if you put some
effort into it . . .   **45**

Roller Skating
At any normal pace . . .   **45**

Rowing
Rowing lazily round a lake . . .   **60**
Competing in a race . . .   **up to 150**

Running
Sprint-for-a-bus style, fast and furious . . .   **105**
Jogging – at a steady pace that can be kept up for quite a
long time . . .   **90**
Running upstairs – much higher expenditure here
because you are moving your body against gravity . . .   **165**

Sailing
Will vary very much with the size of boat and how much
manual work needs to be done.
Sitting holding the sail . . .   **30**
More strenuous sailing tasks . . .   **90**

Scrubbing Floors
With a will . . .   **60**

Sewing
Mending, embroidery, dressmaking . . .   **15-30**

Shopping
With a light load, 5 kg (10 lb) or under . . .   **45**
With a heavy load, over 5 kg (10 lb plus) . . .   **60+**

Sitting
Whether watching television, pounding a typewriter or
just resting . . .   **15**

Skiing
Depends on your pace . . .   **75+**

Skipping
One of the best calorie-burners of all . . .   **150**

Squash
A very strenuous sport if played hard . . .   **150**

Sunbathing
You burn up no more calories than when you are lying in
bed . . .   **15**

Swimming
Often considered the ideal form of
exercise since it uses all the
muscles. Gentle swimming, easy
strokes . . .   **up to 75**
More strenuous swimming, the
competitive kind . . .   **up to 150**

Table Tennis
If you play an average game, not too fast . . .   **45**
If you are a demon player . . .   **60+**

Tennis
An average game with a reasonable amount of running about . . .   **60**
A hard game with a lot of running and retrieving . . .   **90**

Vacuum Cleaning
The cleaner does more work than you do. If you move furniture out of the way, you will burn off more . . .   **45**
If you do not move furniture, you could be using . . .   **under 30**

Volleyball
Moving about the court at average speed . . .   **60**

Walking
Calorie expenditure depends on how slowly or briskly you walk. It can be one of the most valuable everyday activities of all.
Strolling – ambling slowly at an easy pace . . .   **30-45**
Comfortable pace, unhurried walking . . .   **60+**
Purposeful pace – walking quickly but comfortably . . .   **60-75**
Walking uphill slowly . . .   **75**
Walking upstairs and down again without taking a rest . . .   **90**
Brisk walking – quick and steady but enough to make you want to stop for a breather sometimes . . .   **90+**

Washing
Dishes . . .   **under 30**
Clothes by hand. The heavier they are, the more calories you burn . . .   **45**

Windsurfing
The more you fall off, the higher your calorie expenditure . . .   **up to 90**

Yoga
With average bending and stretching . . .   **45**

WHICH EXERCISE?

The calorie expenditure chart on pages 214 to 221 tells you which activities burn up the most calories, but when selecting an exercise in order to increase your calorie-burning potential you also need to take into account the length of time you will be able to continue doing it.

Here is a chart which shows the average time each week most people would spend on each exercise or activity. Athletics and team games such as basketball are not included because if you are involved in these you are unlikely to need to increase your activity level; and if you are not already involved in them it will take some time to reach a standard whereby you start burning up the average calorie expenditure. Also excluded are everyday activities, such as bedmaking, as you are unlikely to increase the time spent doing these. Deducted from each of the calorie calculations is the 1 calorie per minute that you would use up if you spent the time sitting around doing nothing. You need to burn up an extra 3,500 calories to lose 1 lb, but if you are trying to speed up your weight loss every little extra effort is helpful.

AVERAGE CALORIE EXPENDITURE PER WEEK
Over 400 calories
Jogging . . . 45 minutes each day . . . 1,575 calories
Cycling . . . 30 minutes each day . . . 1,290 calories
Cross country running . . . 3 hours . . . 1,080 calories
Brisk walking . . . 30 minutes each day . . . 1,050 calories
Dancing . . . 2 hours . . . 480-580 calories
Home decorating . . . 4 hours . . . 480 calories
Skiing . . . 2 hours . . . 480 calories
Badminton . . . two 1-hour sessions . . . 480 calories

300-400 calories
Gardening . . . 2 hours . . . 380 calories
Golf . . . 2 hours . . . 360 calories
Skipping . . . seven 5-minute sessions . . . 315 calories

200-300 calories
Circuit training . . . 30 minutes . . . 270 calories
Bowls . . . two 1-hour games . . . 240 calories
Fishing . . . 4 hours . . . 240 calories
Horse riding . . . 1 hour . . . 240 calories
Ice skating . . . 1 hour . . . 240 calories
Table tennis . . . 1 hour . . . 240 calories
Yoga . . . two 1-hour sessions . . . 240 calories
Darts . . . 30 minutes each evening . . . 210 calories

100-200 calories
Sailing . . . 1 hour . . . 180 calories
Cricket . . . 2 hours . . . 140 calories
Running upstairs . . . seven 2-minute sessions . . . 140 calories
Archery . . . two 30-minute sessions . . . 120 calories
Billiards or snooker . . . two 1-hour games . . . 120 calories
Canoeing . . . 1 hour . . . 120 calories
Croquet . . . two 30-minute games . . . 120 calories
Roller skating . . . 1 hour . . . 120 calories

CROWDING OUT CRAVINGS
For me, the solution was Keep Busy. . . . Instead of eating as soon as I got home from work, leaving a long, empty evening ahead, I got into the habit of filling the gap with a low-calorie snack, then going out for a brisk walk or jog, playing badminton or swimming. Anything to keep my mind and fingers off chocolate!

A WORD OF WARNING

DON'T OVERDO IT: Don't suddenly start a strenuous exercise programme. Physical activity increased gradually is good for all of us; instant marathons are not. Enthusiastic but ignorant would-be athletes have been given official warnings from bodies concerned by an 'epidemic' of 'aerobic' injuries. Sudden strenuous activity, especially for weight loss purposes, is very unwise; it should not be undertaken by anyone who is unfit, or out of practice. For anyone who's fat – certainly for anybody 2 stone or more overweight – it's likely to be dangerous.

TAKE IT SLOWLY: Increase your activity level gently, especially if you are overweight. See that you are taught or led by experienced, properly trained people. Get your doctor's approval if in the slightest doubt. At the end of any active session, wind down gradually; never stop suddenly.

DISABLED DIETING: If you can't exercise because you are physically immobile, losing surplus weight will be more difficult for you than for someone who is able to be active. But don't be discouraged: the right diet will eventually work. Many disabled people in *Slimming Magazine Clubs*, for instance, achieve target weight. Get your doctor's approval before you start, especially if you are receiving any treatment or medication.

Check your answer to question 6 on the questionnaire.
DON'T BE FOOLED! How tired an activity makes you feel is, alas, often no real guide to its effectiveness as an aid to weight control. You can feel exhausted after tackling a big pile of ironing; but because only limited arm movement is involved, the calorie output may well

disappoint you.

Largest expenditures come about when you move your body weight against gravity – when you climb stairs, for instance.

MENTAL ACTIVITY DOESN'T COUNT: When we feel worn out after a hard day's mental slog, it doesn't seem fair that working the brain, unlike the muscles, burns up no extra calories. The brain does use up some calories – about one fifth of the one calorie a minute used in just keeping the body functioning when we are at rest. However, just like some computers which use little more electric current when calculating than when idling, the busy brain uses little more energy than the idle brain.

When the brain cells get fatigued they transmit a general feeling of tiredness to the body. Often, doing a few purely physical exercises when you are suffering from brain fatigue will lift this tiredness and make you feel much livelier.

GET PHYSICAL! Physical activity is a term which embraces all bodily movement. It includes the sports which we usually think of as 'exercise' but it also takes in housework, trailing around the shops, climbing the stairs, even walking across the room to switch on the television. The sum total of little movements during the course of an average day can have a most significant effect on calorie expenditure.

ON THE MOVE: Most people who move a great deal are slim, while most people who don't move a lot are overweight. Overweight people often think they move a lot, but usually they don't. You can observe the truth of this yourself. Almost certainly among your acquaintances is a woman who is often described as being 'full of nervous energy'. She is almost invariably lean. Watch her for a while next time you visit her home. See how many times she gets up from her seat either to do or to get something. Observe how brisk her movements tend to be.

ACT SWIFTLY! Increase your calorie expenditure by physical activity simply and gradually, and it will eventually become effortless. You can start tackling the task of increasing your daily calorie output in the very simplest of ways. Begin by concentrating on making every movement more swiftly.

Check your answer to question 7.

QUICK MARCH! The speed at which we walk is very much a habit, so make sure you get into the habit of walking more quickly. Train yourself to walk faster. Is there a regular journey that you do on foot? Next time you step out on this journey make a note of how long it takes you and thereafter try to walk a little faster.

If you do not walk regularly, try to incorporate a short walk into your day. If the bus stop is practically outside your place of work, allow yourself a little extra time and get off the bus the stop before. Or leave your car at least 10 minutes' walk from the station.

Check your answer to question 8.

CHANGE YOUR ATTITUDE! Instead of complaining that you have left that book upstairs, and even sending someone else to fetch it, start to welcome that extra little climb as an opportunity to burn up a few calories. Again, try to speed the rate of ascent, but start slowly as running upstairs is very strenuous, especially if you are overweight.

Check your answer to question 9.

TAKE UP A SPORT: Having worked at moving faster through the day you may find that you reach a stage when it seems a good idea to take up some sporting activity. Unfortunately, many women who have been plump as children still remember the horror of those humiliations in the school gym or on the playing fields. There still lingers a fear of making a fool of yourself, of being the one no others pick to be on their team. Well, try to forget all that nonsense instilled at school that sports need to be done well.

Find some like-minded friends and have a go at anything you fancy and just have a good time. Play some tennis or golf and have a good laugh. Your regular get-together could become one of the fun occasions of the week. And however badly you play the game you will be burning more calories to add to your total output.

DON'T AIM TOO HIGH: Don't try to be a perfectionist when starting your campaign to boost calorie output. A resolution to do a daily three-mile jog is just as doomed to disaster as a resolution to eat absolutely nothing all day to make up for the sins of yesterday. Do it gradually. Give yourself a plus mark every time you take a brisk climb upstairs when you would normally avoid it. Establish habits, which by their very nature become effortless.

FIND EXERCISE PARTNERS: It will give you more incentive to stick to an exercise plan if you find someone else to join you. If you have older children, promise to take them swimming at least once a week and challenge them to a few races across the pool. If you can't swim, why not find a friend who will join you in taking some swimming lessons?

DISCOVER THE GREAT OUTDOORS: Instead of cooking an enormous Sunday lunch, then sitting around watching television all afternoon, plan a drive to the country with the family. Pack up a picnic lunch – you'll find lots of low-calorie salads and sandwiches in the diet section – then get out of the car and persuade everyone to go for a long walk. If you don't own a car, take the train to a local beauty spot or to the seaside. During the summer there are often special excursions – just enquire at your local station. If you can't get the family interested in walking with you, check with your local library to see if there is a ramblers' association that you can join. You could make new friends as well as get more exercise.

INCLUDE SMALL CHILDREN IN FLOOR WALKING: Your toddler will think it great fun when you get down to his level and do this exercise with him. It is an excellent calorie burner and also helps tone up tummy and bottom. Sit on the floor with legs straight in front of you. Move forwards briskly, 'walking' on your bottom, swinging your arms backwards and forwards to help you move your body along. When you come close to a wall, reverse the action and floor-walk backwards. Keep going for as long as you can.

BORROW FROM THE CHILDREN: Use the children's skipping ropes, rackets, climbing gear. Don't be afraid of having a go at any activity; it really doesn't matter if the children fall about laughing at your efforts as long as you are enjoying yourself. Skipping is one of the best calorie burners of all. Start off slowly and just do about 25 forwards skips, then try to build up gradually to 50 or more skips at one go. When you have got into the swing of things, try skipping backwards. Hold your arms straight out at shoulder level as you circle the rope backwards and you will firm up your arms at the same time.

PLAN FAMILY RUNS: See if you can get family and friends to join you in a regular run. Take it very gently at first if you've not exercised for a long time. At first your run may only be to the end of the street and back, but every little extra activity will help to solve your weight problem. If you set a time – say, before dinner every evening – and ask the family not to accept or make any excuses, there is less chance that you will be tempted to put off the run.

TAKE YOUR PARTNER DANCING: Disco and country dancing are particularly good for burning up calories, but even ballroom dancing will burn up as many calories as playing tennis or ice skating. Remember to watch your drink consumption, though. Discos don't always sell low-calorie soft drinks and lots of fizzy and alcoholic drinks could undo all your efforts.

LAUGHABLE LIFELINE

A skipping rope has been my lifeline. My family fall about laughing when I dash out into the garden for my regulation 30 skips, but who cares when I'm burning up calories instead of sitting around adding on more weight with some calorie-laden nibble.

*F*ADS AND FALLACIES

Aerobics
AEROBICS DON'T MAKE YOU SLIM: 'Aerobic' means 'with oxygen',
meaning exercise tough enough to make you puff. It may be a relief
for you to learn that in a carefully conducted research programme,
'aerobic exercise' was found not to be as valuable for weight loss as
some theories suggest. Research subjects did 40 minutes a day of
'aerobic exercise' which was sufficiently hard work to produce a
sustained heart rate of 120 to 150 beats a minute. They burned off
an extra 200 calories or so as a result, the amount to be expected.
But, in terms of weight reduction, this is a poor return for such
strenuous effort; other factors being equal, you would probably take
more than 17 days to shift a single surplus pound. Aerobics are a
poor bet if you are relying on these exercises alone to shift surplus
weight in a reasonable space of time.

Exercise machines
ARE YOU EQUIPPED? Exercise bikes, rowing machines and other home
exercise equipment will certainly firm flabby muscles and burn up
extra calories if you use them regularly. But before you spend
pounds on expensive equipment, be quite honest with yourself. Are
you really going to get on that bike every morning and evening for at
least a 10-minute session? Do you have space to keep the
equipment ready assembled? If you have to unpack your rowing
machine every time you want to use it, you'll find you can't be
bothered to do it often.

FIGHT BOREDOM: Cycling away in the middle of your sitting room can
be very boring. A tip to keep you going is to place your bike
opposite the television so you can view as you pedal.

GREAT EXPECTATIONS: Although any kind of exercise is certainly good
for your general fitness and well-being, don't expect exercise
machines to speed up your weight loss dramatically. If you spend 20
minutes a day on an exercise bike instead of just sitting around, you

will burn up around 1,000 extra calories a week (depending on your weight and how strenuously you pedal). That is equivalent to about an extra 1 lb weight loss in three weeks. It makes better sense to increase permanently the energy used in all your everyday activities than to exercise with costly gadgets.

Spot-reducing
PASSIVE ACTION: Passive exercise machines, which feature pads that are clamped to problem areas, can help to improve muscle tone. However, active exercise gives you a definite mental lift that no machine can duplicate. Remember, you won't be burning up extra calories by just lying there and letting the machine do all the work.

FEELING THE PINCH: Vigorous underwater pinching may relieve your feelings, but it won't help unwanted flesh disappear. All it is likely to do is to add black and blue bruising to the problem area.

EXERTING PRESSURE: Bouncing up and down on fat thighs won't break down fatty tissue as some beauty 'experts' claim. If you could reshape your body by external pressure – kneading, pummelling, bashing, slapping, and so on – then the perfect figure, however you define it, would be commonplace rather than a rarity.

Surgery
UNKIND CUTS: Removing fatty bulges surgically does not guarantee a permanent solution; bulges can actually build up again. Surgery is never an 'easy' option: you can't cut tissue without cutting nerves, which causes great shock and discomfort to the system. Most experts agree that surgery is no substitute for slimming. If, however, you are serious about surgery, it is essential that you see your GP first. Don't take risks by going directly to a private clinic that invites applications from the public by advertisement. Some clinics may have experienced surgeons; others may be staffed by people of dubious qualifications. Your best introduction to a suitable surgeon is via your GP.

SHAPE UP

The following anytime exercises don't call for classes, leotards or sweat-bands and are therefore the spot-trimmers you are most likely to stick to, making them extra-effective for helping you to get into shape and stay that way.

Exercise

Morning Thigh-Trimmer

As you stumble into the bathroom first thing in the morning, hang on to the door frame and do this quick exercise. It's hard work but done every morning it will firm those lazy thigh muscles in weeks.

1. Stand close to the frame of the open doorway and grip it lightly at waist level with both hands. Make sure you are standing straight. This means head up, shoulders down, pelvis forward. Place feet comfortably wide apart, toes turned outwards. Keep back and legs straight. You are now in the correct position to begin.

2. Still gripping the frame and keeping heels flat on the floor, drop loosely down on your haunches as far as you can. Don't worry if you can't get right down to begin with, but don't let the heels come up. Keep the body straight and knees as wide apart as possible. You'll feel a firming stretch in the muscles of both inner and outer thigh. Keep this position while you count to 3.

3. Still holding the door frame, come upright, keeping pelvis forward. Let go of the door frame and stretch high. If you are tall enough, or your door frame is low enough, grip the top of the frame and pull yourself upwards so that you get a really good stretch. That's enough for the first day, but gradually build up to doing the exercise 8 times a day.

1

2

3

Exercise

Exercise

Lunchtime Thigh-Trimmer

Before you sit down to lunch, hold on to the dining chair and do this thigh toner. It helps to loosen hip joints, too.

1. Stand up straight and hold on to a chair with your right hand. Keeping your right leg straight and your foot flat on the floor, swing your left leg forwards.

2. Then swing it back. Repeat 10 times. Keep standing upright and do not bend forwards as you swing.

3. Turn around and hold the chair with your left hand and swing your right leg forwards and back 10 times.

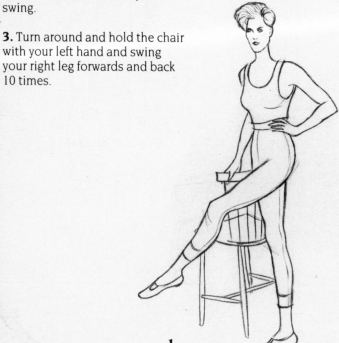

1

3

2

Exercise

Exercise

Lunchtime Waist-Whittler

1. Sit down on a chair, making sure that your bottom is well back and you are sitting straight with shoulders down. Your feet should be flat on the floor. Place your hands on your shoulders, and raise your elbows up to shoulder height. Stay relaxed, and check that your shoulders are still down.

2. Keeping your back straight and eyes forward, swing your body rhythmically from right to left, then left to right: back and forth to a count of 8. Pause to rest, then repeat the exercise. Start gently and gradually build up the number of times you repeat the exercise.

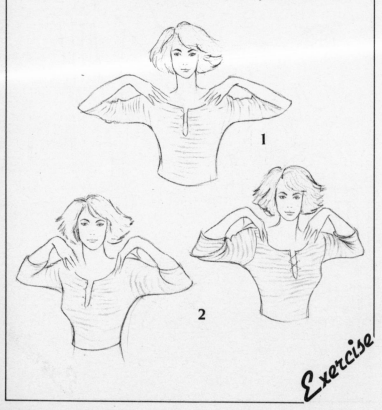

Exercise

Exercise

Limber Up

If you want to tone up your hips and bottom, try this exercise.

1. Stand straight with your feet apart, then drop your body forwards from the hips, letting the head flop down and allowing the knees to bend a little.

2. Push your arms backwards through your legs.

3. Straighten up slowly from the waist. Repeat up to 5 times.

2

Exercise

Exercise

Cupboard Tidying Arm Toner

The next time you are tidying up the airing cupboard or stacking away dishes in wall cupboards, try this exercise which is great for firming under-arm sag.

1. Stand with feet apart. Put the dish in the cupboard then stretch your arms out straight horizontally from the shoulders, palms upwards.

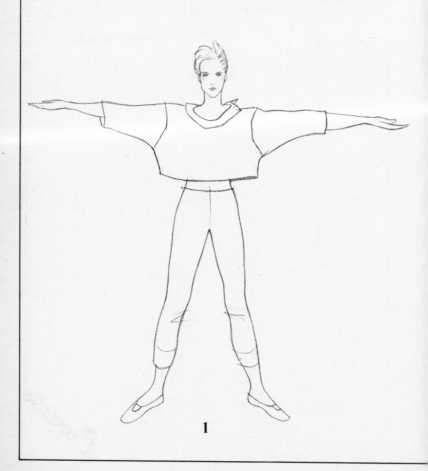

1

2. Bend your arms at the elbows and, keeping your forearm at right angles to the upper arm, move your arms up and down in this position 5 times.

3. Pick up the next item for your cupboard and repeat the arm exercise when you have deposited it.

4. Continue this exercise until you have stacked everything away or until your arms begin to tire.

2

Exercise

Exercise

Kitchen Craft

Don't just stand there in the kitchen waiting for the kettle to boil, fight bottom droop and thigh sag with this exercise.

1. Stand up straight, feet apart, tummy held in, hands on hips.

2. Keeping your body straight, bend the right knee and lurch sideways over it keeping the left leg straight. Do not let the right knee or foot roll inwards.

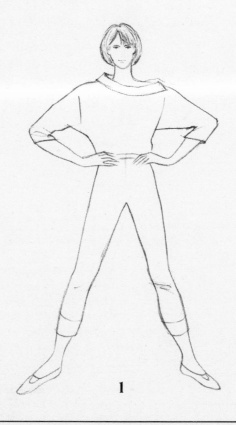

1

3. Return to starting position, then bend left knee and lean sideways over it, keeping the right leg straight. Do not let the left knee or foot roll inwards.

4. Repeat until the kettle boils.

2

Exercise

Exercise

Trim ankles and calves as you chat

Keep a large book or directory by the telephone and kick off your shoes when you get a call. Doing this exercise for just a few minutes a day will get your ankles and calves into good shape quickly.

1. Stand on the book, with your heels hanging over the edge. Steady yourself with the back of a chair if necessary.

2. With feet together, rise up on tiptoe, then lower gradually, pushing the heels down as far as possible.

1

3. Repeat the same movements standing first with toes turned out, then with toes together and heels out.

4. Repeat the whole exercise 5 times to begin with, and then see if you can gradually keep it going for the whole of your telephone conversation.

2

Exercise

Exercise

Window Cleaning Waist and Hip Toner

The neighbours may think you're mad if they catch sight of you but this simple exercise is good for toning the hips and waistline.

1. Stand up straight with legs together. Raise your arms at the side to shoulder height, keeping them straight.

2. Keeping your shoulders and arms still and your legs straight, swing your hips from side to side 10 times.

1

3. Lower your arms. Clean the windows stretching up and out as far as possible without moving your feet.

4. Raise your arms to shoulder height again and swing your hips from side to side another 10 times.

2

Exercise

Exercise

Anytime Bosom Firmer

Breasts have no muscles to be braced, but if you tone their supporting pectoral muscles you should get at least a little lift. With your elbows at waist level, clasp your hands in front and press your palms together hard to a slow count of 5. Relax for another 5; repeat as often as you can.

Exercise

Instant Midriff Minimizer

A fully-stretched spine means instantly minimized midriff.
Whenever you're able, sit or stand with a bean bag, soft plastic pack
of dry rice or something similar balanced on top of your head,
constantly aiming to make the bag hit the ceiling. After a while you
can stand and sit extra-tall by imagining the bag is there.

Spare Tyre Twister

Speed flab from the diaphragm area when you're stuck at a desk,
sink, counter, and so on, by reaching out with your right hand for
anything you need that's to your left – and vice versa – whenever
you conveniently can. By using the less-handy hand you'll work
twists into your day.

When you have a pile of washing to sort through, stand with your
feet about a foot apart, with your right foot against the pile of
clothes. Now bend your knees as you twist and pick up an item of
clothing with your left hand. Turn around and do the same with your
right hand. Repeat until you have sorted out the washing!

Tummy and Seat Trimmer

When waiting for a bus, drying up dishes or doing anything that lets
you stand up straight, pull your tummy in hard, hold for a count of
5, then let go. Repeat as often as possible, provided you are upright
so that the tummy is pulled in and up.

Tone up while watching TV, too, with your hands clasped behind
your head, the small of your back pressed into the chair and feet
resting lightly on the floor. Now tense your buttocks, gathering the
whole pelvis in an upward tilt as if you intended lifting your seat off
the chair, without taking the weight on your legs. Hold to a count of
3, then relax; repeat rhythmically 10 times, gradually building up to
as many as you can manage.

Exercise

Before Bed Buttock Firmer

It will only take a few minutes to do this exercise before you jump into bed, but if your bottom is a little flabby it will help to firm it.

1. Kneel on the carpet holding on to the edge of the bed.

2. Extend your left leg diagonally behind you, with the left knee slightly bent.

3. Lean to the left over the extended leg.

4. Now roll your left hip forwards. Raise and lower the left leg about 3-4 inches from the floor. If you are doing the exercise properly you'll only be able to raise the leg a little and you'll feel the pull on the muscles from the back of the knee to the top of the leg. Don't move your body or lean away from the extended leg as you roll the hip forwards.

5. Repeat the exercise with the other leg and gradually build up to doing the exercise 5 times with each leg.

Bathtime Shape-Ups

Bath exercises aren't a tedious, sweaty or even time-consuming affair. In fact, it takes only a few extra minutes in the bath to bring beautiful benefits to your body.

1. Before You Start

Get yourself a rubber mat for the bottom of the bath – otherwise you'll find yourself slipping around.

2. Pamper Yourself

Make yourself feel good all over. Immerse your body in masses of scented bubbles, and totally r-e-l-a-x. When you're feeling up to it, *gently* rub over your heels, soles and elbows with a pumice stone to smooth the skin.

Exercise

3. Diaphragm Twister
Throughout your bathtime, make a conscious effort to reach out with your right hand whenever you want something situated on your left, and vice versa. This will help twist away extra inches around your diaphragm.

4. Waist Away
Now the works starts. Sit up with your back straight, your legs slightly apart and your feet resting on the bottom of the bath. Now clasp your hands behind your head and twist slowly to the right – as far as you can manage. You should feel a good stretch. Keep this position for a count of 3, relax for another 3, and then twist to the left and hold for 3. Repeat this sequence as often as you can up to 10 times.

5. Tummy Trimmer

Lie back in the bath with your knees bent, and feet resting on the bottom of the bath. Relax your hands and arms at your sides. Now pull in your stomach muscles; squeeze hard as if trying to make your navel touch your spine. Stay in this position for a count of 3, and then relax. Repeat 5 times. You will find it easier if you breathe out before you pull your muscles in, and breathe in as you relax. So far so good.

6. Bathroom Shuffle (to tighten those thighs)

Still lying back, with your hands on the bottom of the bath, bring your right heel towards your bottom. Now straighten your right leg out again, while bringing your left heel towards your bottom. Repeat this shuffle sequence 10 times with each leg.

7. Buttocks Firmer

Still lying back with your knees bent, legs comfortably apart and feet resting on the bottom of the bath, relax your arms at your sides. Now tuck in your buttocks and slowly raise your pelvis towards the ceiling. Try not to arch your back. Hold this position for a count of 5, then *slowly* lower your body from upper to lower back, buttocks touching the bath last. Repeat 5 times.

8. Bust and Arm Bracer

When you have finished bathing, grab a towel and work on your arm tops and under-bust muscles. Hold your towel at the ends, and move it briskly back and forth across your back, working downwards from your neck to your knees. Be sure to stretch your elbows after each movement.

As with all exercises, begin gently, build up gradually, and **persevere**!

Beauty and the Beach

TAKE AWAY TENSION: Sitting up straight with your hands resting loosely in your lap or standing erect with arms dangling, lift your shoulders to meet your ears – as near as you can manage. Hold them hunched up for a slow count of 5, then slump them down for 5. Repeat 10 times now and whenever tension is getting a grip. Feel the tension and frown lines gradually fading.

Exercise

DO INNER THIGHS A FIRMING FAVOUR: Take a big bolster-shaped holdall. Lie flat on your back, legs at full stretch, an instep clasping either end of the bag about 5 inches up. Now squeeze your insteps together as hard as possible while counting slowly to 10. Relax and repeat. If you do not have a bolster bag, squeeze a deck chair's legs.

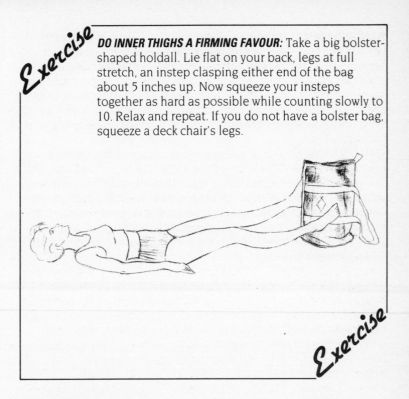

Exercise

NEW SPRING IN YOUR STEP: Scrunch up a 'footful' of sand as you stand on the shore, clenching and working your toes as if they were flexible fingers. First give one foot a minute's work-out, clenching and releasing, then the other. Stride through the surf for 20 paces on tiptoe, then take 20 steps walking on the outer edges of your feet; repeat the sequences as often as you can – your toes will soon start to feel more supple.

GIVE YOURSELF A GLOW: Run or jog or at least take very brisk beach walks. What's sheer slog when you're pounding hard city pavements feels super on sand. If plenty of beach days are possible, build up speed and distance until you can cover a lot of ground before feeling breathless. This sort of exercise is great for developing stamina and burning calories.

NEAR A SEA WALL? Try some wall press-ups which strengthen the whole upper part of your body. Stand with your feet together at arms length from the wall. Rest your palms flat on the wall at shoulder level, fingers pointing inwards. Keeping heels on the floor and spine straight, breathe in, then breathe out as you bend your arms and allow your body to move towards the wall. Straighten your arms until you are upright again. Repeat as many times as you can.

FIRM LEG MUSCLES: Stand in a swimming pool or in the sea with water at about waist height and feet placed firmly on the bottom of the pool or on the seabed. Place feet hip-width apart and turn them outwards. Stretch out your arms at shoulder level, bend your knees and sink down until the water is lapping around your neck. Tighten your buttocks and breathe in as you straighten your legs and rise high on your toes. Breathe out as you lower yourself again. Repeat up to 10 times. Treading water is also good for firming leg muscles.

STRENGTHEN YOUR BACK AND DEVELOP GOOD POSTURE: Sit on your beach towel with the soles of your feet touching. Put your hands on your ankles and pull your feet as close to your body as possible. Sit up straight and lengthen your spine. Relax your shoulders down, and keeping your hands on your ankles, breathe calmly. Gradually allow your thighs to relax down towards your towel. Hold this position for as long as you can while you soak up the sun.

STILL SITTING ON YOUR BEACH TOWEL? Try a tummy tightener. Lie down with your knees bent and feet flat on the towel about hip-width apart. Breathe in. As you breathe out pull your abdomen firmly down towards the sand. Curl up your upper body slowly, reaching forward with your hands. When you can feel your abdominal muscles working well, hold at that point for a count of 2 to 4 depending on what you can comfortably manage. Breathe in as you curl down to the sand again. Repeat 5 times if you can, but build up to this number gradually.

DO SOME ANKLE CIRCLES: To keep ankles supple, do the following exercise. With feet flat on the ground and knees bent, cross the right knee over the left. Keeping your arms by your sides and your shoulders relaxed, circle your right foot 10 times to the right, then 10 times to the left. Change legs and repeat with the other foot.

Slide your feet along the floor until your legs are flat. Let your feet and knees flop outwards. Relax!

Take Time to Relax

If you are tired, bored or anxious, your automatic reaction may be to turn to food for comfort. Learn this relaxing exercise routine and you will probably be able to avoid stress-eating. Take your time over the routine and concentrate on every movement.

1. Begin by standing up straight and tall, feet together, head high, shoulders down. Now shake your arms, then your legs. Turn your body from right to left.

2. Sit in a chair with spine straight and shoulders relaxed. Breathe in and, as you breathe out, slowly lower your chin towards your chest, or until you can feel the stretch at the back of your neck. Breathe out slowly and release your neck tension. Breathe normally as you hold this position for a while, then breathe in as you lift the head slowly upwards.

3. Sitting straight in the chair, draw in your chin. Still facing forward, tilt your head to the left. Hold this position and breathe as before, feeling the stretch up the right side of your neck. Repeat to the right.

4. Now very slowly turn your head to look over your right shoulder as far as you can go; hold, and then slowly turn to look over the left shoulder and hold. Turn your head slowly from side to side several more times.

5. Sit or stand, whichever you prefer, and try this exercise to relax shoulders. Stretch both arms high above your head, then lower them to the sides to shoulder height. Make a loose fist with both hands and pull your shoulder blades together. Now, keeping your arms straight, press both arms back with short, firm movements allowing your chest to open and go forward with the movement. (See the illustration on page 254.) Breathe freely and repeat until your arms feel well worked. If your neck begins to feel tense, allow your chin to drop slightly forward.

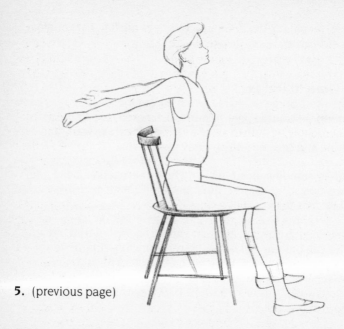

5. (previous page)

6. If you are sitting on a chair, sit forwards. Or do this exercise standing. Place your hands on your ribcage with elbows bent, shoulders relaxed down. Try to get your elbows to touch behind your back by pushing them firmly back with vigorous swinging movements. Breathe freely.

7. For this following sequence you'll need to position yourself facing a wall. Lie on your back, arms by your sides, then bend both legs and rest your feet on the wall. Straighten your legs by sliding your feet up the wall. Allow your legs to slide apart to where you feel a good stretch along the inside thigh. Close your eyes and rest for a few minutes, breathing calmly.

8. Bring both feet together to rest on the wall, then push off by straightening your legs and tilt your pelvis, tightening your buttocks, abdominal and pelvic floor muscles as you do so. Hold, then lower your pelvis, bend your legs and repeat several times. Make sure that your arms, hands and face remain completely relaxed while you are doing these exercises.

9. Roll your pelvis from side to side: lie with your legs slightly bent, feet on the wall. Push away from the wall with your left foot as you roll to the right; straighten your left leg, tighten the right buttock as you roll that way. Hold for a moment and then repeat. Reverse the movement using the right leg. Breathe freely.

10. When you have brought your legs down from the wall exercise, continue to lie on your back with your knees bent up, feet off the ground. Hold your knees with your hands, then gently circle them to the right, then to the left. This will help to release any tension in your lower back.

11. Allow your knees to fall apart, then slowly circle your feet at the ankles 6 times to the right, then 6 times to the left. Roll on your side with knees bent to sit up.

12. Massage your feet for a few minutes: sit on a chair or, if you prefer, remain sitting on the floor. If sitting on the floor, bend your left leg so your foot is flat on the floor. Rest your right ankle on your left knee. Allow your foot to hang freely. Clasp this foot with two hands and circle it slowly round several times. Using your two thumbs, massage up the sole from heel to toe and down again. Circle and stretch each toe individually. Now repeat the whole sequence with the left foot.

13. Lie flat on the floor and just relax for a few minutes, breathing evenly in and out.

CHAPTER 5

GOING STRONG

HOW DO YOU STAY SLIM?

1. What do you now weigh?..............

2. How much weight have you lost?..............

3. How often do you check your weight?..............

4. Do you know how many calories per day you need to maintain your weight? YES/NO
   If yes, write down the total here..............

5. Are you resolved never to be tempted by high-calorie foods again? YES/NO

6. Which foods are your diet enemies?..
   ....
   ....
   ....

7. Which low-calorie foods have you 'discovered' while dieting that you will continue to eat now you are slim? ....
   ....
   ....
   ....

8. List the times when you know you are most likely to overeat
   ....
   ....
   ....
   ....
   ....

9. Which foods will you save for treats and to satisfy cravings?

....

....

....

10. What interesting things do you plan to do now you are slim?

1. ....

2. ....

3. ....

4. ....

5. ....

11. List the joys of being slim and why you'll never get fat again.

....

....

....

....

....

Check your answers to questions 1, 2 and 3.

A NEW WAY OF LIFE: Just because you have now reached target weight, it doesn't mean you can slip back into old eating habits – after all they were the ones that made you fat in the first place. The happier and more confident you are, the easier you will find staying in shape. Keep working at your attitudes to food, to life, to yourself.

NO GOING BACK: You've stepped on the scales and the needle stops exactly where you want it. You are at target weight. The first staying-there fact to swallow is this: unless you had only a half stone or less to lose, you can never go back to 'eating normally'.

PERMANENT CHANGES: In a way, 'going on a diet' is an unfortunate phrase: it implies you can one day simply come off it. But your pre-diet normal was what made you overweight. Go back to it and you'll get fat again. So, for you, normal must have a new meaning: at least a few of your old eating habits must alter for ever.

Check your answer to question 4.

GO SLOWLY: To slim you probably reduced your calorie count to 1,500 or 1,000. Ms Average should maintain weight by eating around

2,000 calories a day. That's the theory, but it doesn't mean it is wise to start eating that total immediately target day dawns. You need to go slowly. Your body and you both have adjustments to make as you come to terms with a new stay-slim lifestyle.

2,150? 2,000? 1,500 OR LESS?: The Department of Health's Recommended Dietary Allowance (RDA) is 2,150 calories daily, but this is based on an average. The weight-prone woman probably needs fewer calories than the norm. Accept that you may have been a bit misled by official guidelines about what's 'average': they may have implied to you that you 'ought' to be able to eat more than you do without surplus-weight gain. In fact, women prone to gain surplus weight easily may have to settle for a maintenance allowance of around 1,400 calories daily if they lead a sedentary life. But they could afford a higher calorie intake if they significantly increased their physical activity.

KEEP MOVING: A good habit to hang on to is to keep up your daily activity level. Keeping slim is much easier if you keep moving: seek stairs to climb and ways to boost the distance you walk.

Check your answer to question 6.
AVOID 'EMPTY' EXTRAS: When you come to add calories to your diet think hard about the kind of extras you indulge in. On a strict diet, nutritionally 'empty' extras such as sweets and alcohol will necessarily have been very much limited. If you got into the habit of going without a lot of them, it is obviously a pity for your health's sake to indulge to a pre-diet extent again.

Check your answer to question 7.
THE HEALTHY WAY: Ideally, take most of your extra calories from additional fruit and vegetables and increase your intake of fibre-rich cereals, too.

FAT CONTROL: Even people without a surplus weight problem should cut their fat intake as a good health measure. Continue to use skimmed or semi-skimmed milk, for instance. Carry on using low-fat spreads instead of butter or margarine. Keep to the habits of your diet days regarding no fried food, no pats of butter as a vegetable garnish, cream kept as a rare menu item, and so on.

READ THE LABELS: You can get a good idea about the content of cans and packets if you get into the habit of reading the label. The label's compulsory list of ingredients must be stated in descending order of weight – main ingredient listed first, then the second weightiest one and so on. This can be important label language if you are watching, say, your sugar or salt intake.

Check your answer to questions 8 and 9.

SPECIAL OCCASIONS: Enjoy special celebration meals or alcoholic parties in moderation, but realize that they may show on the scales unless you watch what you eat before or after (before is better) in order to compensate. Make this saving up or paying back in a calorie sense completely automatic; it should become stay-slim second nature.

DON'T FEEL GUILTY: It's perfectly natural to succumb to temptation. It is not perfectly normal to keep to a rigid, low-calorie count through every birthday, every Christmas, every celebration that comes your way – or box of chocolates that's opened before your eyes, or cake that's handed to you on a plate. The difference between the woman who remains slim and the one who doesn't is that the successful dieter takes an occasional bad day in her stride with common sense and humour. She doesn't become guilt-stricken, and she doesn't make it an excuse to regain lost weight.

ALLOWING FOR THE INEVITABLE

When I get a really strong urge to gobble chocolate, I give into it. I've found the sooner I satisfy my craving (and count it into my daily calorie total), the sooner I can put it out of my mind, and get back on with my diet.

WATCH FOR WARNING SIGNALS: A binge does not appear out of the blue; it is always triggered off by physical, emotional or social factors and there are advance warning signals which you must learn to recognize. You may find that overeating is triggered off by acute boredom, a dull and rainy day, a quarrel or pre-menstrual tension, to name but a few common examples. Anticipating trouble means that you can side-step any hazardous situations instead of walking straight into them.

GET AWAY FROM TEMPTATION: Deciding whether or not to go on a binge when you are standing beside a pantry full of food is clearly not weighting the scales in your favour. Getting away from the source of temptation reduces the chances of a binge occurring.

WAIT BEFORE INDULGING: Remember that the feelings and situations that signal a likely binge are not permanent. Like lethargy or anger, these sensations wax and wane. Just waiting for a binge urge to pass may be among your best counter-measures.

IF I EAT A LITTLE, I'LL EAT A LOT: This usually turns out to be what psychologists call a self-fulfilling prophecy. This means that if you strongly believe that you will lose all control once you start eating a favourite food, then it's very likely that you will. For this reason it is much better to decide to avoid your favourite high-calorie foods as much as possible, rather than make the somewhat unrealistic resolve: 'I will never eat this again.'

LABEL SHOCKER

I label biscuit tins right across the top, 'Eat me and you'll be sorry' or 'Do you want to be fat and ugly all your life?'

MONTHLY CRAVINGS: One out of three women experiences a strong craving for foods just before menstruation. No one understands what triggers these biological and psychological urges, and there's no medical cure. Arm yourself against this difficult time of the month by recognizing the problem and being prepared. Keep a note of your period dates and of the days when you may experience some strong pre-menstrual eating urges. The following tips may help you cope:

BISCUIT BARGAINING: If your eating urges lead you to crunching biscuits, the solution may be to substitute them instead of one of your meals. If you eat a packet of biscuits instead of lunch it will cost you fewer calories than lunch *and* biscuits. There's no harm in eating biscuits or chocolate instead of nutritious meals for just three or four days a month.

IN CREDIT: Try banking some extra calories for this difficult time of the month. On days when it is easy for you to keep to a strict calorie intake, do so, and you will have calories to spend on indulgences on difficult days.

THINK BACK: Sometimes just the thought of what you were like when you were fat is good enough to stop you giving in. Sometimes it isn't. Great standbys are cups of coffee or a glass of a fizzy, low-calorie mixer drink whose bubbles help make you feel full!

SATISFY YOUR CRAVING: When it's a really 'uncontrollable' craving, give in and satisfy it – but cleverly. Buy and eat the tiniest possible amount – a mini-bar of chocolate, a small cake, the smallest packet of crisps.

FEELING LOW: There are bound to be times when you feel mentally low, and often for obvious reason. Whatever the problem, it needs attention.

MAKE LIFE MORE INTERESTING: If your life lacks sufficient interests, hobbies and satisfaction, it is easy to magnify any small setback into a major disaster.

CULTIVATE A BALANCED OUTLOOK: A sense of priority and a proper self-regard can help to prevent blue moods and periods of depression leading to comfort eating.

KEEP BUSY: The habit of eating in response to a bad mood is difficult to break. You will certainly not beat it if your only plan is to sit down and tell yourself over and over again that you are not going to eat, while watching the clock tick. Action is your best line of defence, so keep busy.

A MINOR PROBLEM: A binge is a momentary lapse and no more. Obviously, food eaten during a binge is not going to help you stay in shape, but the actual weight gain resulting from this kind of occasional indulgence will be very small.

TAKE THEM IN OR THROW THEM OUT: When your weight loss plans start to work, don't hang on to those old, baggy clothes 'just in case'. It's a sneaky way of saying to yourself: 'One day I could be fat again and might need them.' If you stick to your dieting resolutions, you won't need them. So either take them in or throw them out.

NEVER SELL YOURSELF SHORT: Many women short-circuit enriching opportunities all their lives by saying 'Oh no, I'm the wrong age/sex/ shape/weight/height/type.' Or: 'It's too late for me to do that now.' In the main these are barriers that they have erected for themselves; no one else is stopping them from having a go. Always hold on to a dream and never stop trying to make it come true.

SAD TRIGGER

A disappointment in my life really triggered off my final success. It made me realize that I should start doing more for myself, rather than only concentrating my efforts on doing things for other people. I became more aware of myself as a person, and started to want to slim very much indeed.

STRENGTHEN YOUR RESOLVE: Check your answers to questions 10 and 11 on the questionnaire whenever you feel your will weakening!

TEN DIETING ENEMIES

For every one person in your life who supports your diet efforts or simply leaves you to get on with them, there are at least TEN trying, deliberately or unwittingly, to ruin your slimming plans! To forearm the unsuspecting, these enemies must be studied in all their guises.

But just be aware that many of your foes may be ones you almost invite to attack; they often spring from situations you can avoid. Remember, too, that it's a common human trait to feel inadequate in the face of someone else's determined plan for self-improvement: it can uncomfortably emphasise one's own inertia. So expect to find 'enemies' when you start to slim, and be prepared.

ENEMY NUMBER ONE in this league is the husband or partner who heartlessly eats everything (particularly chocolate, chips and anything guaranteed to ruin your diet!) in front of you, asks you to cook demon dishes – and then wonders why, after salivating enviously for half an hour, you either give up your diet or become extremely edgy.

TELL YOURSELF: 'Losing surplus weight is so sensible that I'm entitled to my partner's help – or, at least, no hindrance. I think (I hope) he's simply unaware rather than meaning to be obstructive, so I'll try to communicate my needs a bit better. But I am in charge of myself. I decide what I eat. And I'm sticking to my diet.'

TELL HIM: 'It's very important to me to get slim you know, so please help. Your support means such a lot to me . . . I've bought some frozen chips that you just pop into the oven yourself whenever you fancy them.'

ENEMY NUMBER TWO is the doting granny, mother or auntie who still has it in her head that you love jam roly poly and cream (because you once cleared two platefuls at the age of four) and insists on making it for you every time you stay with her. She butters stacks of crumpets with a generous hand, bakes cakes especially for you and you would rather gain a stone in weight than hurt her feelings! She thinks calories are some sort of modern additive and kindly assures you that there are none in her cooking. As for dieting, she cannot see the point of it, even if she is a little on the plump side herself . . .

TELL YOURSELF: 'I love her very much and would hate to hurt her. But it's crazy to stay fat out of kindness – and she wouldn't want something that distresses me to continue. I can find other ways for her to express her affection for me.'

TELL HER: 'I do appreciate all you do for me, but this will have to be the last time I drool over your jam roly poly; the doctor wants me to be strict over what I eat for a while, and I know you'll help me. What I'm very much hoping is that you'll help me knit this sweater – and isn't it lovely that I'll soon be able to wear a smaller size!'

ENEMY NUMBER THREE is the one who says, in utter astonishment: 'Dieting? But you aren't fat!' She doesn't seem to realize that if you are slightly plump, there is really as much reason for you to go on a diet as there is for someone who is grossly overweight. You have to watch this particular enemy, especially when you have achieved your loss. Seeing you beautifully slender, she can't believe you have a weight problem at all. It never occurs to her that you need to keep an eye on your food intake all the time to prevent surplus pounds reappearing.

TELL YOURSELF: 'What a compliment – she thinks my shape 'just happens'. It's proof of my diet's success. And it makes me all the more set on staying in good shape.'

TELL HER: 'Thank you! You are right: I don't need drastic diets. But that's because I keep an eye on what I eat. If I didn't do this, I would need to diet.'

SELF-REGARD

❝ *When faced with food temptation, I say strongly, loudly and clearly: 'I like my new slimmer self too much to eat this.'* ❞

ENEMY NUMBER FOUR: the partner who keeps telling you he likes you as you are. It may be that he does – or is it just that he can't bear the sight of you weighing little bits of cheese, or the sound of your tummy rumbling in bed? This enemy is especially hard to resist, particularly when he's the kind of man who shows his love for you by buying you boxes of chocolates rather than flowers.

TELL YOURSELF: 'He may like me as I am, but I don't. And I feel it's of more importance that I'm happy with myself. If I remain dissatisfied with my weight, both of us will be affected.'

TELL HIM: 'It gives me a glow to hear you say you like me the way I am – thanks! But I can promise that you're going to like me even more when I'm slimmer'.

ENEMY NUMBER FIVE is the one who kills your efforts with her misplaced sympathy. She is usually a friend or colleague who holds out her toffees or crisps at least ten times a day, only to retract them swiftly with sighs of: 'Oh, I'm sorry – I keep forgetting that you can't have these.'

TELL YOURSELF: 'It's mildly annoying to be offered this constant stream of sweets. I'll count the odd toffee into my calorie allowance just to confuse her!'

TELL HER: 'It's not so much that I can't have them – most of the time, I simply don't want them.'

ENEMY NUMBER SIX is the older-generation woman who has lived through hard times and so, for children and adults alike, equates health with plumpness. She cannot bear to see a slice of bread left 'wasted' on a plate. The very idea of dieting seems completely crazy to her. 'Look at me, I don't diet,' she scoffs, as though to be dissatisfied with a less than sylph-like figure denotes some profound ingratitude for one's health and food supply. If you are half a stone overweight, she will tell you that you are over-slim already – if you are at your correct weight, she thinks that you are wasting away.

TELL YOURSELF: 'Her ideas are well-meant and I understand how she acquired them, but they are totally out-of-date or downright ignorant. I know I am much better informed.'

TELL HER: 'You're so lucky not to have to diet. But my correct weight is so-and-so and I feel much better at this weight.'

ENEMY NUMBER SEVEN, who tells you every time she sees you, not how marvellous you are looking, now that you have lost ten bulgy pounds, but how ill, pale and tired you appear. 'Don't you think you're taking this diet thing a bit too far?' she probes. By the time she has finished, you feel so haggard and sorry for yourself that you buy a bar of chocolate on the way home.

TELL YOURSELF: 'I probably look different – that's rather the idea! I know I'm fitter and feel much better at my proper weight. A lot of people get you comfortably pigeon-holed as a fatty and hate to reassess their image of you – they'll try to get you back to their idea of normal. It doesn't matter what she says, I'm pleasing myself.'

TELL HER: 'It's nice of you to be concerned about me, but I go by how I feel and I feel fine!'

ENEMY NUMBER EIGHT is the partner who makes you feel positively guilty about dieting. Calorie charts, bathroom scales and any talk of fibre and fats are dismissed as nonsense. He insists on eating his Yorkshire pudding while you eat your salad, which he disparages as fit only for rabbits and generally keeps pointing out all the negative aspects of dieting.

TELL YOURSELF: 'Understanding is the key here. For a person to work so hard at putting down what I know to be a sensible plan, he must feel secretly very frightened or threatened. Is he afraid the new me won't find him attractive enough? I'll try to make him more secure, but I won't give up dieting or feel guilty any more.'

TELL HIM: Nothing! Silence is always an option. Just smile serenely, refuse to react defensively to taunts, etc. and carry on slimming.

ENEMY NUMBER NINE is the family who insist that you do all the shopping, cooking and table-clearing. This means that you are tempted by contact with food all day – and probably feel so resentful at being the only washer-upper that you finish the pudding in a lonely rage in the kitchen to cheer yourself up. This enemy also chooses the first day of your diet to throw tantrums, break startling bits of news and generally cause the sort of emotional upheavals that can't be tackled on a lettuce leaf and two ounces of cottage cheese.

TELL YOURSELF: 'It's my fault if I've reared a family that has no concept of fair shares: and I realize that, for their sake and mine, I've got to get things on a fairer footing. Meanwhile, it's ridiculous for me to feel resentful about a situation my mishandling has set up.'

TELL THEM: 'Look, it's time for some chore-sharing. Being lumbered with the lot is making me resentful and keeping me fat. So let's draw up a rota.'

ENEMY NUMBER TEN is the family member who is responsible for more diet failures than anyone else. He is the fussy toddler who asks for something very fattening to eat, then doesn't finish it. He may even 'order' and toy with, a succession of snacks, all of which you finish for him 'to avoid waste'.

TELL YOURSELF: 'I know best, and sometimes it is right for me to say no. He won't get starved of food or affection! Besides, it's unfair to him (not to mention my figure) to let him 'order' food items to an unreasonable degree.'

TELL HIM: 'Sorry, but you can't have that again so soon because you hardly touched the last lot. We'll wait a while.'

> ### LEFTOVERS
> Do not be embarrassed to leave food on your plate. It does the plate no harm at all.

HOW TO <u>STAY</u> IN SHAPE

HOW EXACTLY DO SUCCESSFUL SLIMMERS STAY IN SHAPE?
In a revealing survey, 300 women who had slimmed successfully were asked to give precise details of how they maintained their ideal weight. The answers may surprise you.

THE SUCCESSFUL SLIMMER ISN'T A SAINT: She wasn't ever a saint. She didn't take to dieting like a duck to water. She tried and tried and tried again before a slimming programme finally clicked and she found she was able to stick it out until every surplus stone and pound was shed.

SHE DOESN'T HAVE AN IRON WILL: She isn't now, and never was, blessed with extraordinary willpower, and she's the first to admit there were dieting times when it took real determination to see it through, times when she slipped – though less and less as she experienced the marvellous confidence that came as the excess pounds rolled away. If she had failed repeatedly in her bids to slim, she invariably found the support of a slimming club made the vital difference that led to success.

SHE KEEPS A CONSTANT CHECK: She keeps a careful check on her shape and weighs herself once a week. She makes allowances for a temporary gain of a pound or two before her period and when she knows she has been rather indulgent with high-calorie foods.
The most she ever permits herself to gain is 3 lb. At this danger point, she is quick to get on to a strict diet until she is back to her ideal weight.

SHE KNOWS HOW TO DIET WHEN SHE MUST: When she sets out to lose a few extra pounds, she doesn't just 'cut down'. She knows from past dieting experience that she can't afford to be haphazard and make guesses. She doesn't bother with gimmick methods. Because she's dealing with a very few extra pounds, she goes for the tried and trusted 1,000 calories a day. Sometimes she follows a favourite diet and sometimes she uses everyday foods and counts the calories. Whichever it is she is meticulous about weighing and measuring precise calorie-counted quantities. And she sticks with the diet until her weight is normal.

SHE EATS REGULAR MEALS: Though she thinks nothing of skipping a meal when she's too busy to stop or when she's not hungry, she's essentially a three-meals-a-day person. Whether it's breakfast-lunch-dinner or lunch-dinner-and-snack, she organizes things so that she eats at about the same times every day.

SHE PLANS: She doesn't find she has run out of low-calorie mixers, for instance. She doesn't normally follow a specific diet or count every calorie. She eats much the same as everybody else, but less of the high-calorie items. She is very aware of which foods are low-calorie and which aren't.

BREAKFAST: Her favourite breakfast is a couple of pieces of toast or a bowl of cereal.

LUNCH: During the week, her lunches are light; a sandwich or something on toast with a bowl of soup and a piece of fruit is about the most she wants.

MAIN MEAL: She likes to save most of her calories for the evenings and the family meal. Even at dinner, the main meal of the day, she gives herself smaller helpings of high-calorie items like meat pie and selects more vegetables.

DESSERT: She knows that by far the most useful foods in helping her stay slim are fresh fruits and vegetables. Because of their natural sweetness, she finds fruits like apples, pears and grapes very satisfying substitutes for all the high-calorie, creamy, gooey desserts she used to love.

SHE MAKES SUNDAYS SPECIAL: On Sundays she lets herself go. She enjoys the Sunday roast with all the trimmings from Yorkshire pudding to roast potatoes and gravy, and a dessert to follow. Her other meal will be lighter – a salad with cold meat or canned fish, or sandwiches and a piece of cake.

SHE HAS SNACK SENSE: Her snack meal sandwiches have low-calorie fillings like lean meat or prawns instead of high-calorie cheese. For dessert she chooses fruit salad and ice cream or jelly. Nowadays, she very seldom touches pastry, even when she bakes pies for the family; if she does have any, it will be a very small helping with plenty of fresh fruit to fill her up.

SHE NIBBLES ... WITH A DIFFERENCE: She still indulges in, and enjoys, the odd between-meal snack. But now she's careful. 'Eating amnesia' is a thing of the past. Nowadays, she's conscious of every single mouthful.

HER TRAINING PAYS OFF: She can, and does, throw leftovers from other people's plates away without a second thought.

SHE'S CULTIVATED KEEP-SLIM HABITS: Many of the habits she developed when she was aiming to shed weight have become so automatic that she follows them without thinking. She always buys low-calorie varieties of items such as salad dressing, mayonnaise, soft drinks, unsweetened juices and canned fruits.

SHE'S DEVELOPED FOOD AWARENESS: She's very aware that fats are dieting enemy Number One and that sugars come a close second. But, of all the foods she had to cut down on, she found using less butter or margarine, and taking no sugar in drinks, to be the easiest to adapt to. She uses skimmed milk and actually prefers drinks without sugar. In fact, she now finds she can't stand the taste of sugar in tea or coffee, and tends positively to dislike whole milk's 'fatty' texture.

SHE DOESN'T BAN BREAD AND POTATOES: She's not afraid of them! She knows that bread and potatoes are a valuable and nutritious part of a healthy diet, and are not particularly high-calorie in themselves. But, again, she's careful about the quantity she eats and the toppings she uses.

SHE CAN COPE WITH CRAVINGS: She knows all about food cravings! There are times when she passionately longs for a favourite food, and the foods that set off the longing are the very same that she craved when she was fat.

SHE USES TACTICS: One tactic she uses to control cravings is to eat something which is low-calorie. If she craves chocolate, for example, she eats an apple. Her most useful tactic, she says, is keeping busy getting on with an activity that takes her mind off food. Favourite anti-craving ploys are telephoning friends, going for a walk, having a bath and knitting.

SHE'S NO KILLJOY!: If you met her at a party, you'd never guess that she works at staying slim. She's free to enjoy the food and drinks (though you won't find her taking either in excess) because she plans for special occasions.

SHE'S CANNY ABOUT CONVENIENCE FOODS: When she was trying to get her weight down, she found individual, calorie-controlled, frozen meals and boil-in-the-bag fish portions a godsend. She still falls back on them sometimes when she's eating alone, but she finds it more convenient to eat what the rest of the family is having. She makes full use of frozen vegetables when they're better value than fresh, because she knows that greens in unlimited quantity and substantial amounts of root vegetables aren't going to make her fat. On her keep-slim diet, she can afford both. Her favourite family convenience foods are baked beans and fish fingers.

SHE KNOWS HER KEEP-SLIM 'ENEMIES': She bans peanuts, cheesecake and cream completely, because she knows if she starts on them it will be difficult to stop. But she doesn't sacrifice all treats: she still loves chips, chocolate, crisps, biscuits and cake and because she finds these extremely high-calorie foods so palatable, allows herself a certain ration of them.

SHE HAS A RELAXED ATTITUDE TO EXERCISE: She has incomparably more energy and zest for life than she ever had, but she's certainly no keep fit fanatic! She is, however, physically active throughout her day; she doesn't dodge stairs or sit slumped for hours on end. She walks everywhere, often very fast, and thoroughly enjoys the exercise.

SHE'S SET ON STAYING SLIM: She's fitter, happier, healthier than ever before. Her social life, which used to be dull, is now fun. Her sex life is better, she has more confidence in herself and in her looks. She adores going into a shop and walking out with a size 12 off the rack; she loves wearing jeans and buying clothes. She's more active, has more interests, feels more popular. Who'd want to give all that up?!

KEEPING <u>SLIM</u> AIDS

Family, friends and colleagues can be splendid aids in keeping you slim. Here are some 'dos' and 'don'ts'.

DON'T ask anyone to pop upstairs or into the next room to bring you something you want, to save your getting up from your chair. The sum total of lots of little movements throughout the day makes a very big difference to your calorie output.

DON'T apply the above rule if you happen to need something from the kitchen. Here it's usually safer to send a messenger than to risk a nose-to-nose confrontation with the biscuit tin.

DO tell people that you appreciate their thoughtfulness in not flaunting their fish and chips in front of your quivering nostrils!

DON'T hesitate to warn them, however, that choruses of "We saw you eating a cream cake, ya boo", will so infuriate you that you might have three more helpings 'just to show them'.

DO announce that from now on children are expected to clear the table after every family meal and scrape unstorable little leftovers which might otherwise end up in your mouth straight into the bin.

DO get your family to help you through the major hazard of the weekend shopping by, for instance, going into the baker's for supplies, to prevent you succumbing to extra impulse buys.

DO ban biscuits from the house, if you yourself are irresistibly tempted by biscuits.

DO encourage children to leave their bedroom doors open at night. The dread of hearing that little voice trilling: "Mummy, where are you going?" is the greatest deterrent to sneaking off down to the kitchen for that extra bowl of muesli.

▼
▼

SLIMMING AIDS THAT AREN'T

YOU CAN'T PUMMEL AWAY FAT: It is a fallacy that fat can be pummelled away. Neither can it be pressed, hosed or heated away. Some slimming centres claim they can break down fatty tissues by 'improving circulation and mobilizing fatty tissue', or 'break down fatty tissue' with steam and jets of water. Save your money – it's all nonsense.

STOP TAKING THE TABLETS: Stop swallowing claims that lecithin helps to dissolve excess fat in your body. Lecithin is important to you; its chief body function is to help move fat around. For example, it carries fat from the intestine into storage cells by breaking it up into tiny droplets. What lecithin-sellers don't point out is that your body makes all the lecithin it needs. Even if you did need more lecithin in order to break up the fat into even tinier droplets, the fat would still stay inside the cells of your adipose (fatty) tissue. No convenient seepage takes place; if you were to lie down nude on a roll of kitchen paper, you wouldn't arise slimmer leaving a greasy mark behind! Incidentally, you will have some fat stores, even when you are at an ideal weight. Without such a compact energy reserve, we would have to eat all day and all night to keep alive.

BAN THE BLOCKERS: In spite of the fact that America (where it came from commercially) has banned the so-called 'starch blocker' pill from the market, it is still sold here in health food stores. Claimed to 'help you lose weight' by 'blocking' the normal body process which turns starchy foods into digestible sugars, this pill might give the impression that the slimming process will take care of itself in spite of a person's indulging in too many calories. It won't! Scientific trials set up here showed that the starch blocker pill does indeed prevent starches turning into sugars – but only in the test tube, not in the living gut. This is just as well, because a body loaded with undigested starch would produce very unpleasant side effects! Even if starch blockers did work, they wouldn't necessarily be much use to a slimmer. The highest calorie foods around are not the starchy ones, but the fatty and oily items.

IGNORE THE PINEAPPLE MYTH: Pineapple is a perfectly respectable fruit. But it does not have any special slimming power. No food does. The pineapple does contain an enzyme that breaks up the molecules of protein so that it can be absorbed through the gut wall into the bloodstream, but your gut is already well supplied with a whole range of such enzymes: they cope magnificently on your body's behalf even if you never swallow a single pineapple piece. Extra enzymes won't slim you and pineapple is not endowed with magical slimming properties.

GRAPEFRUIT AND BOILED EGGS ARE ORDINARY FOODS: Any idea that grapefruit has a special knack of breaking down fat by increasing metabolism is nonsense. The Grapefruit Diet works by cutting total calorie intake to a slimming level, not because grapefruit contains an 'anti-fat ingredient'. Yet grapefruit is still credited with some slimming magic. Another misguided idea that crops up concerns hard-boiled eggs; the theory is that these are so difficult to digest that the process uses up more calories than the eggs provide. The truth is that no food does this.

NO CREAM CAN SLENDERIZE: Some surplus fat may pucker under the skin and look like orange peel. Some people refer to this as 'cellulite' but it is really just ordinary fat and does not need any special treatment. Despite the claims of displays in some chemists' windows, slenderizing cream cannot remove body fat nor shift 'cellulite'. Such claims are not allowed in magazine and newspaper advertisements, but are not effectively 'censored' elsewhere. Every slimmer will find that fat lingers in some problem areas longer than in others, but it will certainly go if you manage to get right down to your target weight.

STAY CLEAR OF SWEATSUITS: Claims that plastic sweat-inducing garments can help you lose extra inches should be ignored. When you sweat you lose water, not fat, and you can't wear anything or take anything to reduce a specific area of the body.

SLIMMING TEA DOES NOT EXIST: What most slimmers seek is something that will make surplus fat disappear into thin air without having to restrict their intake. But a slimming tea which, it is claimed, 'acts as a fat-killer', isn't the answer to a slimmer's prayer. Any tea makes a refreshing drink that doesn't cost you any calories unless you add milk and sugar. But it can only help you to lose weight as part of a calorie-controlled diet.

CIDER VINEGAR CAN'T BURN FAT: Cider vinegar is widely claimed to have special healing values for arthritis, and to help the body 'burn up unwanted fat' instead of storing it. But let's take a close look at what cider vinegar actually is. It begins as plain apple juice, which is allowed to ferment (so that some of the sugar in it turns to alcohol) and it becomes apple cider. This is then allowed to undergo a second fermentation whereby some of the alcohol turns into acetic acid, which is exactly the same as the acid in ordinary vinegar. Meanwhile, the minerals in the original apple juice haven't changed, nor have most of the other constituents. In fact, drinking this 'unique folk medicine' is much the same as drinking ordinary apple juice or eating an ordinary apple. Acetic acid does nothing at all for health one way or the other. So if cider vinegar did have a magical effect on surplus weight, arthritic joints, and so on, it follows that you'd get the same effect from eating apples. But it doesn't and you won't!

GARLIC CAN'T MELT AWAY POUNDS: There is a scientific theory which claims that garlic can disperse fats in the blood. Blood fats have a completely different function from stored body fats so, even if the theory is correct, there is no evidence that garlic can help in a slimming campaign.

YOU DON'T NEED GLUCOSE: Glucose tablets could conceivably be useful to an athlete engaged in prolonged and really strenuous activity – a marathon runner, for example – because this exertion could allow the blood sugar level to become abnormally low. Glucose is metabolized more quickly than other sugars; but to take glucose tablets or a glucose drink 'for energy' and to diet at the same time makes no sense at all. Glucose has exactly the same calorific value as sugar, and extra calories are just what the slimmer doesn't need: the whole idea is to get calories from the body's stores of surplus fat. And, in any case, you don't 'need sugar for energy'. Everything you eat and most of what you drink gives you energy, because, in this context, energy is simply another word for calories.

LEAVE ROYAL JELLY FOR THE BEES: There's no doubt that royal jelly is good for baby bees. The question is: does it do anything for us? The truth is that no one has yet demonstrated that human beings benefit from eating royal jelly. But just suppose the special substance which turns an ordinary bee larva into a queen bee rather than a worker did have a similar booster effect on you – bracing you against stress, turning you into a power-house of energy, and so on. In order to get this special effect, it seems logical to expect that you would need to take it in proportions similar to the dose a baby bee is given. That would work out to be around 10 kg (22 lb) a day!

CAPSULES CAN'T CURE FAT: Sunflower seed oil capsules are widely claimed to break down body fat, keep down cholesterol levels and help reduce high blood pressure. But here's a perfect example of a few facts being twisted into unreliable nonsense. Let's follow the 'argument'. It begins with the fatty cholesterol-containing deposits inside the arteries that may increase and possibly cause a heart attack. Many research scientists believe that these deposits – and subsequent heart attacks – are more likely to occur if you eat lots of saturated fats (found especially in meats and butter), and less likely to occur if you eat polyunsaturated fats found especially in some vegetable oils, such as sunflower seed, maize or corn oils. Now we come to the point where the argument gets illogical. 'Taking sunflower seed oil reduces the chances that fatty deposits will form in the arteries' (which perhaps it may); 'so this means that the oil dissolves the fatty deposits' (which it doesn't). And: 'This means sunflower seed oil will disperse excessive fat anywhere in the body' (which it most certainly will not). What is more, taking a small amount of sunflower seed oil without making other changes to the diet is most unlikely to reduce cholesterol levels in blood, and certainly won't do a thing for blood pressure.

HERE'S YOUR YARDSTICK: If you are trying to assess any sort of so-called slimming aid's claims, here are some guidelines. Anything that is supposed to help you to lose surplus weight must either assist you to swallow fewer calories or help you to do an appreciable amount of exercise – or both. The basic fact is this: you can only get rid of excess fat by getting your body to burn it away. So it's no use trying to lose surplus fat by pummelling it or massaging it or warming it or cooling it. It is equally pointless to take things that are supposed to dissolve it or mobilize it. They are all a fat lot of good!

SURPRISE DETERMINATION

For the first time, I was one hundred per cent determined – perhaps because, at 23, I'd never really enjoyed life the way most young people do. I became very realistic and accepted that there was no easy route. I got myself into such a determined frame of mind that I surprised myself.

FACTS AND FALLACIES

FALLACY
As soon as you stop dieting, you regain weight.
FACT
There are hundreds of slim people around who were once
overweight to prove that this isn't true. However it must be
remembered that you gained weight in the first place because you
were eating more calories than you needed, and if you go back to
your former eating habits you will put back those lost pounds. The
answer is to acquire new eating habits during your slimming
campaign which will keep you in shape after you've reached your
target weight.

FALLACY
You do yourself harm by not including milk in your diet.
FACT
Milk is certainly a very nutritious drink and one of the easiest ways
to make sure you get enough calcium in your diet. But no one food
is essential and you can get all the vitamins and minerals contained
in milk from other foods. If you don't drink milk, make sure your diet
includes some meat, fish, eggs or cheese, plus lots of greens and
root vegetables and fruit. Skimmed milk is around half the calories
of whole milk, but still contains as much calcium.

FALLACY
Some foods actually take more calories to digest than they contain
and so are 'slimming'.
FACT
There are no 'miracle' ingredients or 'enzymes' which can remove fat
in any foods. There are no 'minus-calorie' foods, ones said to take
more calories to digest than they contain. Caffeine, found in tea and
coffee and certain cola drinks, can give a tiny boost to one's
metabolism, but the slimming effect is too small to be useful in
practical terms and, in any case, a very high caffeine intake isn't
considered nutritionally desirable.

FALLACY

On some diets you are guaranteed to lose 20lb a month.

FACT

No dieting method can guarantee that every individual will shed a set amount of weight in a given time. The more heavily overweight you are, the more quickly you will tend to shed surplus weight. An average weight loss of 2lb a week is satisfactory; those who are several stones overweight may lose weight more quickly than this, those less than a stone overweight may lose weight less quickly.

FALLACY

Laxatives can make you slimmer.

FACT

Laxatives may temporarily make you feel extra empty, but this has nothing to do with making you slimmer. By the time the laxatives have done their work, your body will have extracted all it needs from the food you have eaten. Induced diarrhoea is a health hazard.

FALLACY

When a former athlete 'runs to fat' it is because well-developed muscles turn to fat if no longer worked so hard.

FACT

Not all athletes eventually put on too much weight, but in the case of the ones who do it is not because less-used muscles turn to fat. It is true, though, that such muscles will become smaller from less frequent use, just as they became much bigger from regular use. Athletes participating in, or training for their sport will need a considerable food intake to provide the energy (calories) that they are expending. As they grow older and become less active some may not reduce their accustomed intake of food – and then the pounds will pile on.

FALLACY

Salt baths can slim you by 'drawing out' body fat.

FACT

Your body stores its fat in living tissues. Apart from surgery to cut lumps of this tissue away (and we don't recommend this) the only way to get rid of surplus fat is to make sure that the stored energy it represents is used by your body. If you soak in salty water, you won't see any fat floating to the surface!

FALLACY

You'll lose weight faster by eating 1,000 calories of foods such as lean meat and cottage cheese than if you eat 1,000 calories' worth of chocolate.

FACT

A surplus calorie supplied by lean meat is every bit as fattening as a surplus calorie supplied by chocolate. A calorie is a calorie. No diet that restricts your eating to one or two foods is to be in any way recommended.

FALLACY

Bread, potatoes and pasta are fattening.

FACT

Any food is fattening if you eat too much of it. But bread supplies around 70 calories per ounce, boiled pasta about 33 calories and boiled or baked potatoes 25 calories. Compare that to over 200 calories per ounce for the high-fat foods such as butter, margarine, lard and cooking oils.

FALLACY

You should cut down on liquids to lose weight.

FACT

Drinking excess water does not affect your weight. Unless you are ill, your body will automatically take its required amount of liquid from the amount you drink and it will expel all the surplus. Only calorie-laden liquids such as milk, alcohol and sweetened soft drinks can affect your weight.

FALLACY

Dieting is bad for you. It creates a state of fatigue, depression, even acute malnutrition.

FACT

If you are silly enough to go on a nutritionally unbalanced diet, you can indeed expect fatigue, depression and, in extreme cases, malnutrition. But if you are healthy apart from being overweight, then any of the above symptoms is a sign that your eating habits – possibly your lifestyle, too – are in need of improvement. If you improve them in a nutritionally sound and generally sensible way, there's no doubt that you will feel much healthier, brighter and better as a result.

FALLACY
If people can't exercise, they must resign themselves to staying fat.
FACT
It may be harder for less active people to lose weight, but the right diet will work. Your body burns up most of the calories you consume just by keeping everything functioning. Even if you are sitting down all day, blood is being pumped around your body, body temperature is being maintained, your heart is beating, your digestive system is coping with all the foods you are eating.

FALLACY
If you slim there is a danger that you will 'catch' anorexia nervosa.
FACT
Anorectics – usually young women, but sometimes young men – are not people who have 'just carried slimming a bit too far'. They are victims reacting to what they feel to be unbearable pressures; something has gone deeply wrong with their most intimate relationships, their perceptions of the world – and of themselves. Others may see that they are painfully thin; they can't accept this and find comfort in clinging to a distorted self-image. 'Anorexia' (literally, 'nervous loss of appetite') is itself often a misleading label: many anorectics eat heartily but then induce vomiting or diarrhoea. Recent research has suggested drugs may eventually play some part in treatment, but a long dose of psychotherapy – identifying individual pressures and helping the sufferer to cope – is the usual path to cure, plus hospital treatment if body weight has gone dangerously low. The best help comes through early diagnosis and prompt professional treatment. Family doctors are now generally far quicker to respond to this problem.

FALLACY
If you crave a certain food it is because your body is missing something the food contains.
FACT
Lots of stories are told which seem to suggest this: a baby picks plaster off the wall because, it is supposed, he is short of calcium; a pregnant woman wanting fresh peaches in January demonstrates, it is said, that she needs extra vitamin C. This doesn't explain, however, why the same baby also fancies furniture polish – and why the pregnant lady doesn't long for a much less expensive orange,

which has even more vitamin C than a peach! Craving a bar of chocolate, cake or ice cream for an energy-boost from the sugar these items contain can't be justified, either! Nutritional instinct works for animals in their native situations; no doubt, it also worked for our ancestors when they hunted and gathered their food. But it can't be relied on at all when we are surrounded by tempting manufactured foods; it certainly doesn't work in an environment of chocolate biscuits, cola drinks, toffees, and other mouthwatering commodities!

FALLACY
You should cut fats right out of your diet.
FACT
You do need to include a little fat in your diet. Fat is a carrier for the vitamins A, D and E and if our bodies didn't have any fat to work with, they could not absorb and utilize these vitamins. Also, animal and vegetable fats contain substances known as essential fatty acids which are just as important as vitamins. The body can't make these acids for itself and has to get them from the fats we eat. However, you can obtain all the fat your body needs for health if you include either lean meats, nuts, cereals, eggs or fish in your diet. Many foods contain 'invisible' fats (see the chart at the back of this book) and it would be virtually impossible to eat a completely fatless diet.

FALLACY
To be healthy you must eat a lot of high-protein foods like meat, eggs and cheese.
FACT
Classifying foods into groups such as 'proteins', 'carbohydrates', 'vitamin-rich', is very misleading. For instance, along with carbohydrates, foods such as bread, potatoes and pulses offer significant amounts of protein, vitamins and minerals. And although meat, cheese and other animal-based foods do contain proteins, minerals and vitamins, many of them also contain a great deal of fat. In fact, some could be classified as 'high-fat' rather than 'high-protein' foods. It is now believed that 40 g of protein a day is quite enough for men, women and children alike. And protein contained in vegetables, beans and pulses is just as good as the protein in meat.

FALLACY
Convenience foods aren't as good for you as real food.
FACT
Nutritionally speaking, there is nothing wrong with a food because it is convenient to prepare and cook. Many ready-made foods are very healthy indeed. Boil-in-the-bag fish, freeze-dried curries and other prepared meat, fish and vegetable dishes can provide a meal which has the same nutritional value as a home-cooked one. Indeed these ready-prepared meals might be better for you than the kind of home-cooking which over-boils vegetables and fries everything else. It doesn't make sense to despise all 'convenience' foods as junk. Simply apply the same rules to convenience foods as you do to any other form of food: avoid the ones that are high in fat and/or sugar and enjoy the others with a clear conscience.

FALLACY
If you miss breakfast your blood sugar level will drop and you'll feel tired and weak.
FACT
If you wish to skip breakfast, there is absolutely no reason why you shouldn't. Recent research has shown that going out on an empty stomach leaves no 'weakening' after-effects at all. If you don't normally eat breakfast there is no reason to start when you begin a weight-loss programme.

FALLACY
Eating at night is more fattening.
FACT
If you only eat once a day and you eat that meal in the evening, there could be a tiny grain of truth in this. Your metabolic rate goes up by 10 to 15 per cent after you've eaten; this means that if you have a basal metabolic rate of 1,500 calories which rises by 10 per cent after you've eaten, you'll be spending about 150 extra calories daily if you eat three meals. If, however, you eat only one meal, you'll probably spend about 50 extra calories. The 100 calorie difference probably doesn't make it worth while changing your eating habits if you prefer to eat just one big meal in the evening. If you don't start eating until midday and still manage to get in three meals before you go to bed, then there would be no calorie difference at all.

FALLACY
White bread is bad for you.
FACT
White bread is made from flour from which the wheatgerm and bran
have been removed, but it still contains some protein, vitamins and
minerals. Calcium and iron are added; in fact, there's more calcium
in white bread than in wholemeal. But wholemeal has more of all
the bread nutrients, and is naturally richer in fibre. It is better for
you than white, but white bread is nutritionally perfectly acceptable.
Incidentally, fibre is added to some 'high-fibre' white bread now.

FALLACY
It's wrong to eat between meals.
FACT
It's *what* you eat, not *when* you eat that counts. If you are a nibbler
who likes to eat little-and-often meals there is no harm in that. The
problem with eating snacks is that few people eat the right sort of
food between meals. If your snacks consist of chocolate, biscuits,
crisps and cakes, then they will overload your diet with fats, sugar
and calories. Choose low-calorie between-meal nibbles, such as raw
vegetables and fruit – as long as you count them into your calorie
allowance for the day, they won't slow your weight loss.

FALLACY
A proper hot meal is more nourishing than cold food.
FACT
The meat plus two vegetables followed by a pudding is a British
tradition, yet about 90 per cent of the well-fed people in the world
have probably never experienced this sort of meal. Whether you eat
your food cold or hot is a matter of personal preference. It wouldn't
make any difference to your health if you lived on cold food, as long
as you chose a nutritious selection.

FALLACY
You need sugar for energy.
FACT
Everything you eat and most of what you drink gives you energy –
because, in this context, energy is simply another word for calories.
A small slice of bread will give you as much energy as two rounded
teaspoons of sugar – and will be better for you.

FALLACY
Brown sugar is better for you than white.
FACT
If you relied on brown sugar for any vitamin or mineral, you'd have to consume such vast amounts that you'd find yourself suffering from dental decay and obesity. Brown sugars may look wholesome and 'good for you' but they only have tiny traces of a few vitamins and minerals, and, because sugar is the prime cause of tooth decay, these are far better obtained from other food sources.

FALLACY
Food is better for you raw than cooked.
FACT
You may feel virtuous when eating raw vegetables and fruit and believe that they are better for you than the cooked variety. But, nutritionally, it is very debatable if raw is better than cooked. Vegetables and fruit are very important sources of fibre, but the amount of fibre you get from the same quantity eaten raw or cooked is, for practical purposes, identical. However, 'quantity' does raise another question: would you really eat comparable amounts of raw and cooked foods? A serving of crunchy salad composed of an ounce of shredded cabbage, a large grated carrot and half a finely chopped leek goes a long way. So even if your salad holds maximum amounts of vitamins and minerals, and so on, you won't be getting much of them, and your fibre intake will be about 5 g. But take the same vegetable assortment coming to the table cooked. You may well have no trouble at all in eating 6 oz cabbage, 4 oz carrots and 4 oz leeks if they are pleasingly presented. This means you'll be getting 12 g fibre (over twice the raw mix's amount) and, unless the vegetables have been cooked and served in a way which wastes nutrients, you will also take in far more minerals and vitamins. Steam your vegetables to preserve the nutrients.

FALLACY
Men who have a 'beer belly' can get rid of it by switching to drinking shorts.
FACT
'Beer belly' doesn't imply a special condition caused exclusively by beer. If you weigh too much and have a 'tum', then you have to reduce your total calorie intake of all you eat and drink to a level

that provides all the nutrients you need but makes your body start using up its excess fat reserves. Calories in any kinds of alcohol are 'empty' ones, so it is not a good idea to include too much in your diet allowance. But whether you drink beer, wine or spirits, what counts in the end is the total calories you consume.

FALLACY
Most people will benefit by taking vitamin supplements on a regular basis.
FACT
If you eat a varied healthy diet it is not necessary to add extra vitamins or minerals in the form of pills from chemists or health stores. Taking in more vitamins than you need won't do you good, and could, in fact, do you harm. Very large doses of vitamin A, D, B_6 and C can be toxic, but your body extracts just as much as it needs from other vitamins and any excess is lost through the urine.

Stop looking for excuses

It's very easy to find an excuse to stop dieting. But before you decide to abandon yet another weight loss programme, check the following list. These are some of the excuses Slimming Magazine readers have confessed using.

IT WAS ALL HER FAULT: So you are visiting mother-in-law. Having visited her about five thousand times before, you know whether or not she is likely to offer you a huge array of home-baked pies. If she is, you could telephone and tactfully ask her not to offer you food. Or you could time your visit for after dinner or after some other meal. If she absolutely refuses to co-operate, you could even put off your visit. . . . There are a few situations when you just cannot help visiting someone who, despite all requests, will insist on flaunting food under your nose. But MOST of these situations can be avoided, and if you work at avoiding most of them you can succeed in keeping to your diet.

MINI-DRAMAS: The most common excuse for diet-breaking is the 'unexpected happening', some little drama or out of the ordinary event which knocks you out of your routine. But life is simply full of all sorts of mini-dramas, which makes this type of excuse-making far too easy. In fact, it's fairly rare for a week to go by without a little mini-drama occurring. So if mini-dramas are used as constant let-out clauses from your dieting, there are going to be very few weeks in which you will feel inclined to keep to your diet at all.

GET IN THE PARTY MOOD: If you have to attend a dinner party or some other social function where you will be tempted by food, save calories in advance. Have a very low-calorie day and then go to the party with the idea of eating in moderation rather than with the unrealistic intention of eating virtually nothing. Save willpower for saying no to second helpings, not to first ones!

I COULDN'T RESIST IT EXCUSES: If you see it, smell it, walk past it, you ARE going to be tempted to buy it and eat it. So avert your eyes, cross the road or start running.

SELF-PITYING EXCUSES: If you're on a diet and you're having a trying day (or week) it's the hardest thing in the world not to reach out and grab the nearest fattening food to cheer yourself up. But eating out of self-pity is one of the most vicious eating traps to fall into. The more you eat, the more miserable you become because you're eating. But as the negative feelings which pushed you into the breadbin or biscuit tin in the first place are still there at the end of every binge, you're not solving your problems – merely drowning them in food and setting yourself up for more self-pity in the future.

BLAMING HUSBAND EXCUSES: There are many ways in which a husband can sabotage a diet. He can do it by offering you tempting food, eating your favourite things in front of you, reassuring you that you don't need to diet, or acting as a diet watchman, infuriating you with comments such as: "Thought you weren't supposed to be eating those!" So, before you start to diet, consider what your husband is likely to do to make things difficult. If he means well, have a friendly chat and tell him what he can do to help. If he seems resistant to your dieting, remind yourself that you really want to be slim, and that he will probably lose his reservations when you have achieved your target weight.

TIME OF THE MONTH EXCUSES: Pre-menstrual tension does make dieting during these days very difficult for many women. To that extent, it is a reasonable excuse. Keep busy and stay away from food temptations as much as you can. Go to the cinema or visit a friend rather than sit at home feeling miserable. Having taken all practical steps to 'distance' yourself from food, it may help to accept that a few 'easy' days needn't ruin your diet. It's when you decide that just because you didn't diet during those tense days, there's no point in going on that it becomes a poor excuse.

THE WORLD'S WORST EXCUSE: Without any hesitation at all, we would rate eating food because you can't bring yourself to throw it away as the most pointless excuse for diet-breaking. Make sure you're never caught using it!

SPEED-UP TACTICS

If you have been dieting for a little while and suddenly find that you seem unable to lose another single pound, however hard you try, it could be time to recheck your dieting plan.

ARE YOU SETTING YOUR GOALS TOO HIGH?: Remember that 2 lb a week is a very good weight loss, and even if you only manage to lose 1 lb some weeks those pounds will soon mount up.

IT TAKES TIME: It probably took you more than a few weeks to gain your excess weight, and it will take some time for it to disappear.

DON'T GIVE UP: Every slimmer wants to lose all those extra pounds instantly, so it's not unusual to feel disheartened if things seem to be happening rather slowly, but don't give up.

THE REWARDS OF STICKING TO IT: If you are following a healthy pattern of eating you will be gradually retraining your food preferences. If you once had a very sweet tooth, you will find that very gradually you will start preferring less sweet things. And fatty foods will also lose their attraction. Many slimmers who have successfully reached their target weight are often surprised at how much their food likes and dislikes have changed during their diet.

CHECK YOUR BATHROOM SCALES: Are your scales reliable? Sometimes a balance scale needs to be 'settled' before it weighs accurately. Step on and off the scale about three times to move the balance up and down. Then step on again for your correct weigh-in. Check that your scales are standing on a firm and level surface and that you are using them correctly (see pages 24 to 25).

WEAR THE SAME CLOTHES: Are you wearing the same sort of clothing each time you weigh? And are you weighing yourself at the same time of day? Different outfits and different weighing times can mask a weight loss.

WEIGH ONCE A WEEK ONLY: Are you weighing yourself too often? Don't expect to see a lost pound every time you step on the scales if you weigh yourself every morning. For a true indication of how the pounds are disappearing, weigh once a week only.

DON'T EXPECT A CONSISTENT WEIGHT LOSS: Weekly weight loss rarely remains absolutely steady. Most slimmers will appear to lose more pounds on some weeks than others. This is a very important point to bear in mind, otherwise you might be tempted to give up after the discouragement of a disappointing weigh-in. Weight fluctuations are often caused by minor, natural variations in the body's fluid level. If consistently poor weight losses are recorded by a still-overweight person who is following a reducing diet, then the action is to reduce calorie intake towards a very strictly counted 1,000 calories per day.

DON'T TRY TO DROP YOUR CALORIE INTAKE TOO LOW: Although specialists in obesity clinics are known to put some heavily obese patients on minimal calories, this is only ever done under the strictest medical supervision. For the ordinary person leading a normal life, it can be damaging to health to attempt to diet for more than a few days on near-starvation levels like these.

A SHORT-TERM EFFORT: It is just about possible to make a 750 calorie diet based on 'normal' foods nutritionally sound, but at that low calorie level it is difficult to make sure you get adequate amounts of some nutrients. So never be tempted to follow a diet that is this low in calories for more than a few days and treat it very much as an emergency diet boost, rather than a long-term plan.

GET BACK TO BASICS: The reason why people are overweight is that at some time in their lives they have taken in more calories in solids and liquids than their bodies can use up or burn off. If you are not losing weight, then you must be taking in just the correct number of calories to maintain your weight. Try checking your diet plan more carefully. We'll show you how to check below.

HOW CLOSE ARE YOU TO YOUR TARGET WEIGHT? If you have just a few pounds to go and have stuck there, it could be that you are trying to go too low. Even if you are not in absolutely perfect shape you may well have achieved your ideal weight. The answer is to work at firming up any flabby areas with exercises, while also working out a maintenance plan that will allow you to keep in trim.

KEEP A RECORD: When your weight has stuck, it is a good idea to keep a food record again, just for a few days. This time make the record very simple, for all you are checking is the calories you are consuming. If you are not following a specific diet plan that has already counted the calories for you, check any food items against the calorie chart at the back of this book. Make sure you really do write everything down when you eat it – it is very easy to forget certain items, particularly drinks and snacks, after several hours have lapsed. This chart will help you to see if you really are keeping to the number of calories you think you are.

Daily Record of Food Intake.

	Food & Drink Items	Cals/Fat units	Food & Drink Items	Cals/Fat units	Food & Drink Items	Cals/Fat units
MON						
TUE						
WED						

Strengthen your RESOLVE

THINK POSITIVE: It is very important if you are to succeed in getting to your target weight that you start thinking positive again.

TAPE IT: Make a tape recording of all the reasons why you want to be slim (check your list on page 10). Describe how good you will feel when you get to your target; repeat that you really do want to be slim. Play that tape back at least once each day – preferably when you are sitting relaxed, feet up, eyes closed. You *can* lose weight if you really want to.

ENJOY LIFE: Give top priority to seeing what you can do to get more fun and pleasure from your daily life. Once you begin to enjoy things, you'll find your self-esteem and sense of proportion come back and slimming will be far easier.

BE REALISTIC: To say that you will instantly give up treats you have enjoyed in the past is placing tremendous and unrealistic strain on your willpower. The dieter who denies herself the luxury of any indulgence in favourite foods becomes so obsessed with the idea of them, that sooner or later there's a slip, and usually a bad one. But if your diet allows you to indulge a little in your passion for chocolate or cheesecake or chips as part of a calorie-controlled eating plan, you'll most probably find those treats don't acquire an 'evil glamour'.

ARE YOU CONTENT WITH YOUR LIFE? If, as so often happens, problems seem to loom larger than life – if people seem unfair or unreasonable, if circumstances are difficult, if you dislike your job, or your home or the way you are spending your days – these factors could be having an adverse effect on your ability to conquer your weight problem. The key question to ask is: what can I do to improve things?

Try answering these simple questions which will help clarify your thoughts.
1. What would I like to see happen in my life?
2. What can I do to make it happen?
3. What is stopping me from making it happen?
4. What is likely to happen if I don't make any change at all, but just carry on as I am?
5. Which is likely to make me happier in the long run: staying as I am without changing a thing, or taking steps to achieve some of the changes which I would really like to see?

MAKE A NEW RESOLUTION: Say to yourself: 'I will start making it easy for myself. I'll make up menus of super low-calorie meals that I'll enjoy eating; I'll enjoy getting slim. I'll discover lots of nice new dishes to work into a way of calorie-conscious eating that will help make and keep me slim.'

Take this positive approach and your dieting will be pleasant and positively rewarding.

SAVE YOUR PENNIES: It might be an idea to keep a 'penny pot' by you. An old coffee jar is ideal. Each time you're tempted to eat and resist, put a copper coin in it. It can be a nice surprise to see how quickly the pence mount up to become pounds.

ADOPT A NEW HABIT: The habit of viewing each day cheerfully and thinking about life hopefully can be made to grow just like any other good habit. So, from now on, set out to get the most out of each day as it comes. Don't let yourself complain (even to yourself!) about anything – not your weight, nor even the weather. Positive people are always more attractive to be with than negative ones; and they get things done. Why not be one of them?

RESPECT YOURSELF: Your value as a human being doesn't depend on your fatness or slimness. Your emotional well-being depends on the realization that surplus weight does not mean failure, just as being slim does not guarantee success. Think, now, of your plus points. Being a good partner, parent, colleague, neighbour, friend . . . just being somebody who is nice to have around . . . These qualities are what give you value as a person, not how much or how little you weigh. Use your imagination. List – in writing, if you like –

all the things you are good at, and the things other people might value you for. It's probably going to be a pretty impressive list! From now on, remind yourself daily that being a success or failure in life has little to do with the bathroom scales.

DON'T WAIT TO BE SLIM TO START 'LIVING': To imagine that losing weight will solve everything – mend a marriage, boost your career and so on – is unrealistic. If becoming slim works no miracles, disappointment can turn to anger and resentment, and it's easy to tell yourself: 'The weight loss just wasn't worth it. I may as well get fat again.' Work some nice small changes into your daily life alongside your slimming regime, and you will find dieting much easier to keep up – because you are getting rewards and enjoyments from so many other areas of life.

TAKE PRIDE IN YOUR APPEARANCE: Never mind what the scales say or what shape your figure is, could your clothes flatter you more, your hairstyle do more for you? How's your make-up? Look as good as you know how, not just today but every day. It's a terrific morale-booster to know that the colours you wear flatter your skin, your hair shines, your make-up is right and your hands are well-groomed. Looking as good as you can is a wonderful incentive to carry on a diet – and life – with growing confidence. (See 'Create an Illusion', pages 309 to 341.)

ENJOY AT LEAST ONE INDULGENCE A DAY: At each day's end, ask yourself: 'What have I done today that made me feel really good and gave me real pleasure?' If the answer is: 'Nothing', that's bad news! So think of some simple pleasure you enjoy: maybe it's walking in the sun . . . tackling a crossword . . . reading a book . . . listening to music you love . . . having a swim or a long scented bath. From now on, work at least one of your enjoyments into each of the days ahead. And watch for times when you think: 'I can't be bothered to make the effort.' These are exactly the times when you need the mental and physical refreshment that your pleasures can bring you.

ARE YOU BEING TOO PESSIMISTIC? This is the first week that you haven't lost weight and if you tend to be a pessimist you may say: 'I knew I'd never lose weight. That's the way I am and I can't help it.' Learn to be an optimist. Say to yourself: 'Well, I've already lost over

I stone and I'm certainly not going to let it creep back on again. It could be that the scales aren't registering my real weight loss this time; but if I stick to my diet, by the end of next week I could be in for a very nice surprise.'

SEVEN ESSENTIALS

Write out these resolve-strengthening words and pin them up wherever you will see them first thing in the morning – on your wardrobe, the fridge door, anywhere that these seven essentials meet your gaze.

1. ALL I'M TACKLING IS TODAY
I won't make any long-term vows. I'm simply dieting today. Each 'good hour' gone by is yet another tiny triumph.

2. I'M LOSING WEIGHT FOR MYSELF
What anyone else thinks about me is of secondary importance: it's my own opinion of myself that matters. And I've decided to be slim.

3. I WON'T POSTPONE PLEASURE
I'll stop putting off that fashion buy, new hairdo, outing, till I'm in better shape. I'm worth my treat today.

4. MY MOOD STAYS POSITIVE
I'll bite back every 'Oh I couldn't.' I'll think positively about everything I tackle.

5. I'M GOING TO KEEP MOVING
No more 'saving my legs', seeking short cuts. I'm grabbing every chance to climb stairs, walk further, move faster.

6. I'LL TAKE SETBACKS IN MY STRIDE
Being human, I'll slip up occasionally – even quite often. I won't feel bad about it, but just get right back on track.

7. NOTHING CAN STOP ME
I'm responsible for my life and my body, and I choose to improve both. I'll accept the truly unchangeable and make the best of it. But I'm improving everything else. Day by day. Ounce by ounce.

HOW TO AVOID COMMON CALORIE MISTAKES

ALWAYS WEIGH BREAKFAST CEREALS CAREFULLY: Don't just tip your cereal straight into your breakfast bowl. Your bowlful of light cornflakes will probably not be much more than 100 calories' worth, but a bowlful of muesli could easily be over 400 calories.

NEVER CUT A CHUNK OF CHEESE AND GUESS ITS WEIGHT: Cheese is very deceptive and 25 g (1 oz) doesn't look like much. Always weigh cheese very carefully, particularly the higher calorie hard sort.

SPREAD SPARINGLY: Refrain from automatically spreading your bread with butter or margarine when you are going to make a sandwich with a moist filling. Just a tiny scraping of butter could cost you at least 50 extra calories.

ALWAYS USE SKIMMED MILK: Don't be tempted to use a full-cream milk in drinks when you have run out of skimmed milk, thinking it won't make much difference. Full-cream whole milk is almost double the calories of skimmed.

REMEMBER TO COUNT DRINKS CALORIES: You can, of course, drink as much as you like of plain water, black tea and coffee, and low-calorie soft drinks as they contain no or very few calories. But you must make sure that any other sort of drinks are included in your daily calculations. Drinks calories are the easiest to develop a 'slimmer's amnesia' over.

BEAR IN MIND THAT ALL FOODS SUPPLY CALORIES: All foods supply energy, too – because calories are the small unit measurement of energy, 'calories' and 'energy' mean precisely the same thing in a slimming context. Food manufacturers understandably often prefer to describe products as 'high-energy' – but remember this must always also mean 'high-calorie'.

BE AWARE THAT ALL SURPLUS CALORIES ARE EQUALLY FATTENING: A surplus calorie supplied by lean meat or cottage cheese, for instance, is every bit as fattening as a surplus calorie supplied by sugar. But it is much easier to forget about that extra spoonful of sugar in your cup than it is to absent-mindedly cut yourself an extra slice of meat. Remember, also, that a level spoonful is one that is flat on top so that you could draw a knife across it. A rounded spoonful is double the amount of a level spoon and a heaped teaspoon is treble the amount and calories.

RESIST THE TEMPTATION TO NIBBLE: Are you absent-mindedly dipping into the biscuit barrel or cake tin while you are waiting for the kettle to boil? If so, make sure those tins are put in a cupboard well out of harm's way – or, better still, kept empty!

OUT OF REACH
In my house, I make sure all the fattening goodies are on the top shelf of my highest cupboard, so I can't reach them without standing on a chair. And if my husband or children catch me doing that, I don't live it down for days.

BE STRICT WITH YOURSELF: If you grate yourself a little too much cheese, do you pile it on top of your salad anyway? You probably think that little extra won't make much of a calorie difference but those little 'mistakes' add up if you make them often enough. Grated cheese freezes perfectly well, so why not keep a small box in your freezer into which you can add even the tiniest cheese leftover? When you have filled the container you will be able to weigh it and calculate how many calories you have saved.

GRILL FATTY FOODS WELL: A lightly grilled sausage or beefburger can cost a lot more calories than we allow for in our calorie chart. If you resent the way your sausage shrinks when well-grilled, look out for low-fat or lean meat sausages which will shrink less.

USE NON-STICK PANS: If you grease a pan, the food cooked in it will absorb the fat and its calories. So if you cook a pizza, for example, you must add on to its basic calories the amount of any oil you have used on the baking tray. If you use non-stick pans it is often unnecessary to grease with fat or oil.

DON'T ADD KNOBS OF BUTTER: Are you putting a knob of butter on food when your diet doesn't mention any additions? It is important not to add anything to any food unless your diet tells you to do so.

AVOID CREAMY MASH: Mashing your potatoes with extra milk and butter is another habit that's often hard to break. A little skimmed milk is all that you need – and some slimmers report that they just mash their potatoes in a little cooking water. Boiled new potatoes – cook them in their skins for extra flavour – are delicious even when they aren't smothered in a butter topping.

THROW IT AWAY: Are you still eating little extras because you can't bear to throw food away? That extra slice of toast, spoonfuls of baby dessert, someone's unwanted Yorkshire pudding, could all add up to enough calories to slow down, if not stop, your weight loss.

KEEP GRAVY FAT-FREE: Are you cooking your meat on a rack so that the fat drips into the pan below, then making gravy with the fatty juices? If so, your gravy will now contain all the fatty calories you lost from the meat.

ARE <u>YOU</u> HOLDING ON TO BAD HABITS?

DO YOU BELIEVE BREAD MUST HAVE BUTTER? If your snack or sandwich would be too dry without any spread, any of these low-calorie alternatives makes it 'moist' for a fraction of the calories: cottage cheese (27 calories an ounce), curd cheese (54 calories an ounce), ½ oz processed cheese triangle (40 calories); or, specially good for salad sandwiches, a thin layer of low-calorie mayonnaise (about 40 calories per tablespoon). Lose the butter-with-everything habit, and you could save over 300 calories a day.

ARE YOU LEAVING ALL THE FAT IN A CASSEROLE OR MINCED MEAT DISH? There's a worthwhile calorie difference between ordinary mince and ground (leanest) mince: consider paying a bit more for the average 20-calorie-per-ounce saving which ground beef gives you. But even when you've trimmed off all visible fat from stewing steak or bought the leanest mince available, a lot of hidden fat can still find its way into the cooked dish – unless you take extra care. Fat floats to the top of a casserole. You can skim off quite a bit by dabbing lightly with absorbent kitchen paper across the hot surface. Even better, let the dish go cold so that the congealed fat is easy to see and can be removed entirely before you reheat and serve.

These tactics don't work quite so well with minced meat because fat clings to the tiny surfaces and gets 'buried'. Beat the problem by gently pre-frying the mince in a non-stick pan (no extra fat needed) and draining off the liquid fat before you add any other ingredients.

ARE YOU PRESERVING THE PUDDING HABIT? You probably grew up to expect apple pie or rice pud or something similar to follow the main savoury course as surely as night follows day.

If you're trying to lose surplus pounds, the traditional sweet course can be a real calorie hazard because it tempts you to eat more just by being different. How often have you greeted the suggestion of more vegetables with a heartfelt: 'No, thanks, I couldn't'? Then along comes the pudding, and suddenly you have room for those extra calories! It isn't hunger that drives you. It's the anticipation – and temptation – offered by a different taste sensation. There's nothing wrong with wanting to end a good meal with something sweet, but it doesn't have to be a heaped helping of dessert. Break the pudding habit by serving delicious fresh fruit instead. And satisfy your sweet-tooth craving with one or two figs, dates or a few raisins.

ARE YOU HAVING CALORIE-LADEN DRINKS WHEN YOU'RE THIRSTY? When the body says it's thirsty, it is asking for water. It isn't demanding sugary tea or coffee, or coke or lemonade or gin, or any other drink. It's habit that makes us seek liquid extras to please the eye and the palate – and perhaps there's no particular snag (except expense) provided the drinks you take are low-calorie. Just the same, it's a good idea to quench your thirst with no-calorie water before you move on to any other kind of drink.

This habit of drinking water first is particularly useful at parties and in pubs. It's thirst, rather than a taste for the strong stuff, that so often leads to a higher alcohol intake than sense or slimming would sanction.

ARE YOU PUTTING TOO MUCH FOOD ON YOUR PLATE? By 'too much', we mean more than you truly want or need to eat at the time. It's so easy, isn't it, to add that extra little cheese chunk or that extra spoonful because they look so more-ish? Make a new habit of serving yourself small portions. You can always go back for more if, after eating slowly, you are still hungry. But the chances are that you won't need to, because your eye – like your stomach – will learn to be satisfied with less.

ARE YOU GOING FOOD-SHOPPING WITH NO CLEAR IDEA OF WHAT YOU WANT TO BUY? If your eye is easily tempted and you have a weight problem, letting yourself loose in the supermarket 'on spec' is a highly dangerous habit. Before you know it, you've filled the trolley with all sorts of high-calorie goodies which you, your figure and your family don't need.

ARE YOU EATING BY THE CLOCK? Time for elevenses . . . for lunch . . . for tea . . . for dinner . . . for supper . . . for a bedtime snack. Have you ever thought just how much eating is dominated by what the clock says – and not by your hunger? For the adult person in normal health, regular mealtimes are a social habit rather than a health or hunger requirement, and an awful lot of superfluous calories get eaten because the hands of the clock say it's time to drop everything and get to the table! One of the best get-slim-and-stay-slim habits you can form is to eat only when you're hungry. Don't be afraid to postpone or skip a meal you don't actually crave. And don't let the clock bully you into thinking you're hungry because the time says you 'should be'! Don't use a meal or snack as a punctuation mark during your day when a simple sit-down with just a cup of tea or coffee is sufficient to mark the end of a task or provide a break.

TRY FIVE MEALS A DAY: You could give your diet a tiny boost by switching to a five meal a day eating plan. The advantages aren't very great, though. After a meal, the body's metabolic rate speeds up and burns up calories at an appreciably faster rate. This effect lasts for an hour or two and tails off gradually over the next few hours. The larger the meal, the higher the speed-up rate, and vice versa. Research has not yet come up with cast-iron figures, but the indications are that after a really substantial meal, the metabolic rate might well speed up by as much as 20 per cent; but after a meal or snack the rate is much lower – probably only around 5 per cent. It is a case of swings and roundabouts. Eating little and often gives a longer but relatively lower metabolic speed-up rate. Eating a large meal gives a shorter but relatively higher speed-up rate. A dieter who eats little-and-often throughout the day could burn up something in the region of 100 calories a day more than someone who just eats one big meal a day. This estimated increase in calorie expenditure would take about five weeks to produce the loss of one extra pound of body fat, but is perhaps worth a try if you really are finding the going tough.

BINGE-BEATERS

When that irresistible urge to eat something that is not included in your diet plan strikes, try one of these binge-beating tactics.
Tactic 1: Run a bath, toss in lots of scented bubble bath or bath essence, jump in and relax. Lie back as far as you can, knees bent, feet flat on the bottom of the bath. Now inhale deeply, then exhale,

breathing rhythmically. Breathe in through the nose and exhale through the mouth. Close your eyes and picture yourself sitting in a sunny garden, smell the flowers and imagine the sounds of the birds and perhaps a trickling of a little waterfall. Stay relaxed in the bath until that garden image starts to drifts away. Your urge to eat should have drifted away with it.

Tactic 2: It's almost impossible to eat if you have just painted your nails. So get out your favourite nail polish – you're less likely to risk spoiling that than a polish you don't really care for – and slowly and carefully paint your nails.

Tactic 3: Keep an emergency skipping rope in the kitchen and, as soon as an eating urge strikes, grab your rope and do a 10-minute strenuous skipping session. Work really hard so that sweat appears on your brow. Not only will you have beaten the binge but you will also have burned up some extra calories.

Tactic 4: Go for a walk, but make sure you don't automatically head in the direction of the shops! It could be that your eating urge happened because you were bored or tired, and a good brisk walk is a wonderful way to lift your spirits as well as a way of getting away from the kitchen.

Tactic 5: Get out your knitting or sewing, etc. and promise yourself you won't get up from your seat until you have done at least 10 minutes' work. By the end of the 10 minutes you may well find that you have become so absorbed in your task that you just carry on and forget all about your urge to eat.

Tactic 6: Sort out your drawers. You are bound to have at least one drawer that has got itself into a muddle. Tip everything out – not in the kitchen, please! – and throw away any unwanted items, tidily putting back what you need to keep. If you find tidying a bit boring, the best way to overcome this is to throw yourself into the task with enthusiasm. If you attack a tedious chore with only half your mind on it, it will seem extremely boring. If you give a routine job your full attention, it makes it much more interesting.

Tactic 7: Call at the local library and find out the names and addresses of any activity groups you have often thought of joining but never got around to doing. Have you often thought you would like to take part in amateur dramatics, learn to play bridge, join a rambling club? Now is the time to take the first step and find out who your local contacts are.

Tactic 8: When you have taken 10 minutes to try Tactic 7, you can go on to follow up your interests and write to club contacts for further details of meetings, etc. Or look in your local yellow pages to see if you can find anything of interest listed under clubs or schools. While you have got out your pen and paper, why not write to some of those friends and relations you haven't seen for a long time? Telling them all the latest news will keep your mind concentrated on something other than food.

Tactic 9: Try on new clothes that you have bought since you started to lose weight, and tell yourself that there is no way you are going to allow yourself to get fat again. If you are still at the beginning of your dieting campaign, try to dig out some clothes that are too small for you and promise that you will stick to your diet until you can easily slip into them again.

Tactic 10: Try this pick-you-up which will help release any tension as well as keep you away from the kitchen.

1. First stand up and shake the whole of your body, breathing slowly and deeply. Imagine you are a rag doll as you shake out arms, legs, head and body – make yourself aware of any tension areas as you move.

2. Sit down, preferably in a chair which supports your head as well as your back. Open your mouth wide a couple of times as if yawning.

3. Close your eyes and give yourself this short face massage. Place your finger tips on either side of your nose, just under the eyes. Now gently draw your fingers outwards, ending at the slight hollow at the temples. Press and circle fingers gently, then lift off. Repeat by beginning each stroke slightly lower down your face but always ending at the temples. Breathe calmly throughout. Now spread your fingertips and place them just above the eyebrows. Stroke your forehead up to the hairline, smoothing out any frown lines. Rest your fingers on the hairline and rock the scalp forwards and backwards several times. Repeat these strokes from the eyebrows several times.

4. Check that you are sitting up with a straight spine and relaxed shoulders. Breathe in and, as you breathe out, slowly lower your chin forwards to your chest, or until you can feel the stretch at the back of your neck. Breathe out slowly and completely, letting go of any tension you may have felt in your neck. Breathe normally as you hold this position for a while, then breathe in as you slowly lift your head up again. Feeling nicely relaxed? If not, repeat the whole sequence again.

CHAPTER 6

CREATE AN ILLUSION

HOW <u>CAN</u> YOU <u>LOOK</u> SLIMMER?

1. What are your measurements? Get out a tape measure and write them in below.
Bust: ....
Waist: ....
Hips: ....
Thighs: ....
Ankles: ....

2. How tall are you? ....

3. Tick what you consider to be your problem area(s).
Bust: ☐
Waist: ☐
Hips: ☐
Thighs: ☐
Legs: ☐
Bottom: ☐

4. Now list what you consider to be your good points.
....
....
....
....
....

5. When was the last time you checked your bra size? ....

6. Which is your favourite dress or outfit? ....

7. Which is your least favourite dress or outfit? ....

8. What is your favourite colour? ....

9. Are you using the same make-up you did over five years ago? ....

10. When was the last time you had your hair restyled? ....

PAY ATTENTION NOW: Don't wait until you are right down to target weight before you start paying attention to how you dress and look. Wearing becoming clothes and having an air of confidence go a long way towards making you feel attractive.

Check your answer to question 3.
COME TO TERMS WITH YOUR PROBLEM ZONES: Turn to the exercise section on pages 232 to 251 and concentrate on those exercises which are designed for your particular problem area. Take a few tips from the Dress Sense section (pages 314 to 319) which will give you ideas on which styles to avoid and which to adopt as the most flattering.

Check your answer to question 4.
MAKE THE MOST OF ALL YOUR GOOD POINTS: Maybe you have lovely hair, a creamy skin, or a particularly nice smile. You probably have more things going for you than you think and the good points are as much a part of you as the one imperfect feature you dwell on.

LEARN BODY LANGUAGE: If you are in some way ashamed of how you look, you could unconsciously be sending out 'keep away' signals through body language, such as hunched shoulders, hands dug deep in pockets, eyes always looking towards the floor, unrelaxed and nervous gestures, as signs that you don't want to be approached.

BE BOLDER: A woman who dresses in a colourless and nondescript way is asking not to be noticed.

▼▼ **P**ROBLEM-<u>SOLVERS</u>

HAVE YOU SOMETHING TO HIDE? You'd be a very unusual person if you felt everything about you was perfect. Even top models and glamorous film stars have hang-ups about small eyes, crooked mouth, fine hair or lots of tiny things you'd probably never notice.

MUM'S THE WORD! The first lesson in disguising a problem is not to mention it to anyone. If you go around complaining about your flabby arms or large ears you will be drawing attention to something that – probably to your great surprise – others would not have noticed.

PLAY UP YOUR ASSETS, PLAY DOWN YOUR FAULTS: If you are not entirely happy with your neck, for example, draw attention away from it by emphasizing an attractive waistline or good legs.

CLEVER CAMOUFLAGE: Camouflage small problems then forget about them. Cover up the odd spot with a medicated concealer cream. Choose a shade that matches your skin, and blend it in with your foundation.

Tiny broken veins can be hidden with an opaque tinted fluid or cream; again match your skin tone but avoid a rosy shade. Dab on the fluid with your fingertip and powder over. For a more covering effect, dab on colour, wait for a minute or two, then dab on a little more.

For dark under-eye shadows that often result from too little sleep and exercise, choose a light shade of spot concealer. Provided it is paler than your foundation, it will 'lift' out the shadows and highlight your eyes. For best effect, look straight ahead into a well-lit mirror and slowly dip your chin. You will notice those shadows get gradually deeper – and, at the can't-bear-any-more stage, use your little finger to pat and blend the concealer gently into your foundation. Finish off with a dusting of translucent powder to take away any shine.

Scars can be covered up by a concealer cream or thick stick make-up (making sure you blend in the edges).

A too-rosy skin can be cooled with a green-tinted foundation or face powder.

Freckles and moles can be toned down with foundation and powder, but why not make a feature of them instead? Turn a well-placed mole into a beauty spot by emphasizing it with a touch of eye pencil and leave your face freckles uncovered and emphasize your eyes.

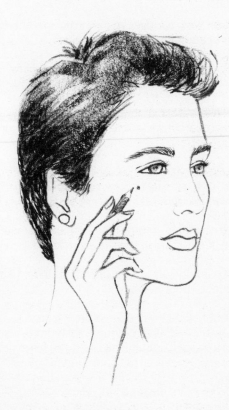

DRESS SENSE

IF YOU ARE SHORT-WAISTED: Wear dresses and non-waisted garments as often as possible. If wearing separates, choose a belt that tones with your top rather than your skirt or trousers and you will give the illusion of a lower waistline.

THE GOLDEN RULE: Wear a loose top or bottom, never both, otherwise the effect isn't beautifully casual, just baggy.

NO BREAKS: Elongate your outline by banning all hard, horizontal breaks; go for long lines everywhere.

LONG LEGS: Trousers and matching boots give a lovely long leg-line. On the other hand, trousers tucked into contrasting boots will make your legs seem shorter.

USE COLOUR CLEVERLY: Pale colours tend to enlarge, dark ones to diminish. Use this basic rule to disguise problem areas. Too large hips? Wear a dark-coloured skirt. A heavy bust and slim hips? You could wear a dark top and light trousers if you are tall. Contrasting colours shorten the body, though, and a small person is better choosing a top and bottom in the same shade.

GENTLY DOES IT: Gentle waist pleats are much kinder to a flabby tum than a plain front or front pockets.

FLATTERING COLLAR: A starkly collarless dress is hard to wear, especially if you are over 40. Much more flattering is a shirt-collar style. It acts as a frame for your head and if you leave buttons undone to cleavage level it gives a long slimming line.

KEEP IT SIMPLE: If you are buying a suit, choose a firm, light fabric (tweed can look lumpy) and a single-breasted jacket with long lapels. If you are short don't wear an overlong jacket as this will make you seem even shorter.

TAKE CARE WITH TOPS: Avoid boatnecked, batwinged tops – they are very broadening.

TOP HEAVY: High buttons make a bosom seem larger and lower and shoulders heavier. It pays in this instance to unbutton a bit. To disguise a large or low-slung bosom your best aids are a good bra and an open collar.

Check your answer to question 5.
THE RIGHT BRA: When was the last time you were fitted for a bra, or re-checked your measurements? If you have lost weight you can't just assume that you will take the same cup size in a smaller bra.

MEASURING UP: It's worth being measured up by a professional fitter if you can, but otherwise use this guide. First measure your chest below the breasts. If the number of inches you measure is even (eg, 32, 34, etc) add 4 inches to its total; if it's odd (eg, 33, 35) add 5 inches. The final number is your correct bra size. Next place the tape around the fullest part of your bust. The difference between this measurement and the first one determines what size cup you need. If the measurements are the same (eg, both 36) you take an A cup; if 1 inch more, you take a B cup; 2 inches more a C cup, 3 inches a D cup and 4 inches more means a DD cup.

UPPER ARM COVER: Very short sleeves or sleeveless dresses don't flatter the over-50s. The upper arm is often the first part of a woman's body to let her down. Unless you exercise regularly, flesh here goes either fattish or flabby.

BIG IS NOT BEST: Any big design, hard shine or glitter is enlarging. So is a soft stretch material. And wearing anything strained, tight and crumpled is always unflattering.

TAKE CARE WITH ACCESSORIES: If you have a short neck don't wear dangling earrings; wear studs instead. Only the tiniest waist can wear a wide belt. A huge shoulder bag doesn't suit a small lady, and remember that tucking an evening clutch bag under your arm will make any upper arm flab widen. A classic handbag with double handles slung over the arms is ageing; a neat shoulder bag has a much younger look.

BOOT OUT STODGY SHOES: Whatever your leg shape, plain courts are the most flattering style of all. Straps, especially at the ankles, have a foreshortening and fattening effect.

FIRM SUPPORT: Support tights can give the legs a long, firm line and youthful smoothness, especially in the calf and knee area. There isn't the slightest 'surgical' appearance about the support tights you can buy now and they are worth considering if your legs are at all flabby. Choose a darker shade to slim legs more.

Check your answer to question 6.
WEAR YOUR FAVOURITE CLOTHES: Resolve not to leave your favourite dress or outfit hanging in the wardrobe for special occasions, but wear it as much as possible. You'll always look your best if you feel good in what you are wearing.

Check your answer to question 7.
THROW AWAY YOUR SHOPPING MISTAKES: Are there any items in your wardrobe that you feel don't do you justice? Get rid of them now. Give them to a good cause if you can't bear to throw them away. There is no point in hanging on to mistakes – we all make them – they won't do your confidence any good at all.

PLAN AHEAD: Instead of buying the odd dress or skirt just because you like the look of it, try to plan in advance how it will fit into your wardrobe as a whole.

START WITH THE BASICS: You'll immediately improve your fashion image if you put your effort into planning workday outfits rather than spending weeks aiming to look wonderful at a wedding or a big event. So start planning a new basic wardrobe for when you are down to your slim target.

Check your answer to question 8.

COLOUR IS THE KEY: Colour is important; it is best to buy some basic items such as a skirt, jacket, trousers, coat in a neutral colour so that you can team different coloured blouses, jumpers and skirts with them. Choose grey, navy, black, white and beige which will tone with lots of other colours. If your favourite colour is a primary colour such as red or yellow, select a sweater, blouse or scarf in this colour to wear with a suit or choose a dress in this colour if your shape will take it. Keep shoes in neutral colours, too. Grey shoes, with grey tights and a grey skirt give a long waist-to-toe line.

SMILE! A youthful look is light, uncluttered and apparently casual. Your best aid to looking good at any age is an air of confidence and a happy smile.

FACE FACTS

Check your answer to question 9.

THINK THIN ABOUT MAKE-UP: Thick make-up lodges in any lines and wrinkles and emphasizes them. Use the thinnest possible layer of moisturizer, foundation and powder. Aim at a natural-looking, healthy glow.

SWITCH TO A BEAUTY SPONGE: Fingers don't make the best applicators for face foundation; their tips simply haven't a broad enough spread to apply a really fine covering layer with minimum pressure. You should apply foundation with a slightly dampened sponge (soaked in water first, then wrung nearly dry). Using this method, it's much easier to achieve a very light, yet even, film of foundation all over your face and fade it away at the edges. The result is a much more natural look.

TEST BEFORE CHOOSING: Names and shade cards are useful but always test a foundation before selecting a shade. Colours may look quite different on your skin from when they're in the bottle. Match your skin tone, or, if in doubt, choose a beige. Foundation 'warms' on some skins and any extra colour you need can be added by using blusher. Make-up will last much longer if you apply powder on top of your foundation. Use translucent, untinted powder which won't add colour.

SHAPE WITH BLUSHER: Blusher can be used to shape as well as to add colour. A dark colour will thin an area, while a light colour will emphasize it. Tone blusher with your lipstick.

GIVE YOUR FACE A GLOW: Glamour Queen Marlene Dietrich used to shed decades at a stroke by lightly brushing blusher all around her hairline down to the jawline either side to give her face a youthful glow. Done subtly, this trick instantly uplifts the whole face and helps take away a pale, tired look. Use a natural, not a vibrant, shade of blusher, and apply very lightly with a big, soft brush.

USE EYELINER SPARINGLY: A heavy line around eyes makes them appear smaller and can be hard and ageing.

AVOID 'DOWN' LINES: As you get older you can't afford a build-up of liner and shadow, and so on, to get caught in a downward crease at the eye's outer corner. Down lines are always ageing. Stroke a cotton bud upwards at the eye corner to take surplus colour away and so let liner and shadow end with a lift.

GET THOSE LIGHTS RIGHT: You may achieve a beautiful after-dark make-up when studied under your own lights, but if you've worked with illumination from an overhead lamp, colours and shadows won't stand later scrutiny. Apply make-up in the light of lamps, preferably unshaded, sited either side of your dressing table, so that your face is evenly and brightly lit. Bright dressing-table lights with easily removable shades are best. The less kind your lighting now, the better you'll look later. You can set forth absolutely confident that your face has already faced the worst.

CHEAT AWAY THAT CHIN! Posture can make all the difference: a head held high instantly diminishes a heavy chin. Shading tricks rarely work in daylight, and a camouflaged area can attract attention because of its apparent grubbiness. But in artificial light, lose years by being bolder; a brown blusher or shader gently stroked on a double chin can play it down effectively.

EYES

WHITE MAGIC FOR BIGGER EYES: For a wonderfully wide-eyed look, draw white kohl pencil gently along each eye's inner rim, just above the bottom lashes. This simple trick has the effect of 'extending' eye-whites, making your eyes look larger and suggesting an added sparkle. When making up the delicate eye area, go carefully: make sure the pencil is soft and don't apply pressure. Kohl pencils are available in most beauty ranges.

PUT UP A SMOKESCREEN: If you have deepset, small or older eyes, push aside those turquoise, blue and other colourful eye shadows. Investigate instead the way in which gentle greys – soft bronzes and browns, too – can put up a smokescreen to disguise faults. If your eyes are set in smudgy brown pools, they gain extra sparkle by contrast: the whole effect of using gentle colours is enlarging, glamorous, soft.

DROP IN EXTRA SPARKLE: Eye drops can help take away a tired, sore look. Apply as directed – but not for a special occasion without practice. You need to learn the knack of using the drops without messing up your make-up.

RESHAPING EYES

SMALL EYES: Shade along the socket line, beginning a little way in from the inner eye. Brush colour upwards and outwards. Stroke a very pale colour along the upper lids and blend into the socket shading. Shade finely under the outer bottom lid. Highlight the centre of the upper lid with a pale or pearly colour.

DEEP-SET EYES: Highlight the upper lid generously. Blend a deeper but neutral sludgy shade from the socket line upwards to fade near the brow.

CLOSE-SET EYES: Widen them with eyeliner at the outer corners and shading drawn outwards.

ROUND EYES: Shade strongly at the outer corners, blending up and outwards.

NOT-SO-YOUNG EYES, DROOPY LIDS: Shade upwards at the outer corners. Highlight softly at the centre of the lids.

SHAPELY EYEBROWS: Well-shaped eyebrows give your face an instant lift. The most flattering brow extends from just above the eye's inner corner to a point found by extending a pencil from your nostril past your eye's outer corner. Pluck out any hairs growing beyond these points. Don't alter brow shape dramatically: this very rarely works well. Aim to define the natural curve by tidily tweezing out any stray hairs from underneath the natural arch. A face can lose years in a twinkling if any hairs that give a downward droop at the brows' outer edge are tweezed out.

To thicken skimpy brows, sketch in individual hairs with brown and grey pencil strokes (use black only if brows are naturally very dark). This is far more effective than drawing one hard line.

AWARD YOURSELF THICKER LASHES: In the days of cake-and-spittle mascara, make-up artists used to thicken stars' eyelashes with face powder. It's an instant trick still worth trying if lashes aren't as lushly clustered as you'd like – and it's cheaper than lashbuilding mascaras. Apply a first coat of ordinary mascara, allow to dry, then use a cotton bud covered in translucent powder to give lashes a dusting. Now apply a second coat of mascara.

MOUTH

GIVE YOUR MOUTH A LIFT: Using a lip brush or pencil, neatly extend the line of your top lip just a tiny way upwards at each corner. It gives a hint of a smile, a lovely lift. Put lip and eye pencils in the freezer for 15 minutes: they can then be sharpened more easily.

PRETTY LIPS: Shape the upper lip by outlining from the centre to the outer corners. Outline the lower lip from corner to corner. Fill in the outline with lip colour, using your lipstick or painting with a lip brush. The experts use a lip brush to achieve a precise outline, but you may find it easier to do this with a lip pencil. These are available in several colours; your outline should be a slightly darker shade than the inside colour. For correcting lip shape, use a beige brown for the outline.

LIPS TOO THIN? You can make lips appear plumper by using stronger colour. Outline fractionally outside the natural lip line. Colour in with toning lipstick. For a more subtle effect, blot after colouring by placing a tissue between your lips and pressing the lips together. Paint on a softer colour up to the lip line.

LIPS TOO THICK? Outline with brownish pencil just inside the natural lip shape. Colour in with lipstick.

DROOPING MOUTH? Make your lower lip fuller by lining with brownish pencil outside its natural contour. Lift the colour slightly at the upper lip corners. Colour in with lipstick.

WRINKLED LIPS? Stretch lips with finger and thumb, then outline with a skin-toned pencil to help prevent lip colour smudging into lines outside the mouth. Release lips and colour in with lipstick. Or try using a lip fix cream to prevent colour smudging.

HAIR

Check your answer to question 10.
HAIR TONIC: Now and then every woman knows she needs a change of hair shape and style, a tonic to give self-confidence and extra sparkle.

PEAK CONDITION: Whatever style you choose, make sure your hair is in good condition or it won't look its best. Oily hair may need frequent washing, but make sure you use a mild shampoo. Do not use very hot water because this can stimulate the oil glands and make your problem worse. If you have dry hair make sure you always condition it well.

DANDRUFF TREATMENT: Frequent shampooing may help to alleviate very mild dandruff, but it usually pays to switch to anti-dandruff products. A dry scalp may be mistaken for dandruff; this can be dealt with by massaging in warm oil before shampooing.

GIVE HAIR A NEW GLOSS: If hair feels dry, frizzy or generally out-of-condition, simply massage oil well into your hair and your scalp, combing through to ensure all the hair is covered. (You can use olive oil if you wish, but sunflower, corn or any other cooking oil will do just as well.) Then wrap your head in steaming hot towels (this helps hair absorb the oil and discourages oily drips). Let the oil do its work for as long as possible – at least twenty to thirty minutes, then wash the oil off thoroughly. You will only need to give your hair this sort of oil bath once every few weeks.

TRANSFORM YOUR HAIR SHADE: Unless you're very sure, don't attempt a total colour transformation, but going lighter or richer can do a lot for a mouse. (Going darker is for under-45s only as the contrast is too harsh for a less vivid older skin.) Do-it-yourself colours can work very well. Provided you don't have bleached or heavily grey hair, a semi-permanent, shampoo-in colourant provides a pleasant colour change which fades away in about four to six weeks. For a longer-lasting effect, use a permanent colourant or lightener. You can preview its effect by trying on a wig in a big store. Home treatments are twice as easy if you tackle them with a deft friend.

A LIGHTER LOOK: If you have fairish hair a gentle lightener can turn it into something new and exciting. You can have your hair lightened professionally by a hairdresser or use a do-it-yourself kit.

TEST FOR ALLERGIES: It is important to read the instructions about doing a skin test to make sure you aren't allergic to the product you intend to use. (This is a rare possibility, affecting only about one person in a million.) If your hair has already been coloured or permed, make sure it is safe to treat your hair.

TRY A NEW HAIRSTYLE: A new hairstyle can make a great deal of difference to how you look. If you don't regularly go to a hair stylist, ask a friend whose hair you admire for her stylist's name or arrange a consultation at a salon of your choice before you decide how you want your hair restyled. There is no point in wearing the latest fashion if it does nothing for your looks and the style you choose must also suit your hair texture. If your hair is fine and straight it won't take a curly style unless you have it permed. Thick, curly hair needs very careful cutting and wouldn't stay in a sleek bob.

CHOOSE WITH CARE: The hairstyle you choose can add width, height and soften features. Here are four basic face shapes and the styles that suit each.

FOR A LONG FACE: A soft, full style to add width.

FOR A ROUND FACE: Height is needed to slim the face. Hair can be kept longer at the back.

FOR A SQUARE FACE: Gentle movement and height.

FOR STRONG FEATURES OR A NOT-SO-YOUNG FACE: Soften with curved sweeps and tendrils.

NAILS

NEGLECTED NAILS: If you have decided that your nails are a disgrace, what do you do? First, decide if you can afford to treat yourself to a professional manicure. Look up the telephone number of any beauty clinic in your area and ring to ask how much they charge. If there are no beauty clinics listed you may find that some hairdressers also do a manicure service. If you get your nails done professionally you will pick up some tips for doing your own manicures at home.

SELF-HELP: Also consider how you could care for your nails yourself. Do you wash up wearing protective gloves? If not, detergent and hot water could be making your hands rough, your nails split and broken. In future plan to wear gloves for any wet work and massage your hands with a moisturizing cream afterwards.

DIY Manicure

1. If you are already wearing polish, use cotton wool to rub nail polish remover on all nails. Remove the polish, one nail at a time, working in a circular direction. Take care to remove polish from around cuticles.

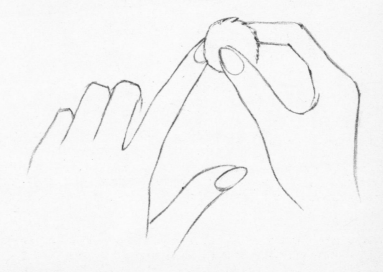

2. File nails one way only, as see-saw movements encourage splitting. File from the sides to the centre, rounding off the nail tip. Avoid filing nails low down at the sides or they will split. Use the darker side of the emery file to start with, then finish using the finer, lighter side.

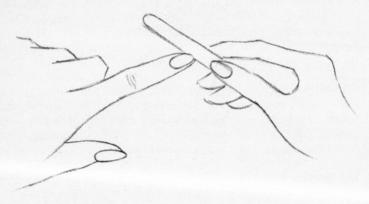

3. Massage cuticle cream into the cuticles.

4. Soak nails for 5 minutes in warm, soapy water or water with 2 teaspoons of oil added (helps flaky nails).Dry nails or wipe away traces of oil.

5. Wrap a wisp of cotton wool around the end of a manicure stick and very gently scrape around the cuticles to remove any flakes of skin or other débris. Carefully trim off loose skin or hangnails. Draw the manicure stick behind nail tips without applying pressure.

6. Dip fingers in water; flutter them dry. Check that all loosened skin has disappeared from around cuticles.

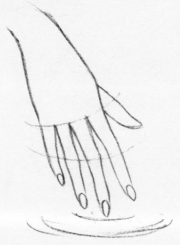

7. Massage in hand cream.

FIRST BASE: Apply a base coat before using coloured polish. It makes top polish more durable and provides a smooth surface by glossing over dents and ridges.

TAKE YOUR TIME: A professional polish takes time. It is a mistake to apply nail polish too thickly because it then takes a long time to dry. Watch a well-trained manicurist. She uses the minimum of polish, applying it in thin coats, allowing each to dry thoroughly before the next is applied.

CHOOSE COLOURS CAREFULLY: Pale nail polish shades do more than dark, moody tones to make hands and nails appear longer and slimmer. Colours which reflect skin tone look more elegant than those that clash with it. Chooose pink polish or rosy red if skin has a natural pink tinge, chestnut or coral if it is sallow or tanned.

CHILL POLISH: Keep polish in the refrigerator. It's easier to apply and dries more quickly when chilled.

EASY OPENING: Keep the bottle-top free of polish so that you won't have to wrench the cap to remove it next time. Loosen hardened polish with cotton wool dabbed with remover, but take care it doesn't remove the polish from your nails while you're doing it.

How to apply nail polish
1. Stroke the brush on the inside of the bottle to remove surplus polish. You should be able to hold up the brush without it dripping.

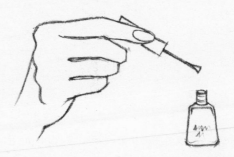

2. Paint a stripe in the centre of the nail, from cuticle to tip.

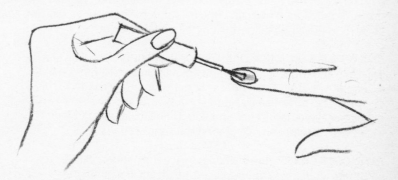

3. Paint either side of this stripe, flexing the brush lightly to spread the colour to the outer corners of the nail.

4. Allow nails to dry for about 10 minutes before applying a second coat of polish.

MAKE YOUR NAILS LOOK LONGER: Give your nails a flatteringly longer look by playing this colour trick with two shades of polish. Apply your favourite colour in the usual way, taking it down to the nail bed but not taking it right out to the sides. Then, when this is dry, paint a brush-width of a paler, toning shade down the centre of each nail. Instant extension! If you can't find a complementary toner, use any colourless pearl polish for the lengthening line.

STRENGTHEN WEAK NAILS: Only very strong nails are proof against breakage and the strength or frailty of nails is something you tend to inherit. Weak nails can be strengthened but they need continuous care. Polish by rubbing backwards and forwards across the palm of your hand whenever you use hand cream, and manicure to improve the appearance of even the shortest nails.

FOR GLEAMING NAILS: Run a white pencil gently under nail tips to give them an instant super-spruced-up gleam. If nail pencils specially made for this beauty trick aren't easy to find, pencils from children's colouring sets will work just as well, provided the white tip is not too hard.

SOFT SOAP: Remember to protect your nails' pale-tipped prettiness by digging them into a soft bar of soap before you do any grubby job. Afterwards, the soap washes instantly away, and your nails stay super-clean.

FEET

DON'T NEGLECT YOUR FEET: Any pain in your feet shows instantly in your face and will spoil any efforts to look good. Throw out any badly fitting shoes now as they can build up calluses and corns. Take any foot troubles to a chiropodist immediately. Give yourself a regular pedicure.

DIY Pedicure
1. Soak feet in soapy water for 10 minutes. Rub away hard skin with a pumice stone or waterproof emery paper.

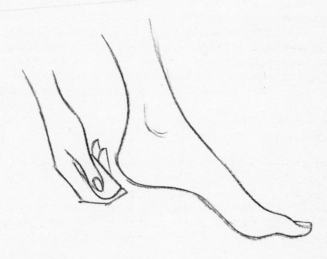

2. Dry feet and cut nails straight across with clippers or small scissors. Round off sharp corners slightly, but do not cut your nails too short as this can encourage an ingrowing toe nail.

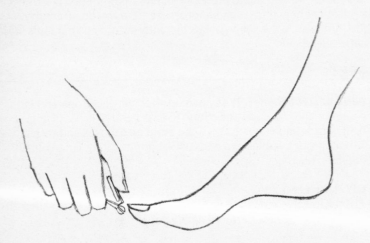

3. Massage in cuticle cream and gently ease round the cuticle with a manicure stick wrapped in cotton wool. Ease the stick around the sides of large toe nails to free any build-up of skin. Scrape lightly behind the tops of nails.

4. Sponge feet to remove any débris and dry thoroughly.

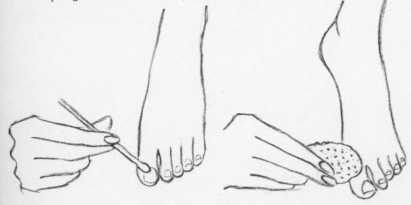

5. Apply polish as for fingernails or buff nails to make them shine. Rubbing in almond oil or a paste polish will give them a rosy hue.

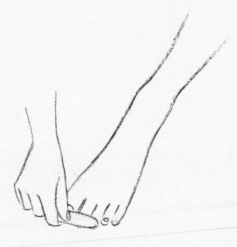

6. Massage feet with hand lotion to leave them soft and silky. Stroke from toes to ankle on top of foot. Place fingers under feet, thumbs above, and pull along foot and up over heel.

CHART OF BASIC FOODS

Many of these figures are based on original research by *Slimming Magazine* and *cannot* be reproduced without permission.

Below you will find the calories, fibre and fat units in most basic foods. Where no figure is given, this means information on this food is presently unavailable. Some sweet foods and drinks do not contain fat but are still high in calories and could severely hamper your weight loss if you consume too much. We have, therefore, accorded them an equivalent fat unit count.

Abbreviations: C=calories; GF=grams fibre; FU=fat units; n/a=not available

A

	C	GF	FU
ALMONDS			
Shelled, per 28 g/1 oz	160	4.1	5.5
Ground, per 15 ml/1 level tablespoon	30	0.8	1
Per almond, whole	10	0.2	0.5
Per sugared almond	15	0.2	0.5
ANCHOVIES			
Per 28 g/1 oz	40	0	
Per anchovy fillet	5	0	
ANCHOVY ESSENCE			
Per 5 ml/1 level teaspoon	5	0	0

	C	GF	FU
AUBERGINES			
Raw, per 28 g/1 oz	4	0.7	0
Sliced, fried, 28 g/1 oz raw weight	60	0.7	2
Whole aubergine, 198 g/7 oz	28	5.0	0
Whole aubergine, sliced, fried, 198 g/7 oz raw weight	405	5.0	14
AVOCADO			
Flesh only, per 28 g/1 oz	63	0.6	2.5
Per half avocado, 106 g/3¾ oz	235	2.1	8.5

	C	GF	FU
ANGELICA			
Per 28 g/1 oz	90	0	1
Per average stick	10	0	0
APPLES			
Eating, per 28 g/1 oz, flesh only	13	0.6	0
Cooking, per 28 g/1 oz, flesh only	11	0.7	0
Medium whole eating, 142 g/5 oz	50	2.7	0
Medium whole cooking, 227 g/8 oz	80	4.3	0
Apple sauce, sweetened, per 15 ml/1 level tablespoon	20	0	0
Apple sauce, unsweetened, per 15 ml/1 level tablespoon	10	0	0
APRICOTS			
Canned in natural juice, per 28 g/1 oz	13	0.4	0
Canned in syrup, per 28 g/1 oz	30	0.4	0
Dried, per 28 g/1 oz	52	6.8	0.5
Fresh with stone, per 28 g/1 oz	7	0.5	0
Per dried apricot	10	1.3	0
ARROWROOT			
Per 28 g/1 oz	101	0.8	0
Per 5 ml/1 level teaspoon	10	0	0
ARTICHOKES			
Globe, boiled, per 28 g/1 oz	4		0
Jerusalem, boiled, per 28 g/1 oz	5		0

	C	GF	FU
ASPARAGUS			
Raw or boiled, soft tips, per 28 g/1 oz	5	0.4	0
Per asparagus spear	5	0.4	0
B			
BACON (see also *Gammon*)			
Per 28 g/1 oz			
Back rasher, raw	122	0	4
Collar joint, raw, lean and fat	91	0	3
Collar joint, boiled, lean only	54	0	1
Collar joint, boiled, lean and fat	92	0	2.5
Streaky rashers, raw	118	0	4
1 streaky rasher, well grilled or fried, 21 g/¾ oz raw weight	50	0	1
1 back rasher, well grilled or fried, 35 g/1¼ oz raw weight	80	0	1.5
1 bacon steak, well grilled, 99 g/3½ oz average raw weight	105	0	1.5
BAKING POWDER			
Per 28 g/1 oz	46	0	0
Per 5 ml/1 level teaspoon	5	0	0
BAMBOO SHOOTS			
Canned, per 28 g/1 oz	5	0.1	0

	C	GF	FU
BANANAS			
Small whole fruit, 115 g/4 oz raw	55	2.3	0
Medium whole fruit, 170 g/6 oz	80	3.4	0
Large whole fruit, 198 g/7 oz	95	4.0	0
BARCELONA NUTS			
Shelled, per 28 g/1 oz	181	2.9	6.5
BARLEY			
Pearl, raw, per 28 g/1 oz	102	1.8	0
Pearl, boiled, per 28 g/1 oz	34	0.6	0
Per 15 ml/1 level tablespoon raw	45	0.8	0
BASS			
Fillet, steamed, per 28 g/1 oz	35	0	0
BEAN SPROUTS			
Raw, per 28 g/1 oz	8	0.3	0
Boiled, per 28 g/1 oz	7	0.3	0
BEANS			
Per 28 g/1 oz			
Baked, canned in tomato sauce	20	2.1	0
Black eye beans, raw weight	93	7.2	0
Broad, boiled	14	1.2	0
Butter, boiled	27	1.4	0
Butter, raw, dry weight	77	6.1	0
French, boiled	10	0.9	0
Haricot, boiled	26	2.1	0
Haricot, raw weight	77	7.2	0
Red kidney, canned	25	2.3	0
Red kidney, raw, dry weight	77	7.0	0
Mung, raw, dry weight	92	6.2	0

	C	GF	FU
Rump steak, well grilled, 170 g/6 oz raw	290	0	5.5
Rump steak, rare grilled, 170 g/6 oz raw	310	0	6
Silverside, salted, boiled, lean and fat	69	0	1.5
Silverside, salted, boiled, lean only	49	0	0.5
Sirloin, roast, lean and fat	80	0	2
Sirloin, roast, lean only	55	0	1
Stewing steak, raw, lean only	35	0	1
Stewing steak, raw, lean and fat	50	0	0
Topside, raw, lean only	35	0	0.5
Topside, raw, lean and fat	51	0	1
Topside, roast, lean and fat	61	0	
Topside, roast, lean only	44	0	0.5
BEEFBURGERS			
Beefburger, fresh or frozen, well grilled, 57g/2 oz raw weight	115	0.2	3
Beefburger, fresh or frozen, grilled 113 g/4 oz raw weight	240	0.4	6
BEETROOT			
Raw, per 28 g/1 oz	8	0.9	0
Boiled, per 28 g/1 oz	12	0.7	0
Per baby beet, boiled	5	0.4	0
BILBERRIES			
Raw or frozen, per 28 g/1 oz	16	0	0

	C	GF	FU
Runner, boiled	5	0.9	0
Runner, raw, green	10	0.9	0
Soya, dry weight	108	1.2	1.5
BEECH NUTS			
Shelled, per 28 g/1 oz	160		5
BEEF			
Per 28 g/1 oz			
Brisket, boiled, lean and fat	92	0	2.5
Brisket, raw, lean and fat	71		2
Ground beef, very lean, raw	45	0	0.5
Ground beef, very lean, fried and drained of fat	55	0	0.5
Ground beef, lean, fried and drained of fat, per 28 g/1 oz raw weight	40	0	0.5
Minced beef, raw	74	0	1.5
Minced beef, well fried and drained of fat	82	0	1
Minced beef, well fried and drained of fat per 28 g/1 oz raw weight	60	0	0.5
Rump steak, fried, lean only	54	0	1
Rump steak, raw, lean and fat	56	0	1
Rump steak, grilled lean only, 28 g/1 oz	48	0	0.5
Rump steak, medium grilled, 170 g/6 oz raw	260	0	4

	C	GF	FU
BISCUITS			
Per average biscuit			
Chocolate chip cookie	60		1.5
Digestive, large	70	0.8	0.5
Digestive, medium	55	0.6	0.5
Digestive, small	45	0.4	0.5
Fig roll	65	0.7	0.5
Garibaldi, per finger	30	0.2	0.25
Ginger nut	40	0.2	0.5
Ginger snap	35	0.2	0.25
Jaffa cake	50		0.5
Lincoln	40	0.1	0.5
Malted milk	40		0.5
Marie	30	0.2	0.25
Morning coffee	25	0.2	0.25
Nice	45		0.5
Osborne	35	0.2	0.25
Petit Beurre	30		0.25
Rich tea, finger	25	0.2	0.25
Rich tea, round	45	0.2	0.25
Sponge finger	20		0.5
BLACKBERRIES			
Raw or frozen, 28 g/1 oz	8	2.4	0
Stewed, without sugar, per 28 g/1 oz	7	1.8	0

	C	GF	FU
Muffin, 64 g/2¼ oz	125		0.5
Pitta, 71 g/2½ oz	205		0.5
Scone, plain white, 57 g/2 oz	210	1.2	3
Soft brown roll, 50 g/1¾ oz	140	2.7	1
Soft white roll, 50 g/1¾ oz	150	1.4	1
Tea cake, 57 g/2 oz	155	1.2	1.5
Per 15ml/level tablespoon			
Breadcrumbs, dried	30	0.7	0
Breadcrumbs, white, fresh	8	0.1	0
Bread sauce	15	0.1	0.5
BREAKFAST CEREALS			
Per 28 g/1 oz			
All Bran cereal	70	8.0	0.25
Bran flakes	85	4.2	0
Cornflakes	100	0.5	0
Muesli or Swiss style	105	2.1	0.5
Porridge oats	115	4.3	0.5
Puffed wheat	100	4.3	0.5
Sultana bran	85	3.6	0.25
Weetabix or whole wheat biscuits, per biscuit	65	2.4	0.25
BROCCOLI			
Raw, per 28 g/1 oz	7	1.0	0
Boiled, per 28 g/1 oz	5	1.1	0
BRUSSELS SPROUTS			
Raw, per 28 g/1 oz	7	1.2	0
Boiled, per 28 g/1 oz	5	0.8	0

	C	GF	FU
BLACKCURRANTS			
Raw or frozen, per 28 g/1 oz	8	2.4	0
Stewed without sugar, per 28 g/1 oz	7	2.1	0
BLOATERS			
Fillet, grilled, per 28 g/1 oz	71	0	1.5
On the bone, grilled per 28 g/1 oz	53	0	1.5
BRAINS			
Per 28 g/1 oz			
Calves' or lambs', raw	31	0	1
Calves', boiled	43	0	1
Lambs', boiled	36	0	1
BRAN			
Per 28 g/1 oz	58	12.5	0.5
Per 15ml/1 level tablespoon	10	1.2	0
BRAWN			
Per 28 g/1 oz	43	0	1.5
BRAZIL NUTS			
Shelled, per 28 g/1 oz	175	2.5	6
Per nut, shelled	20	0.3	0.5
Per buttered brazil	40	0.3	0.5
Per chocolate brazil	55	0.3	0.5
BREAD			
Per 28 g/1 oz slice			
Black rye	90		0.5
Brown or wheatmeal	63	1.5	0.25
Currant	70	0.5	0.5

	C	GF	FU
Enriched, e.g. cholla	110	0.8	0.25
French	85	0.8	0.5
Fruit sesame	120		0.5
Granary	70		0.25
Light rye	70		0.25
Malt	70	1.4	0.5
Milk	80		0.5
Soda	75	0.65	0.25
Vogel	65		0.25
Wheatgerm, e.g. Hovis and Vitbe	65	1.3	0.25
White	66	0.8	0.25
Wholemeal (100%)	61	2.4	0.25
Rolls, buns etc., each			
Baby bridge roll, 14 g/½ oz	35	0.4	0.25
Bagel, 42 g/1½ oz	150		1.5
Bap, 42 g/1½ oz	130	1.2	1.5
Bath bun, 42 g/1½ oz	120	1.1	0.5
Brioche roll, 45 g/1⅝ oz	215		2
Chelsea bun, 92 g/3¼ oz	255	2.3	2.5
Croissant, 71 g/2½ oz	280		5½
Crumpet, 42 g/1½ oz	75		0.5
Crusty roll, brown or white, 50 g/1¾ oz	145	2.9	0.5
Currant bun, 50 g/1¾ oz	150	0.9	1.5
Devonshire split, with cream, 71 g/2½ oz	195	4	
Dinner roll, soft, 42 g/1½ oz	130	1.2	0.5
Hot cross bun, 57 g/2 oz	180		1.5

	C	GF	FU
BUTTER			
All brands, per 28 g/1 oz	210	0	8
C			
CABBAGE			
Per 28 g/1 oz			
Raw	6	0.7	0
Boiled	4	0.7	0
Pickled red	3	0.9	0
CAKES			
Home-made, per average slice			
Butterfly cake, 35 g/1¼ oz	220	n/a	n/a
Cherry cake, 85 g/3 oz slice	335	1.4	4
Chocolate cake, filled with butter icing and topped with chocolate glacé icing. 113 g/4 oz	525	n/a	n/a
Christmas cake or wedding, with marzipan and royal icing, 99 g/3½ oz	350	3.4	4
Eccles cake, 57 g/2 oz	290	2.1	5½
Flapjack, 43 g/1½ oz piece	300	1.2	4
Fruit cake, plain, 85 g/3 oz slice	300	2.4	4
Jam tart, 28 g/1 oz	110	0.5	1½
Madeira cake, 85 g/3 oz	335	1.2	4
Mince pie, 43 g/1½ oz	185	1.6	4
Scone, plain, 57 g/2 oz	210	1.2	3

	C	GF	FU
Sponge sandwich, jam filled, whisked fatless method, 43 g/1½ oz slice	130	0.5	1
Victoria sandwich, jam filled, 57 g/2 oz slice	260	0.6	5½
Fresh cream cakes			
Chocolate éclair, 71 g/2½ oz	275	n/a	3½
Cream doughnut, 71 g/2½ oz	260	n/a	3½
Cream slice with puff pastry and glacé icing, 99 g/3½ oz	420	0.9	5½
Meringue, 71 g/1½ oz	195	0	0
Strawberry tart, 85 g/3 oz	200	n/a	1½
CANDIED PEEL			
Per 28 g/1 oz	90	0	1
Per 15 ml/level tablespoon	45	0	0.5
CAPERS			
Per 28 g/1 oz	5		
CARROTS			
Raw, per 28 g/1 oz	6	0.8	0
Boiled, per 28 g/1 oz	5	0.8	0
Per average carrot, 57 g/2 oz	12	1.6	0
CASHEW NUTS			
Shelled, per 28 g/1 oz	160	4.0	4
Per nut	15	0.3	0.5
CASSAVA			
Fresh, per 28 g/1 oz	43	0.3	0
CAULIFLOWER			
Raw, per 28 g/1 oz	4	0.6	0

	C	GF	FU
Cotswold	105	0	3
Cottage cheese, plain or with chives, onion, pepper or pineapple	27	0	0.5
Cream cheese	125	0	4.5
Curd cheese	54	0	1
Danbo	98	0	2
Danish Blue	103	0	3
Danish Elbo	98	0	3
Danish Esrom	98	0	3
Danish Fynbo	100	0	3
Danish Havarti	117	0	3.5
Danish Maribo	100	0	3
Danish Molbo	100	0	3
Danish Mozzarella	98	0	3
Danish Mycella	99	0	3
Danish Samsoe	98	0	3.5
Derby	110	0	3
Dolcelatte	100	0	3
Double Gloucester	105	0	3
Edam	88	0	2.5
Emmental	115	0	3
Feta	54	0	1.5
Gorgonzola	112	0	2.5
Gouda	100	0	3
Gruyere	117	0	3.5
Ilchester Cheddar and beer	112	0	3.5
Jarlsberg	95	0	2.5

	C	GF	FU
Boiled, per 28 g/1 oz	3	0.5	0
CAVIAR			
Per 28 g/1 oz	75	0	0
CELERIAC			
Boiled, per 28 g/1 oz	4	1.4	0
CELERY			
Raw, per 28 g/1 oz	2	0.4	0
Boiled, per 28 g/1 oz	1	0.6	0
Per stick of celery	5	1.0	0
CHEESE			
Per 28 g/1 oz			
Austrian smoked	78	0	2.5
Babybel	97	0	2
Bavarian smoked	80	0	2
Bel Paese	96	0	3.5
Blue Stilton	131	0	4
Bonbel	102	0	3.5
Boursin	116	0	4
Bresse bleu	80	0	2
Brie	88	0	2.5
Caerphilly	120	0	3
Caithness Morven	110	0	3
Caithness full fat soft	110	0	3
Camembert	88	0	2.5
Cheddar	120	0	3.5
Cheese spread	80	0	3.5
Cheshire	110	0	3
Cheviot	120	0	3.5

	C	GF	FU
Lancashire	109	0	3
Leicester	105	0	3
Norwegian blue	100	0	3
Norwegian Gjeost	133	0	4
Orangerulle	92	0	3
Orkney Claymore	111	0	3
Parmesan	118	0	3.5
Philadelphia	90	0	3
Port Salut	94	0	3
Processed	88	0	2.5
Rambol, with walnuts	117	0	3
Red Windsor	119	0	3.5
Ricotta	55	0	2
Roquefort	88	0	3
Sage Derby	112	0	3
Skimmed milk soft cheese	25	0	0.5
St Paulin	98	0	2.5
Tôme au raisin	74	0	2
Wensleydale	115	0	3
White Stilton	108	0	4
Per 15 ml/level tablespoon			
Cottage cheese	15	0	0
Cream cheese	60	0	4.5
Curd cheese	25	0	1
Parmesan cheese	30	0	3
CHERRIES			
Fresh, with stones, per 28 g/1 oz	12	0.4	0
Glacé, per 28 g/1 oz	60	0	0

	C	GF	FU
Per glacé cherry	10		0
CHESTNUTS			
Per 28 g/1 oz			
Shelled	48	1.9	
With shells	40	1.6	
Unsweetened chestnut purée	30		0.25
CHICKEN			
Per 28 g/1 oz			
On bone, raw, no skin	25	0	0.25
Meat only, raw	34	0	0.5
Meat only, boiled	52	0	0.5
Meat only, roast	42	0	0.5
Meat and skin, roast	61	0	1.5
Chicken drumstick, raw, 99 g/3½ oz average raw weight	90	0	1.5
Chicken drumstick, grilled and skin removed, 99 g/3½ oz average raw weight	65	0	1
Chicken drumstick, grilled, 99 g/3½ oz raw weight	85	0	1.5
Chicken joint, raw 227 g/8 oz average weight	410	0	0.3
Chicken joint, grilled and skin removed, 227 g/8 oz average raw weight	165	0	2
Chicken joint, grilled, with skin, 227 g/8 oz	250	0	5

	C	GF	FU
COCKLES			
Without shells, boiled, per 28 g/1 oz	14	0	0
COCOA POWDER			
Per 28 g/1 oz	88		2
Per 5 ml/level teaspoon	10		0.5
COCONUT			
Per 28 g/1 oz			
Fresh	100	3.8	3.5
Desiccated	171	6.6	6
Fresh coconut milk, per 28 ml/1fl oz	6		0
Creamed coconut	218		8
Desiccated, per 15 ml/level tablespoon	30	1.1	1
COD			
Per 28 g/1 oz			
Fillet, raw	22	0	0
Fillet, baked or grilled with a little fat	27	0	0.5
Fillet, poached in water or steamed	24	0	0
Frozen steaks, raw	19	0	0
On the bone, raw	15	0	0
COD LIVER OIL			
Per 5 ml/teaspoon	40	0	1.5
COD ROE			
Raw, hard roe, per 28 g/1 oz	32	0	0.25

	C	GF	FU
CHICORY			
Raw, per 28 g/1 oz	3	0.4	0
CHILLIES			
Dried, per 28 g/1 oz	85	7.1	0
CHIVES			
Per 28 g/1 oz	10		0
CHINESE LEAVES			
Raw, per 28 g/1 oz	3	0.6	0
CHOCOLATE			
Per 28 g/1 oz			
Milk or plain	150	0	1.5
Cooking	155	0	1.5
Filled chocolates	130	0	1.5
Vermicelli	135	0	1.5
Per 5 ml/level teaspoon			
Chocolate spread	20	0	0.25
Drinking chocolate	10	0	0
Vermicelli	20	0	0.25
CLAMS			
With shells, raw, per 28 g/1 oz	15	0	0
Without shells, raw, per 28 g/1 oz	25	0	0
COB NUTS			
With shells, per 28 g/1 oz	39	1.7	1.5
Shelled, per 28 g/1 oz	108	0.6	3.5
Per nut	5	0	0

	C	GF	FU
COFFEE			
Coffee beans, roasted and ground infusion	0	0	0
Instant, per 5 ml/teaspoon	0	0	0
COLEY			
Per 28 g/1 oz			
Raw	21	0	0
On the bone, steamed	24	0	0
Fillet, steamed	28	0	0
COOKING OR SALAD OIL			
Per 28 g/1 oz	255	0	10
Per 15 ml/1 level tablespoon	120	0	5
CORNED BEEF, CANNED			
Per 28 g/1 oz	62	0	1
CORNFLOUR			
Per 28 g/1 oz	100	0.8	0
Per 15 ml/1 level tablespoon	33	0.3	0
CORN OIL			
Per 28 g/1 oz	225	0	10
Per 15 ml/1 level tablespoon	120	0	5
CORN ON THE COB			
Average whole cob	155	4.5	0
COURGETTES			
Raw, per 28 g/1 oz	4	0.5	0
Per courgette, 70 g/2½ oz	10	1.3	0

CHART OF BASIC FOODS

	C	GF	FU
CRAB			
With shell, per 28 g/1 oz boiled	7	0	0
Meat only, per 28 g/1 oz boiled	36	0	0.5
Average crab with shell	95	0	1.5
CRANBERRIES			
Per 28 g/1 oz	4	1.2	0
CRANBERRY SAUCE			
Per 28 g/1 oz	65	0	0.5
Per 15 ml/1 level tablespoon	45	0	0.5
CREAM			
Per 28 g/1 oz			
Clotted	165	0	5.5
Double	127	0	5
Half cream	35	0	1
Imitation	85	0	3
Single	60	0	2
Soured	60	0	2
Sterilised, canned	65	0	2.5
Whipping	94	0	3.5
Per 15 ml/1 level tablespoon			
Clotted	105	0	3.5
Double	55	0	2
Half cream	20	0	0.5
Imitation	55	0	2
Single	30	0	1
Soured	30	0	1
Sterilised, canned	35	0	1
Whipping	45	0	1.5

	C	GF	FU
DELICATESSEN SAUSAGES			
Per 28 g/1 oz			
Belgian liver sausage	90	0.1	2.5
Bierwurst	75	0	2.5
Bockwurst	180	0	5
Cervelat	140	0	4
Chorizo	140	0	3
Continental liver sausage	85	0.1	3
Frankfurter	78	0.3	2.5
French garlic sausage	90	0	3
Garlic sausage	70	0	2.5
Ham sausage	50	0	0.5
Kabanos	115	0	3.5
Krakowska	80	0	2.5
Liver sausage	88	0.1	2.5
Mettwurst	120	0	3.5
Mortadella, Italian	105	0	3
Polish country sausage	60	0	1
Polony	80	0	2
Pork boiling ring, coarse	110	0.2	3.5
Salami, Belgian	130	0	4
Salami, Danish	160	0	4.5
Salami, Hungarian	130	0	4
Salami, German	120	0	3.5
Saveloy	74	0.1	2
Smoked Dutch sausage	105	0	3
Smoked pork sausage	130	0	3.5
Smoked ham sausage	65	0	2

	C	GF	FU
CRISPS (potato)			
All flavours per 28 g/1 oz	150	3	3
CUCUMBER			
Raw, per 28 g/1 oz	3	0.1	0
CURRANTS			
Per 28 g/1 oz	69	2.2	1
Per 15 ml/1 level tablespoon	20	0.6	0.25
CURRY PASTE/CONCENTRATE			
Per 28 g/1 oz	40	0	1
CURRY POWDER			
Per 28 g/1 oz	66		0
Per 5 ml/1 level teaspoon	12		0
CUSTARD APPLE			
Flesh only, per 28 g/1 oz	25	0	0
CUSTARD POWDER			
Per 28 g/1 oz	100	0.8	0
Per 15 ml/1 level tablespoon	33	0.2	0
D			
DAMSONS			
Fresh, with stones, per 28 g/1 oz	11	1.0	0
Stewed, no sugar, per 28 g/1 oz	8	0.9	0
DATES Per 28 g/1 oz			
Dried, with stones	60	2.1	0.5
Dried, without stones	70	2.4	0.5
Fresh, with stones	30		0
Per date, fresh	15		0

	C	GF	FU
DRIPPING			
per 28 g/1 oz	253	0	10
per 15 ml/1 level tablespoon	125	0	5
DUCK			
Per 28 g/1 oz			
Raw, meat only	35	0	0.5
Raw, meat, fat and skin	122	0	4.5
Roast, meat only	54	0	1
Roast, meat, fat and skin	96	0	3
DUCK EGGS			
99 g/3½ oz egg	170	0	4
E			
EEL			
Meat only, raw per 28 g/1 oz	48	0	1
Meat only, stewed in water, per 28 g/1 oz	57	0	1.5
Jellied eels plus some jelly, 85 g/3 oz	180	0	4
EGGS, each			
Size 1	95	0	2.5
Size 2	90	0	2.5
Size 3	80	0	2
Size 4	75	0	2
Size 5	70	0	2
Size 6	60	0	1.5
Yolk of size 3 egg	65	0	2
White of size 3 egg	15	0	0

	C	GF	FU
ENDIVE			
Raw, per 28 g/1 oz	3	0.6	0
F			
FAGGOTS			
Per 28 g/1 oz	76	0	2
FIGS			
Dried, per 28 g/1 oz	60	5.2	0.5
Fresh, green, per 28 g/1 oz	12	0.7	0
Per dried fig	30	2.6	0.25
FLOUNDER			
On the bone, raw, per 28 g/1 oz	20	0	0
On the bone, steamed, per 28 g/1 oz	15	0	0
FLOUR			
Per 28 g/1 oz			
Wheatmeal	93	2.1	0.25
White, plain	99	1.0	0
White, self raising	96	1.0	0
White, strong	96	0.8	0
Wholemeal	90	2.7	0.25
Buckwheat	99	0.3	0.25
Cassava	97	0.4	0
Granary	99		0
Maizemeal (96%)	103	0.4	0.5
Maizemeal (60%)	100	0.2	0

	C	GF	FU
GELATINE, powdered			
Per 15 ml/1 level tablespoon	30	0	0
Per 28 g/1 oz	96	0	0
Per 10 g envelope	35		10
GHEE			
Per 28 g/1 oz	235	0	10
GHERKINS			
Per 28 g/1 oz	5		
GINGER			
Ground, per 28 g/1 oz	73		0.5
Ground, 5 ml/1 level teaspoon	8		0
Root, raw, peeled, 28 g/1 oz	18		0
Stem in syrup, strained, per 28 g/1 oz	60		0.5
GOOSE			
Roast, on bone, per 28 g/1 oz	55	0	2
Roast, meat only (without skin), per 28 g/1 oz	90	0	2
GOOSEBERRIES			
Fresh, ripe dessert, per 28 g/1 oz	10	1	0
Fresh, cooking, per 28 g/1 oz	5	0.9	0
GRAPEFRUIT			
Per 28 g/1 oz			
Canned in syrup	17	0.2	0
Canned in natural juice	11	0.2	0
Flesh only	6	0.2	0
Flesh and skin	3	0.1	0

	C	GF	FU
Rice	100	0.7	0
Rye (100%)	95	3.3	0.25
Soya, low fat	100	4.0	0.5
Soya, full fat	127	3.4	2.5
Yam	90	0.4	0
Per 15 ml/1 level tablespoon			
White	32	0.3	0
Wholemeal	29	0.9	0
FRENCH DRESSING			
Per 15 ml/tablespoon	75	0	3
Oil-free, per 15 ml/tablespoon	5	0	0
FRUIT			
Crystallised, per 28 g/1 oz	75	0	1
G			
GAMMON			
Per 28 g/1 oz			
Gammon joint, raw, lean and fat	67	0	2
Gammon joint, boiled, lean and fat	76	0	2
Gammon joint, boiled, lean only	47	0	0.5
Gammon rashers, grilled, lean and fat	65	0	1
Gammon rashers, grilled, lean only	49	0	0.5
GARLIC			
One clove	0	0	0

	C	GF	FU
Juice, unsweetened, per 28 ml/1 fl oz	9	0	0
Juice, sweetened, per 28 ml/1 fl oz	11	0	0
Medium whole fruit, 340 g/12 oz	35	1.0	0
GRAPES			
Black, per 28 g/1 oz	14	0.1	0
White, per 28 g/1 oz	17	0.2	0
GREENGAGES			
Fresh, with stones, per 28 g/1 oz	13	0.7	0
Stewed, with stones, no sugar, per 28 g/1 oz	11	0.6	0
GRENADINE SYRUP			
Per 28 g/1 oz	72	0	1
GROUSE			
Roast, meat only, per 28 g/1 oz	50	0	0.5
GROUND RICE			
Per 28 g/1 oz	100	0.7	0
Per 15 ml/1 level tablespoon	33	0.2	0
GUAVAS			
Canned, per 28 g/1 oz	17	1.0	0
GUINEA FOWL			
Roast, on bone, per 28 g/1 oz	30	0	0
Roast, meat only, per 28 g/1 oz	60	0	0

H

HADDOCK
Per 28 g/1 oz

	C	GF	FU
Fillet, raw	21	0	0
Fillet in breadcrumbs, fried	50	0.1	1
On the bone, raw	15	0	0
Smoked fillet, raw	25	0	0
HAGGIS			
Cooked, per 28 g/1 oz	88	0	2
HAKE			
Per 28 g/1 oz			
Fillet, raw	20	0	0
Fillet, steamed	30	0	0
Fillet, fried	60	0	1
On the bone, raw	10	0	0
HALIBUT			
Per 28 g/1 oz			
Fillet, steamed	37	0	0.25
On the bone, raw	26	0	0
On the bone, steamed	28	0	0
Steak, 170 g/6 oz	155	0	2
HAM			
Per 28 g/1 oz			
Chopped ham roll or loaf	75	0	1.5
Ham, boiled, lean	47	0	0.5
Ham, boiled, fatty	90	0	2
Honey roast ham	50	0	0.5

	C	GF	FU
Rollmop herring, 70 g/2½ oz average weight	120	0	3
Whole herring, grilled, 128 g/4½ oz average weight	170	0	3.5
HERRING ROE			
Fried, per 28 g/1 oz	69	0	1.5
Raw, soft roe	23	0	0.5
HONEY			
Per 15 ml/level tablespoon	60	0	0.5
Per 5 ml/1 teaspoon	20	0	0
HORSERADISH			
Fresh root, per 28 g/1 oz	17	2.4	0
Horseradish sauce, per 15 ml/1 level tablespoon	13	0	0
HUMMUS			
Per 28 g/1 oz	50	0	0.5

I

ICE-CREAM
Per 28 g/1 oz

	C	GF	FU
Chocolate	55	0	1
Coffee	50	0	1
Cornish dairy	50	0	1
Raspberry ripple	50	0	1
Soft ice-cream	45	0	1
Strawberry	50	0	1
Vanilla	45	0	1

Food	C	GF	FU
Old smokey ham	65	0	1
Maryland ham	55	0	0.25
Virginia ham	40	0	0.25
Ham steak, well grilled, 99 g/3½ oz, average raw weight	105	0	1
HARE			
Stewed, meat only per 28 g/1 oz raw	55	0	1
Stewed, on bone, per 28 g/1 oz	39	0	0.5
HASLET			
Per 28 g/1 oz	80	0	1.5
HAZELNUTS			
Shelled, per 28 g/1 oz	108	1.7	3.5
Per nut	5	0	0
Chocolate hazelnut whirl, each	40	0	0
HEART			
Per 28 g/1 oz			
Lamb's raw	34	0	0.5
Ox, raw	31	0	0.5
Pig's, raw	26	0	0.5
HERRING			
Per 28 g/1 oz			
Fillet, raw	66	0	2
Fillet, grilled	56	0	1.5
On the bone, grilled	38	0	1
Rollmop herring	47	0	1
J			
JAM			
Per 15 ml/level tablespoon	45	0.2	0.5
Per 5 ml/level teaspoon	15	0	0
JELLY			
Cubes as sold, per 28 g/1 oz	73	0	0
Made up with water, per 142 ml/¼ pint	85	0	0
Per cube	29	0	0
K			
KIDNEY			
All types, raw, per 28 g/1 oz	25	0	0.25
Lamb's kidney, grilled, without fat 57 g/2 oz average raw weight	50	0	0.5
KIPPERS			
Fillet, baked or grilled, without fat, per 28 g/1 oz	58	0	1
On the bone, baked, per 28 g/1 oz	31	0	0.5
Whole kipper, grilled, without fat, 170 g/6 oz	280	0	3.5

L

LAMB
Per 28 oz/1 oz

	C	GF	FU
Breast, boned, raw, lean and fat	107	0	3.5
Breast, boned, roast, lean and fat	116	0	3.5
Breast, boned roast, lean only	71		1.5
Leg, raw, lean and fat, without bone	68	0	2
Leg, roast, lean and fat, without bone	75	0	2
Leg, roast, lean only, without bone	54	0	1
Scrag and neck, raw, lean and fat, weighed with bone	54	0	3
Scrag and neck, raw lean and fat, weighed without bone	90	0	4
Scrag and neck, stewed, lean only, weighed with bone	38	0	1
Scrag and neck, stewed, lean only, weighed without bone	72	0	1.5
Shoulder, boned, roast, lean and fat	89	0	2.5
Shoulder, boned, roast, lean only	56	0	1
Chump chop, well grilled, 142 g/5 oz raw weight	205	0	6

LETTUCE

	C	GF	FU
Fresh, per 28 g/1 oz	3	0.4	0

LIVER
Per 28 g/1 oz

	C	GF	FU
Calf's, raw	43	0	1
Chicken's, raw	38	0	0.5
Chicken's, fried	55	0	1
Lamb's, raw	51	0	1
Lamb's, fried	66	0	1.5
Ox, raw	46	0	1
Pig's raw	44	0	0.5

LOBSTER

	C	GF	FU
With shell, boiled, per 28 g/1 oz	12	0	0.25
Meat only, boiled, per 28 g/1 oz	34	0	0.5

LOGANBERRIES

	C	GF	FU
Fresh, per 28 g/1 oz	5	1.8	0
Canned in natural juice, per 28 g/1 oz	9	1	0

LOW-FAT SPREAD

	C	GF	FU
All brands, per 28 g/1 oz	105	0	4
Per 5 ml/level teaspoon	15	0	0.5

LUNCHEON MEAT

	C	GF	FU
Per 28 g/1 oz	89	0	2.5

	C	GF	FU
Leg steak, boneless, well grilled, 227 g/8 oz raw weight	370	0	7
Loin chop, well grilled, 142 g/5 oz raw weight	175	0	6.5
LARD Per 28 g/1 oz	253	0	10
LAVERBREAD Per 28 g/1 oz	15	0	0
LEEKS			
Raw, per 28 g/1 oz	9	0.8	0
Average whole leek, raw	25	2.2	0
LEMON			
Flesh and skin, per 28 g/1 oz	4	1.5	0
Whole lemon, 142 g/5 oz	20	7.4	0
Lemon juice, per 15 ml/1 tablespoon	0	0	0
LEMON CURD Per 28 g/1 oz	80	0	0
Per 5 ml/1 level teaspoon	15	0	0
LEMON SOLE Per 28 g/1 oz			
Fillet, steamed or poached	26	0	0
On the bone, raw	23	0	0
On the bone, steamed or poached	18	0	0
LENTILS			
Raw, per 28 g/1 oz	86	3.3	0
Split, boiled, per 28 g/1 oz	28	1.0	0

M

	C	GF	FU
MACARONI Per 28 g/1 oz			
White, raw	105	0.8	0.25
Wholewheat, raw	95	2.8	0.25
White, boiled	33	0.3	0
Wholewheat, boiled	30	0.9	0
MACEDONIA NUTS Per 28 g/1 oz	188		6.5
MACKEREL Per 28 g/1 oz			
Fillet, raw	63		1.5
Kippered mackerel	62		1.5
Smoked mackerel fillet	70		2.5
Whole raw mackerel, 227 g/8 oz	320		7.5
MAIZE			
Whole grain, per 28 g/1 oz	103	0.6	0
MANDARINS			
Canned in natural juice, per 28 g/1 oz	11	0.1	0
Fresh, weighed with skin, per 28 g/1 oz	7	0.4	0
Medium whole fruit, 70 g/2½ oz	20	0.9	0
MANGO			
Raw, per 28 g/1 oz	17	0.4	0
Canned in syrup, per 28 g/1 oz	22	0.3	0
Mango chutney, per 15 ml/1 level tablespoon	40		0

	C	GF	FU
MAPLE SYRUP			
Per 15 ml/1 tablespoon	50	0	0.5
MARGARINE			
All brands including those labelled 'high in polyunsaturates', per 28 g/1 oz	210	0	8
MARMALADE			
Per 28 g/1 oz	74	0.2	1
Per 15 ml/1 level tablespoon	45	0.1	0.5
MARRON GLACÉ			
Per 28 g/1 oz	74	0	1
MARROW			
Raw, flesh only, per 28 g/1 oz	5	0.5	0
Boiled, per 28 g/1 oz	2	0.2	0
MARZIPAN (Almond Paste)			
Per 28 g/1 oz	126	1.8	2.5
Petit fours	126		2.5
MAYONNAISE			
Per 28 g/1 oz	205	0	6.0
Per 15 ml/1 level tablespoon	120	0	3.5
MEDLARS			
Flesh only, per 28 g/1 oz	12	2.9	0
MELON			
Per 28 g/1 oz			
Cantaloupe, with skin	4	0.1	0
Honeydew or Yellow, with skin	4	0.1	0
Ogen, with skin	5	0.2	0

	C	GF	FU
Evaporated full cream	23	0	0.5
Homogenised, pasteurised, green top, silver top and sterilised	10	0	0
Instant low fat milk, dry	18	0	0
Instant low fat milk, reconstituted	5	0	0
Skimmed or separated	5	0	0
Canned milk, per 28 g/1 oz			
Evaporated full cream	45	0	1
Condensed, skimmed, sweetened	76	0	0.5
Condensed full cream, sweetened	91	0	1
Condensed, unsweetened	40	0	0.5
MINCEMEAT			
Per 28 g/1 oz	67	0.9	0.5
Per 15 ml/1 level tablespoon	40	0.5	0.5
MINT			
Fresh, per 28 g/1 oz	3	0	0
MINT SAUCE			
Per 15 ml/1 level tablespoon	5	0	0
MOLASSES			
Per 28 g/1 oz	78	0	1
Per 15 ml/1 level tablespoon	45	0	0.5
MUESLI			
Per 28 g/1 oz	105	2.1	0.5
Per 15 ml/1 level tablespoon	30	0.5	0

	C	GF	FU
Watermelon, with skin	3	0.1	0
Slice of Cantaloupe, Honeydew or Yellow, with skin, 227 g/8 oz	30	1.3	0
MILK			
Per 568 ml/1 pint			
Buttermilk	232	0	0
Channel Island or gold top	445	0	10
Evaporated milk, full cream, reconstituted	360	0	10
Goat's	415	0	9.5
Homogenised or red top	380	0	8
Instant dried skimmed milk with vegetable fat, reconstituted	280	0	6
Longlife or UHT	380	0	8
Pasteurised or silver top	380	0	8
Pasteurised or silver top with cream removed, 510 ml/18fl oz	240	0	0.5
Skimmed or separated	200	0	0
Soya milk, diluted as directed	370	0	12
Sterilised	380	0	8
Untreated farm milk or green top	380	0	8
Per 15 ml/1 level tablespoon			
Channel Island or gold top	15	0	0.5
Condensed full cream, sweetened	50	0	0.5
Condensed, skimmed, sweetened	40	0	0.5

	C	GF	FU
MULBERRIES			
Raw, per 28 g/1 oz	10	0.4	0
MULLET			
Raw, flesh only, per 28 g/1 oz	40	0	0.5
MUSHROOMS			
Raw, per 28 g/1-oz	4	0.7	0
Sliced and fried, per 28 g/1 oz	60	1.1	3.5
MUSSELS			
With shells, boiled, per 28 g/1 oz	7	0	0
Without shells, boiled, per 28 g/1 oz	25	0	0.25
Per mussel	10	0	0
MUSTARD AND CRESS			
Raw, per 28 g/1 oz	3	1	0
Whole carton	5	1.6	0
MUSTARD			
Dry, per 28 g/1 oz	128		
Made mustard, English, per 5 ml/1 level teaspoon	10		
N			
NECTARINES			
Whole fruit, medium	50	2.5	0
NOODLES			
Cooked, per 28 g/1 oz	33	0	0
NUTMEG			
Powdered, per 2.5 ml/½ level teaspoon	0	0	0

O

	C	GF	FU
OATMEAL			
Raw, per 28 g/1 oz	114	2	1
Per 15 ml/1 level tablespoon, raw	40	0.7	0
OCTOPUS			
Raw, per 28 g/1 oz	20	0	0
OKRA			
Raw, per 28 g/1 oz	5	0.9	0
OLIVE OIL			
Per 28 ml/1fl oz	255	0	10
Per 15 ml/1 level tablespoon	120	0	5
OLIVES			
Stoned, in brine, per 28 g/1 oz	29	1.2	1
With stones, in brine, per 28 g/1 oz	23	1	1
Per stuffed olive	5	0.2	0
ONIONS			
Per 28 g/1 oz			
Raw	7	0.4	0
Boiled	4	0.3	0
Fried, sliced	98	1.3	3.5
Dried, per 15 ml/1 level tablespoon	10	0.6	0
Whole onion, raw, 85 g/3 oz	20	1.2	0
Pickled onion, each	5	0.2	0
Cocktail onion, each	1	0	0

	C	GF	FU
PARSNIPS			
Per 28 g/1 oz			
Raw	14	1.1	0
Boiled	16	0.7	0
Roast	30		0.5
PARTRIDGE			
Roast, on bone, per 28 g/1 oz	36	0	0.5
Roast, meat only, per 28 g/1 oz	60	0	0.5
PASSION FRUIT			
Flesh only, per 28 g/1 oz	10	4.5	0
PASTA			
White, all shapes, raw, per 28 g/1 oz	105	0.8	0
White, boiled, per 28 g/1 oz	33	0.3	0
Wholewheat, raw	95	2.8	0.25
Wholewheat, boiled	30	0.9	0
PASTRY			
Per 28 g/1 oz			
Choux, raw	60	0.2	1.5
Choux, baked	95	0.4	2
Flaky, raw	120	0.4	3
Flaky, baked	160	0.6	4
Shortcrust, raw	130	0.6	3
Shortcrust, baked	150	0.7	3
PAW PAW			
Canned, per 28 g/1 oz	18	0.1	0
Fresh, flesh only, per 28 g/1 oz	11	0.2	0

	C	GF	FU
ORANGES			
Flesh only, per 28 g/1 oz	10	0.6	0
Flesh with skin, per 28 g/1 oz	7	0.4	0
Whole fruit, small, 142 g/5 oz	35	2.1	0
Whole fruit, medium 227 g/8 oz	60	3.4	0
Whole fruit, large, 284 g/10 oz	75	4.2	0
ORANGE JUICE			
Per 28 ml/1 fl oz			
Canned, sweetened	15	0	0
Unsweetened	11	0	0
OXTAIL			
Stewed, without bone, per 28 g/1 oz	69	0	1.5
On the bone, stewed and skimmed of fat, per 28 g/1 oz	26	0	0.5
OYSTERS			
With shells, raw, per 28 g/1 oz	2	0	0
Without shells, raw, per 28 g/1 oz	14	0	0
Per oyster	5	0	0
P			
PARSLEY			
Fresh, per 28 g/1 oz	6	2.6	0
Parsley sauce, per 15 ml/1 level tablespoon	45	0	0

	C	GF	FU
PEACHES			
Canned in natural juice, per 28 g/1 oz	13	0.2	0
Canned in syrup, per 28 g/1 oz	25	0.2	0.25
Fresh, with stones, per 28 g/1 oz	9	0.3	0
Whole fruit, 115 g/4 oz	35	1.4	0
PEANUTS			
Per 28 g/1 oz			
Shelled, fresh	162	2.3	5
Dry roasted	160	2.3	5
Roasted and salted	162	2.3	5
Peanut butter	177	2.1	5.5
Per peanut	5	0	0
PEARS			
Per 28 g/1 oz			
Cooking pears, raw, peeled	10	0.8	0
Dessert pears	8	0.5	0
Canned in syrup	22	0.5	0.25
Whole fruit, medium, 142 g/5 oz	40	2.4	0
PEAS			
Per 28 g/1 oz			
Frozen	15	2.2	0
Canned, garden	13	1.8	0
Canned, processed	23	2.2	0
Dried, raw	81	4.7	0
Dried, boiled	29	1.3	0
Split, raw	88	3.4	0
Split, boiled	33	1.4	0

	C	GF	FU
Per 30 ml/1 rounded tablespoon			
Dried, boiled	30	1.3	0
Fresh, boiled	10	1.1	0
Pease pudding	35		0
PECANS			
Per nut	15	0	1
PEPPER			
Powdered, per pinch	0	0	0
PEPPERS			
Red or green, per 28 g/1 oz	4	0.3	0
Average pepper, 142 g/5 oz	20	1.3	0
PERCH			
White, raw, per 28 g/1 oz	35	0	0.5
Yellow, raw, per 28 g/1 oz	25	0	0.5
PHEASANT			
Meat only, roast, per 28 g/1 oz	60	0	1
On the bone, roast, per 28 g/1 oz	38	0	0.5
PICKLES AND RELISHES			
Mixed pickles, per 28 g/1 oz	5	0.5	0
Per 15 ml/1 level tablespoon			
Piccalilli	15	0.3	0
Ploughmans	35	0.3	0
Sweet pickle	35	0.3	0
PIGEON			
Meat only, roast, per 28 g/1 oz	65	0	1.5
On the bone, roast, per 28 g/1 oz	29	0	0.5
PIKE			
Raw fillet, per 28 g/1 oz	25	0	0

	C	GF	FU
PLUMS			
Per 28 g/1 oz			
Cooking plums with stones, stewed without sugar	6	0.6	0
Fresh dessert plums, with stones	10	0.6	0
Cooking plums, with stones	7	0.7	0
Victoria dessert plum, medium, each	15	0.6	0
POLLACK			
On the bone, raw, per 28 g/1 oz	25	0	0
POLONY			
On the bone, raw, per 28 g/1 oz	80	0.2	2
POMEGRANATE			
Flesh, only, per 28 g/1 oz	20	0	0
Whole pomegranate, 205 g/7¼ oz	65	0	0
POPCORN			
Per 28 g/1 oz	110	0	1
PORK Per 28 g/1 oz			
Belly rashers, raw, lean and fat	108	0	3.5
Belly rashers, grilled, lean and fat	113	0	3.5
Fillet, raw, lean only	42	0	1
Leg, raw, lean and fat, weighed without bone	76	0	2.5
Leg, raw, lean only, weighed without bone	42	0	1

	C	GF	FU
PILCHARDS			
Canned in tomato sauce, per 28 g/1 oz	36	0	0.5
PIMENTOS			
Canned in brine, per 28 g/1 oz	6	0	0
PINEAPPLES			
Canned in natural juice, weighed with juice, per 28 g/1 oz	15	0.2	0
Canned in syrup, per 28 g/1 oz	22	0.2	0.25
Fresh, weighed without skin and core, per 28 g/1 oz	13	0.3	0
Ring of canned, drained pineapple in syrup	35	0.5	0.25
Ring of canned, drained pineapple in natural juice	20	0.5	0
PISTACHIO NUTS			
Shelled, per 28 g/1 oz	180		5.5
Per nut	5		0
PLAICE Per 28 g/1 oz			
Fillet, raw or steamed	26	0	0.25
Fillet, in batter, fried	79	0.2	2
Fillet, in breadcrumbs, fried	65	0.1	1.5
PLANTAIN Per 28 g/1 oz			
Green, raw	32	1.6	0
Green, boiled	35	1.8	0
Ripe, fried	76	1.6	1

	C	GF	FU
Leg, roast, lean and fat	81	0	2
Leg, roast, lean only	52	0	0.5
Crackling	190	0	4
Scratchings	185	0	4
Pork chop, well grilled, 184 g/6½ oz raw weight, fat removed	240	0	4
POTATOES Per 28 g/1 oz			
Raw	25	0.6	0
Old, baked, weighed with skin	24	0.7	0
Boiled, old potatoes	23	0.3	0
Boiled, new potatoes	22	0.5	0
Canned, new potatoes, drained	15	0.7	0
Chips (average thickness)	70	0.6	7.5
Crisps	150	3.4	3.5
Roast, large chunks	40	0.6	0.5
Sauté	40	0.6	0.5
Instant mashed potato powder, per 15 ml/level tablespoon, dry	40	1.0	0
Jacket-baked potato, 198 g/7 oz raw weight	170	4.9	0
PRAWNS			
With shells, per 28 g/1 oz	12	0	0
Without shells, per 28 g/1 oz	30	0	0.25
Per shelled prawn	2	0	0

	C	GF	FU
PRUNES			
Per 28 g/1 oz			
Dried, no stones	46	4.6	0.5
Stewed, without sugar, fruit and juice without stones	21	2.1	0
Prune juice	25	0	0
Per prune	10	0	0
PUMPKIN			
Raw, flesh only per 28 g/1 oz	4	0.1	0
Q			
QUINCES			
Raw, per 28 g/1 oz	7	1.8	0
R			
RABBIT			
Per 28 g/1 oz			
Meat only, raw	35	0	0.5
Meat only, stewed	51	0	1.5
On the bone, stewed	26	0	0.5
RADISHES			
Fresh, per 28 g/1 oz	4	0.5	0
Per radish	2	0.2	0
RAISINS			
Dried, per 28 g/1 oz	70	2.8	1
Per 15 ml/1 level tablespoon	25	0.7	0.25

	C	GF	FU
SALAD CREAM			
Per 15 ml/1 level tablespoon	50	0	1.5
Low-calorie salad cream, per 15 ml/1 level tablespoon	25	0	0.5
SALMON Per 28 g/1 oz			
Canned	44	0	1
Fillet, steamed	56	0	1.5
Fresh, raw, flesh only	52	0	1
On the bone, steamed	45	0	1
Smoked	40	0	0.5
SALSIFY			
Boiled, per 28 g/1 oz	5	0.1	0
SALT			
Per 28 g/1 oz	0	0	0
SARDINES			
Per 28 g/1 oz			
Canned in oil, drained	62	0	1.5
Canned in tomato sauce	50	0	1
SAUSAGES, each			
Beef chipolata, well grilled	50	0	1.5
Beef, large, well grilled	120	0	3
Beef, skinless, well grilled	65	0	1.5
Pork chipolata, well grilled	65	0.1	2
Pork, large, well grilled	125	0.2	3.5
Pork, skinless, well grilled	95	0	2
Pork and beef chipolata, well grilled	60	0	1.5
Pork and beef, large, well grilled	125	0	3

	C	GF	FU
RASPBERRIES			
Fresh or frozen, per 28 g/1 oz	7	2.1	0
Canned, drained, per 28 g/1 oz	25		0
REDCURRANTS			
Fresh, per 28 g/1 oz	6	2.3	0
Redcurrant jelly, per 5 ml/1 level teaspoon	15		0
RHUBARB			
Raw, per 28 g/1 oz	2	0.7	0
Stewed without sugar, per 28 g/1 oz	2	0.6	0
RICE Per 28 g/1 oz			
Brown, raw	99	1.2	0.25
White, raw	102	0.3	0
White, boiled	35	0.1	0
Brown, boiled	33	0.4	0
ROCK			
Seaside rock, per 28 g/1 oz	95	0	1
S			
SAGO			
Raw, per 28 g/1 oz	101	0.8	0
SAITHE (Coley) Per 28 g/1 oz			
Fillet, raw	21	0	0
Fillet, steamed	28	0	0
On the bone, steamed	24	0	0

	C	GF	FU
SCALLOPS			
Steamed, without shells per 28 g/1 oz	30	0	0
SCAMPI			
Fried in breadcrumbs, per 28 g/1 oz	90	0.3	2
SEAKALE			
Boiled, per 28 g/1 oz	2	0.3	0
SEMOLINA			
Raw, per 28 g/1 oz dry	99	0.8	0
Per 15 ml/1 level tablespoon	35	0.2	0
SESAME SEEDS			
Per 28 g/1 oz	168		5
SHRIMPS			
Per 28 g/1 oz			
Canned, drained	27	0	0
Fresh, with shells	11	0	0
Fresh, without shells	33	0	0
SKATE			
Fillet, in batter, fried, per 28 g/1 oz	57	0.1	1
SMELTS			
Without bones, fried, per 28 g/1 oz	115	0	1

SNAILS	C	GF	FU
Flesh only, per 28 g/1 oz	25	0	0
SOLE Per 28 g/1 oz			
Fillet, raw	23	0	0
Fillet, steamed or poached	26	0	0
On the bone, steamed or poached	18	0	0
SORBET			
Per 50 g/2 oz serving			
All flavours	70	0	0
SPAGHETTI			
Per 28 g/1 oz			
White, raw	107	0.8	0.25
Wholewheat, raw	97	2.8	0.25
White, boiled	33	0.3	0
White, boiled	33	0.3	0
Wholewheat, boiled	30	0.9	0
Canned in tomato sauce	17	0.1	0
SPINACH			
Boiled, per 28 g/1 oz	9	1.7	0
SPRATS			
Fried without heads, per 28 g/1 oz	110	0	4
SPRING GREENS			
Boiled, per 28 g/1 oz	3	1.1	0
SPRING ONIONS			
Raw, per 28 g/1 oz	10	0.4	0
Per onion	3	0.1	0

SWEETCORN	C	GF	FU
Canned in brine, per 28 g/1 oz	22	1.6	0
Fresh, kernels only, boiled, per 28 g/1 oz	25	1.3	0
Frozen, per 28 g/1 oz	25	1.3	0
Whole medium cob	155	4.5	0
SWEETS			
Per 28 g/1 oz			
Barley sugar	100	0	1
Boiled sweets	93	0	1
Butterscotch	115	0	1
Filled chocolates	130		1.5
Fudge	111	0	1.5
Liquorice allsorts	105		1
Marshmallows	90	0	1
Nougat	110		1
Nut brittle or crunch	120		1
Peppermints	110	0	1
Toffees	122		1

T

TANGERINES	C	GF	FU
Flesh only, per 28 g/1 oz	10	0.5	0
Flesh with skin, per 28 g/1 oz	7	1.8	0
Whole fruit, 70 g/2½ oz	20	0.9	0

	C	GF	FU
SQUID			
Flesh only, raw per 28 g/1 oz	25	0	0
STRAWBERRIES			
Fresh or frozen, per 28 g/1 oz	7	0.6	0
Canned, drained, per 28 g/1 oz	23	0.1	0
Per fresh strawberry	2		0
STURGEON			
On the bone, raw, per 28 g/1 oz	25	0	0
SUET			
Shredded, per 28 g/1 oz	235	0	8.5
Per 15 ml/1 level tablespoon	85	0	3
SUGAR			
White, brown, caster, Demerara, granulated, icing, per 28 g/1 oz	112	0	1
Per 15 ml/1 level tablespoon	50	0	0.5
SULTANAS			
Dried, per 28 g/1 oz	71	1.9	0.5
Per 15 ml/1 level tablespoon	25	0.7	0.25
SUNFLOWER SEED OIL			
Per 28 g/1 oz	255	0	10
Per 15 ml/1 tablespoon	120	0	5
SWEDES			
Raw, per 28 g/1 oz	6	0.7	0
Boiled, per 28 g/1 oz	5	0.8	0
SWEETBREADS			
Lamb's raw, per 28 g/1 oz	37	0	1

	C	GF	FU
TAPIOCA			
Dry per 28 g/1 oz	102	0.8	0
TARAMASALATA			
Per 28 g/1 oz	135	0	5
TARTARE SAUCE			
Per 15 ml/1 level tablespoon	35		1
TEA			
All brands, per cup, no milk	0	0	0
TOMATOES Per 28 g/1 oz			
Raw	4	0.4	0
Canned	3	0.2	0
Fried, halved	20	0.8	0.5
Fried, sliced	30	0.8	0.5
Ketchup	28	0	0
Purée	19	0	0
Whole medium tomato, 57 g/2 oz	8	0.8	0
Per 15 ml/1 level tablespoon			
Chutney	45	0.3	0
Ketchup	15		0
Purée	10		0
TONGUE Per 28 g/1 oz			
Lamb's, raw	55	0	1.5
Lamb's, lean only, stewed	82	0	2.5
Ox, lean only, boiled	83	0	2.5
TREACLE			
Black, per 28 g/1 oz	73	0	1
Per 15 ml/1 level tablespoon	50	0	0.5

	C	GF	FU
TRIPE			
Dressed, per 28 g/1 oz	17	0	0.25
Stewed, per 28 g/1 oz	28	0	0.5
TROUT			
Fillet, smoked, per 28 g/1 oz	38	0	0.5
Whole trout, poached or grilled without fat, 170 g/6 oz	150	0	2
Whole smoked trout, 156 g/5½ oz	150	0	2
TUNA			
Per 28 g/1 oz			
Canned in brine, drained	30	0	0
Canned in oil	82	0	2
Canned in oil, drained	60	0	1.5
TURKEY			
Per 28 g/1 oz			
Meat only, raw	30	0	0.25
Meat only, roast	40	0	0.25
Meat and skin, roast	48	0	0.5
TURNIPS			
Raw, per 28 g/1 oz	6	0.8	0
Boiled, per 28 g/1 oz	4	0.6	0
V			
VEAL			
Per 28 g/1 oz			
Fillet, raw	31	0	0.25

	C	GF	FU
WHITEBAIT			
Fried coated in flour, per 28g/1oz	149	0	5
WHITE PUDDING			
As sold, per 28g/1oz	128	0	3
WHITING			
Per 28g/1oz			
Fillet, fried in breadcrumbs	54	0	1
Fillet, steamed	26	0	0
On the bone, fried in breadcrumbs	49	0	1
On the bone, steamed	18	0	0
WINKLES			
With shells, boiled, per 28g/1oz	4	0	0
Without shells, boiled, per 28g/1oz	21	0	0
WORCESTERSHIRE SAUCE			
Per 28ml/1floz	20	0	0
Per 15 ml/1 level tablespoon	13	0	0
Y			
YAMS			
Raw, per 28g/1oz	37	1.2	0
Boiled, per 28g/1oz	34	1.1	0
YEAST			
Fresh, per 28g/1oz	15	1.9	0
Dried, per 28g/1oz	48	6.1	0
Dried, per 5ml/1 level teaspoon	8	1.0	0

	C	GF	FU
Fillet, roast	65	0	1
Jellied veal, canned	35	0	0
VENISON			
Roast meat only, per 28g/1oz	56	0	0.5
VINEGAR			
Per 28ml/1floz	1	0	0
W			
WALNUTS			
Shelled, per 28g/1oz	149	1.5	5
Per walnut half	15	0.1	0.5
WATERCHESTNUTS			
Per 28g/1oz	10		0
WATERCRESS			
Per 28g/1oz	4	0.9	0
WATERMELON			
Flesh only, per 28g/1oz	6		0
Flesh with skin, per 285g/10oz slice	30	0.8	0
WHEATGERM			
Per 28g/1oz	100	0.6	1
Per 15ml/1 level tablespoon	18		0.25
WHELKS			
With shells, boiled, per 28g/1oz	4		0
Without shells, boiled, per 28g/1oz	26		0

	C	GF	FU
YOGURT			
Per 150g/5oz carton			
Low fat, natural	75	0	0.5
Low fat, flavoured	115	0	0.5
Low fat, fruit	135	2.5	0.5
Low fat, nut	150		1.5
YORKSHIRE PUDDING			
Cooked, per 28g/1oz	60	0.3	1

INDEX

Recipe abbreviations: (gc) = good cook's diet;
(hf) = high-fibre diet; (hw) = housewife's diet;
(lc) = low-calorie diet; (lf) = low-fat diet;
(ww) = working woman's diet